Performing Chekhov

David Allen

London and New York

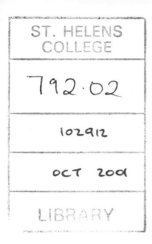
First published 2000 by Routledge
11 New Fetter Lane, London EC4P 4EE

Simultaneously published in the USA and Canada
by Routledge
29 West 35th Street, New York, NY 10001

Routledge is an imprint of the Taylor & Francis Group

Typeset in Garamond by Taylor & Francis Books Ltd
Printed and bound in Great Britain by TJ International Ltd, Padstow,
Cornwall

British Library Cataloguing in Publication Data
A catalogue record for this book is available from the British Library

Library of Congress Cataloging-in-Publication Data
Allen, David
  Performing Chekhov / David Allen.
    p. cm.
  Includes bibliographical references and index.
    (alk. paper)
  1. Chekhov, Anton Pavlovich, 1860–1904 – Stage history.
  2. Chekhov, Anton Pavlovich, 1860–1904 – Dramatic production.
  I. Title.
  PG3458.Z9Z823   1999   99-31944
  792.9'5–dc21   CIP

ISBN 0–415–18934–9 (hbk)
ISBN 0–415–18935–7 (pbk)

Performing Chekhov

Performing Chekhov is a unique guide to Chekhov's plays in performance. Drawing on extensive interviews with actors, directors and designers, it offers in-depth case studies of a number of significant, and often controversial, productions which have challenged and changed our ideas about Chekhov. Bridging the gap between history and practical training, it focuses on the work of key directors in Russia, America and England, including:

- Stanislavski
- The Moscow Art Theatre
- Vakhtangov
- Meyerhold
- Yuri Lyubimov
- Lee Strasberg
- The Wooster Group
- Jonathan Miller
- Mike Alfreds

This practical and accessible book reflects some of the most crucial debates, not only about Chekhov's work, but about the very nature of acting and performance.

Performing Chekhov will be indispensable to students, teachers and theatre practitioners interested, not only in Chekhov, but in the history of the modern stage.

David Allen is a senior lecturer in drama at the University of Wolverhampton. He has written numerous articles on Chekhov, and is the author of *Stanislavski for Beginners* and the forthcoming *Chekhov for Beginners*.

To my father and in memory of my mother

The journey in all acting is to unite the internal and external, the psychological and the physical.

Mike Alfreds

Contents

PART IV
Chekhov in England

Plates

Preface

This book is not a complete historical survey of Chekhov on the stage; instead, I have chosen to focus on a number of significant, and often controversial productions, which I feel crystallise some of the key issues and debates about performing Chekhov. As far as possible, I have gone back to original sources – interviews with the directors actors, designers etc. actually involved in the productions – to try to uncover their ideas about Chekhov's work, and show how these ideas were applied in practice.

The book has its origins, in part, in a PhD thesis I wrote on Chekhov in Britain (*Nothing Happens: Chekhov on the British Stage, 1909–1996*, University of Birmingham, 1996). I would like to thank my supervisors, Gerry McCarthy and Joel Kaplan; and the British Academy and the British Council for their financial support which enabled me to write my thesis, and undertake research in Moscow. I would also like to thank the University of Wolverhampton for sabbatical leave to allow me to write this book.

Part III of the book (*Chekhov in England*) includes material which first appeared, in a much earlier form, in *New Theatre Quarterly*, vol. 2, no. 8: 'Exploring the limitless depths: Mike Alfreds directs Chekhov'; and vol. 5, no. 17: 'Jonathan Miller directs Chekhov'.

Acknowledgements

My thanks to: the late Rodney Ackland, Mike Alfreds, Aleksei Bartoshevich, Birgit Beumers, the late Gwen Ffrangçon-Davies, Miranda French, Marco Ghelardi, the late Warren Jenkins, Galina Klimenko, Charles Marowitz, Vicki Midmer, Patrick Miles, Jonathan Miller, Valentina Ryapolova, Roy and Larissa Sadler, Tatyana Shakh-Azizova, Stephanie Terpant, Jon Trevor, Nick Ward, Stuart Young. And finally, to my wife, Olga.

Acknowledgement is due to Victor Seymour for permission to quote from his PhD thesis, *Stage Directors' Workshop: A Descriptive*

Study of the Actors Studio Directors Unit, 1960–1964 (University of Wisconsin, 1965).

Selections are also included from Laurence Shyer, 'Andrei Serban Directs Chekhov', *Theater* (Fall/Winter 1981). Copyright 1981 Yale School of Drama/Yale Repertory Theatre. All rights reserved. Reprinted by permission of Duke University Press.

Thanks also to Euridice Arratia for permission to quote material from 'Island Hopping: Rehearsing the Wooster Group's *Brace Up!*'; to Susie Mee for permission to quote from 'Chekhov's *Three Sisters* and the Wooster Group's *Brace Up!*'; and the Helen Merrill Agency for permission to quote from 'The Sounds of *Brace Up!*: Translating the Music of Chekhov' by the late Paul Schmidt. All of the above appear in *The Drama Review*, T136, Winter, 1992

Photographs appear courtesy of: Chadwyck–Healey Ltd (productions by Stanislavski, Vakhtangov and Meyerhold); Taganka Theatre Archive (Efros and Lyubimov); George E. Joseph (Andrei Serban); The Wooster Group (*Brace Up!*); V & A Picture Library/The Theatre Museum (Komisarjevsky's *The Seagull*); Sophie Baker (Jonathan Miller's *Three Sisters*); John Haynes (Mike Alfreds' *The Cherry Orchard* at the National Theatre); Sarah Ainslie (Alfreds' *Three Sisters*); and Simon Annand (Alfreds' *Cherry Orchard* for Method and Madness).

Transliteration and translation

The international system for the transliteration of Russian words, used by scholars, is not familiar to most readers. I have used a method which is intended to be accessible to English-language readers with no Russian. я is given as *ya*; ю as *yu*; й as *i*; ы and ый as *y*; и and ий as *i*. э appears as *e*; but no distinction is made between е and ё, which are both given as *e*. In the text, soft and hard signs have been deleted. English spellings of Russian names that have passed into common usage (e.g. Komisarjevsky, Meyerhold and Gorky) have been preserved; but more technically accurate versions are given in the transliteration of Russian titles in the notes and bibliography.

For a number of years, there were at least six different ways of spelling Chekhov (e.g. Tchehov) and there remain various ways of spelling Stanislavski (Stanislavsky, Stanislavskii, etc.). There are also various ways of spelling the names of the characters in the plays (e.g. Ranevsky, Ranyevskaya, etc.). For the sake of clarity, the spelling of these names has been standardised throughout. Unless otherwise specified, all translations are my own.

Introduction

The first production of Chekhov's play, *The Seagull*, in St Petersburg in 1896 was a disaster. Spectators at the Aleksandrinski Theatre shouted, jeered and howled with laughter. 'What nonsense this is!' one of them declared. 'I'm surprised at the directors of the theatre', another fumed. 'How can they put such rubbish on the stage!'[1] A newspaper review the following day concluded: '*The Seagull* has perished. The unanimous hissing of the whole audience has killed it. It was as if millions of bees, wasps and bumble-bees filled the auditorium – the hissing was so strong, so venomous.'[2] Chekhov was devastated. His friend, Aleksei Suvorin, recalled:

> At one o'clock in the morning, his sister turned up at our door, asking where he was. She was agitated. ... He couldn't be found anywhere. He arrived at two o'clock. I went up to him and asked:
> 'Where were you?'
> 'I walked the streets and sat for a while. I couldn't just say to hell with this production. If I live another 700 years, I'll never give a theatre another play. I've had enough. In this area, I'm a failure.'[3]

The hostility of the first-night audience at the Aleksandrinski Theatre is usually blamed on the conditions of the performance. The play was staged after only eight rehearsals, and the actors barely knew their lines. Moreover, it had been chosen by a popular comic actress, Elizaveta Levkeeva, for her benefit night. The auditorium was full of her admirers, expecting an evening of light entertainment with their favourite comedienne. *The Seagull* was hardly a suitable choice for such an occasion, and Levkeeva herself did not even appear in it. The conditions, then, certainly did not help. The Russian critics, however, turned their fire on the *play*, rather than the production. The

Peterburgski listok (*Petersburg Leaflet*) argued that it 'is very badly conceived, and clumsily put together, and its contents are very odd, or rather, there are no contents. ... It's a kind of mess in a bad dramatic form.'[4] Even Suvorin was puzzled by the play. As he wrote in his diary, it seemed to contain 'little action, a lack of dramatically interesting developments in the scenes and a lot of space given to the trivia of life'.[5]

It seems almost incomprehensible now, when Chekhov's work is so popular, that it once provoked so much controversy. What was so shocking was the author's apparent disregard for the fundamental 'laws of drama', the 'most elementary demands of the stage'.[6] Crucially, his work seemed to contain 'almost no action in the usual sense – i.e. the rapid movement of external theatrical events, one after the other'.[7] When his earlier play, *The Wood Demon*, was offered to the Aleksandrinski Theatre in 1889, it was rejected because of the apparent absence of 'action', and the 'tedious' dialogue. It was eventually performed at the Abramova Theatre in Moscow. One critic complained that all the 'action' in the play was limited to eating; the characters just 'talk the whole time, without ceasing ... saying everything that pops into their head'. Another critic said there were no 'events' in the play, but only the portrayal of 'incidents' interweaved among a mass of domestic conversations which were 'extremely long and tedious'.[8]

'Nothing happens': the same criticism was made, again and again, of Chekhov's work (and is still sometimes made today). Drama, by definition, meant 'action'. Audiences went to the theatre to 'see something happen'[9]; and dramatists obliged, presenting as much of the exciting action as possible.

In 1837, Gogol had lamented the way the Russian theatre was dominated by melodramas, which were full of extraordinary events:

> The strange has become the subject matter of contemporary drama. The whole point is to recount a totally new, totally strange, hitherto unheard of and unseen event: murder, fires, the most savage passions, which simply don't exist in modern society! ... Hangmen, poisons – effects, eternal effects.

Only a genius, he concluded, 'can catch everything that surrounds us daily, and is inseparable from us, the ordinary – while mediocrity grabs with both hands at everything unusual and exceptional, that astonishes us by its ugliness'.[10] Similarly, Chekhov attacked contemporary dramatists for their love of external action and sensational, dramatic

Plate 1 Vera Komissarzhevskaya as Nina in the first production of *The Seagull*. Aleksandrinski Theatre, St Petersburg (1896).

events. Plays were filled with everything 'that is most terrible, miserable, sour and dazzling in nature': 'Heroes and heroines throw themselves over a precipice, drown, shoot, hang themselves, or die from a terrible disease, which cannot be found in even the most complete medical textbooks.'[11] Famously, he declared:

> In real life people do not spend every minute shooting each other, hanging themselves or making declarations of love. They don't spend every minute saying clever things. Rather, they eat, drink, flirt, talk nonsense. And that is what should be seen on the stage. One should write a play in which people come and go, eat, talk about the weather and play cards. And not because that is what the author wants, but because that is what happens in real life. ...
>
> ... It is not a question of naturalism or realism. It is not necessary to keep within such limits. It is necessary that life should be shown exactly as it is, and people exactly as they are, and not in a stilted way.[12]

And in 1889 he told Ilya Gurlyand: 'Let everything on stage be just as complicated and just as simple as in life. People eat, just eat, and at the same time their happiness is being decided or their lives ruined.'[13] This implies a rejection of 'extraordinary events' in drama. Rather, the emphasis is on apparently minor or incidental events – 'people come and go, eat, talk about the weather and play cards'. At the same time, the aim is not simply to reproduce the 'naturalistic' surface of life. On the surface, little may appear to be happening; but there is a tension and dichotomy between this lack of 'external' drama, and the significant changes, the *inner* drama, that may be occurring just beneath the surface: 'People eat, just eat, and at the same time their happiness is being decided or their lives ruined.'

It is not true, of course, that 'nothing happens' in Chekhov. However, critics and audiences at first could see only the 'trivia of life' in his work. They could not see beyond the surface to the 'inner drama' within.

Before its first performance, Chekhov read *The Seagull* to an assembly in Moscow, including the theatrical producer, Fedor Korsh, and the actor Lidya Yavorskaya. 'I remember the impression created by the play', Tatyana Shchepkina-Kupernik recalled.

It could be compared to Arkadina's reaction to Treplev's play. 'Decadence' ... 'New forms?' The play surprised with its novelty those who, like Korsh and Yavorskaya, recognised only effective dramas such as those by Sardou, Dumas, and the like. ... I remember the argument, the uproar, Lidya's insincere admiration, Korsh's surprise: 'My dear fellow, it just isn't stageworthy: you have a man shoot himself off-stage, and don't even let him say a few words before he dies!'[14]

Chekhov, then, had offended against the 'laws' of the stage by deliberately eschewing an opportunity for a big dramatic 'effect'. Another dramatist would have filled the scene – 'note, the climactic scene of the play – with the most beautiful and effective words of the man who is saying farewell to this sad world'.[15] Nikolai Efros observed that Chekhov, 'whether he is writing a story or a drama, is economical with words, and extraordinarily laconic'. In *The Seagull* 'the most essential, important moments of drama are restricted to two or three lines, a handful of words, and sometimes simply a stage-direction'. After Nina's exit in Act III, Treplev says a few words 'which seem unimportant, and not even in the spirit of the elevated scene which has just passed in front of the spectator'.

TREPLEV: It wouldn't be good if someone met her in the garden and then told mama. It might distress mama.

Then comes the stage direction: 'Over the next two minutes he silently tears up all his manuscripts and throws them under the desk, then opens the right-hand door and goes out.' Shortly afterwards a shot is heard from off-stage. An inattentive reader, Efros argued, might simply overlook this simple stage direction, and then 'will be surprised – where does Treplev's suicide come from? What motivates it?' In other words, the reader might fail to grasp the 'inner drama'. Chekhov 'does not consider it necessary', Efros said, to do the readers' work; instead, we have to 'read' the meaning for ourselves.[16] The character's feelings are not expressed in words, or exhibited in an obvious, external way. On the surface, the 'action' of tearing the manuscripts might seem casual, insignificant, even trivial. The 'inner action' lies buried in the 'subtext'.

Nina: It's hard to act in your play … There's very little action in it. (Act I, The Seagull)

In 1897, A. Smirnov – with a perception rare among contemporary critics – argued that Chekhov had transferred the 'centre of gravity in his drama from the external to the internal, from the acts and events of external life to the internal psychological world of his characters'.[17] Chekhov once saw a production of *Uncle Vanya*. The actress N.S. Butova recalled:

> In the third Act Sonya went down on her knees on the words, 'Papa, you must be merciful', and kissed his hands. 'You mustn't do that, that isn't what drama is', said Anton Pavlovich. 'All the meaning and all the drama of a person lies internally, not in external manifestations. There was drama in Sonya's life before this moment; there will be drama in it afterwards, and this – this is simply an incident, a continuation of the pistol shot. And the pistol shot is not a drama, either, but an incident.'[18]

Chekhov's comments, then, directed the actor's attention away 'from the external to the internal, from the acts and events of external life to the internal psychological world' of the character. He rejected all obvious ways of exhibiting the character's feelings through 'external manifestations'.

Most acting in the Russian theatre at the time was based on 'visualised' action: the external demonstration of the characters' feelings. The Russian playwright, Leonid Andreev, described some of the methods conventionally employed:

> If you have to express great sorrow, you would start to weep; sorrow abated, you would lay your head on the table. Putting a finger to your lips apparently without meaning to or watching the door after someone makes an exit signifies: a wife is cheating on her husband, something fishy is going on. Clutching your head, dealing out a slap, running, not walking into a room, laughing for joy and sobbing for despair, pursing the lips, knitting the brow, putting dark patches under the eyes and so forth are all part of the conventional *language* of the drama, every bit as generally accepted as the conventional Morse code of the telegraph.[19]

The emotions of the characters, then, were clearly demonstrated, even 'telegraphed' to the audience through external 'signs'.

Chekhov was opposed to the falsehoods and exaggerations of acting he saw in most theatres of his day. In a letter, he wrote:

> where – in streets and houses – do you see people tearing about, leaping up and down, and clutching their heads? Suffering should be expressed as it is expressed in life – i.e., not with your arms and legs, but by a tone of voice, or a glance; not by gesticulating, but by grace. Subtle inner feelings, natural in educated people, must be subtly expressed in an external form. You will say – stage conditions. But no conditions justify lies.[20]

How, exactly, should 'subtle inner feelings' be 'subtly expressed in an external form'? Chekhov offered this advice to Olga Knipper on how to approach playing Masha in *Three Sisters*: 'Don't pull a sad face in any of the acts. Angry, yes, but not sad. People who have long carried grief within themselves and have become used to it just whistle and are frequently lost in thought.'[21]

The writer, then, directed the actor's attention away from obvious 'external manifestations' of sadness. The character does not weep or clutch her head to 'show' her suffering. 'Whistling' could seem simply a trivial action, a piece of 'naturalistic' business. But it is, in fact, a detail which has been carefully selected as a subtle expression of the 'inner drama' taking place in the character.

A new form of drama demanded new methods of acting. Actors at the Aleksandrinski Theatre were at first very puzzled by *The Seagull*. The director of the production was Evtikhi Karpov, who sensed how difficult the play was for the majority of actors. They were only happy, it seemed, if they could 'seize each other by the throat, begin to choke one another or pour poison in a glass, drink it and start to die in convulsions'.[22] In other words, they were used to working through 'external manifestations' which very clearly expressed the feelings of the characters. The problem they faced, in scenes such as Treplev's suicide, was that they could not seize it and act it through in a conventional way.

When he saw rehearsals, Chekhov objected that the actors 'act a lot, there should be less acting'.[23] But as Vladimir Nemirovich-Danchenko observed:

> *how to act, without acting anything* no one could tell them. Least of all the author. 'Everything must be done very simply', Chekhov said, 'just as in life. It must be done as if they spoke about it every day.' It was easy to say that! That is the most difficult thing.

Nemirovich identified the challenge facing the actors: 'How could you say these simple lines simply, and yet make them effective on the stage, and not simply boring?'[24] In other words: How do you communicate the 'subtext' behind the words? How do you express the 'inner drama', in external form?

Maria Chitau, who played Masha, recalled that the actors were intrigued but also puzzled by the play's 'totally new tones'. Abarinova, playing Polina, thought she had found the key to the play; the secret, it seemed, was to be gloomy and 'speak despondently'. And so, 'with tears in her voice, she would say to Treplev: "Well, now you have become a famous writer."' The apparently trivial line, then, would be made 'meaningful' through the actor's tone of voice. But Elizaveta Levkeeva, witnessing rehearsals, was puzzled. '"But it's a good thing that he's become a famous writer", she whispered to me, "so why is Tosha [Abarinova] saying the line as if she were telling him that his favourite aunt had fallen ill?!"'[25]

Clearly, this was not the 'key' to revealing the 'inner drama' in the lines.

Ultimately, Chekhov felt the production failed through 'the disgusting way it was acted'.[26] It seems that later performances were more enthusiastically received; but according to Chitau, the acting was no better. The play was withdrawn from the theatre's repertoire after only five performances. Nemirovich-Danchenko concluded:

> Other actors were necessary for Chekhov, and a different method of acting.[27]

Production notes

The Seagull, directed by Evtikhi Karpov. Aleksandrinski Theatre, St Petersburg; first performance, 17 October 1896.

I Chekhov and Stanislavski

1 'The theatre of mood'
The Moscow Art Theatre

The Moscow Art Theatre was founded by Vladimir Nemirovich-Danchenko and Konstantin Stanislavski in 1898. Nemirovich was a playwright and critic, and also taught acting at the Philharmonic School. Stanislavski had established a strong reputation as an actor and director with the semi-professional Society of Art and Literature. Both deplored the current state of the professional Russian theatre, and were determined to wage war against the clichés and routine 'lies' of the stage.

> We rebelled against the old manner of acting, against theatricality, against false pathos, declamation and artificiality, against bad conventions of staging and decor ... against the whole system of production, and the contemptible repertoire, in theatres at that time.[1]

Stanislavski declared: 'I sought living, real life in the theatre – not ordinary life, of course, but artistic life.'[2] Chekhov and the Art Theatre, he saw, were united in a common desire 'to achieve artistic simplicity and truthfulness on the stage'.[3]

Olga Knipper had trained as an actor under Nemirovich at the Philharmonic School. She recalled how he had infected everyone there with a love for *The Seagull*: they read and re-read it, and could not imagine how it could be acted.[4] Now, Nemirovich wanted the play for the Art Theatre. But Chekhov was hesitant at first; after the debacle in St Petersburg, he declared he would never let the play be performed in Moscow.[5] Nemirovich had to write to him three times before he agreed. 'Perhaps the play will not provoke storms of applause', he wrote, 'but a genuine production with *fresh* qualities, *liberated from routine*, will be a triumph of art – I guarantee it.' Significantly, he suggested that the new production would seek to reveal 'the hidden drama and tragedy in *every* character'.[6]

Stanislavski, however, could not understand the play at first. He thought it monotonous and unsuitable for the stage; 'the people in it seemed to him to be unformed, the passions ineffective, the words perhaps too simple, and the images failed to give the actors any good material'.[7] He could not see the 'hidden drama'. Nemirovich spent many hours trying to explain it to him – stressing the play's lyrical qualities and the 'atmosphere, the aroma and mood, which envelop the characters'.[8] It is clear, then, that Nemirovich was the main mover behind the Art Theatre's production. It was his idea to stage the play, and it was *his* interpretation. Stanislavski, still somewhat uncertain, went away to write a production plan, which he sent in instalments to Nemirovich. He confessed:

> I myself don't know if the plan for *The Seagull* is good, or completely useless. I only know the play is talented, interesting, but I don't know at which end to start. I've come at it haphazardly, so do what you like with the plan. ... In this particular play – the cards are in your hands. Of course, you know and feel Chekhov better and more strongly than I.[9]

Nemirovich, however, declared that the plan 'was bold, different from the kind the public was used to, and very much alive'.[10]

On the first night, the actors were extremely nervous. How would the audience respond to the play? The company had heard that Chekhov was ill with tuberculosis, and they feared if the play failed again it might kill him. No wonder, then, that many of them took valerian drops (a form of tranquilliser) before the performance began. At the end of Act I, the curtain was drawn. And then, silence. Nobody clapped. The actors decided that the production was a failure. 'Then, suddenly, in the auditorium, it was as if a dam had broken, or a bomb had exploded – all at once there was a deafening burst of applause.'[11] Olga Knipper recalled:

> Everything merged into one mad exultation, the auditorium and the stage were one. The curtain did not drop, we all stood as if drunk, tears flowed down all our faces, we embraced, kissed each other, and excited voices in the audience rang out, saying something, demanding that a telegram be sent to Yalta. *The Seagull* and Chekhov the dramatist had been rehabilitated.[12]

'Chekhov's art demands a theatre of mood', Meyerhold declared. The premiere of the play at the Aleksandrinski failed, he argued, because it did not capture 'the mood the author demands'.[13] Now, only two years later, the play was a triumph; and the difference was attributed, in part, to Stanislavski's creation of an emotionally absorbing 'atmosphere'. The *Russkaya mysl* (*Russian Thought*) wrote: 'The play was a great success because the most important thing in it – "the mood" – is correctly captured by the actors, and conveyed in absolutely the right and proper tone.'[14] The Art Theatre production, sometimes seen as the acme of stage naturalism, was in fact a highly *poetic* rendering of the play. The use of lighting, sound and setting was intended less to reproduce the naturalistic surface of life than to soak the play in an overwhelming 'atmosphere'. This is what Stanislavski sought to develop in his production plan or 'score'. He deployed a plethora of aural and visual effects. He paid particular attention to opening and ending of Acts, with the aim of making a strong impression on the audience, and establishing the 'atmosphere'. Here, for example, are his notes for the opening of Act I:

> The play begins in darkness, an evening in August. The dim light of a lantern, the distant singing of a cavorting drunkard, the distant howling of a dog, the croaking of frogs, the cry of a corncrake, and the occasional tolling of a distant church-bell – help the audience to feel the sad, monotonous life of the characters.[15]

The individual sounds are 'naturalistic', but they are combined in a way that is *non-naturalistic*. They are designed less to create a sense of 'real life' than to evoke a feeling or 'mood' in the audience; to help them 'feel the sad, monotonous life of the characters'. In the deep gloom of the evening setting there was a sense of disquiet, in the howling of the dog, in the drunkard's singing. The distant roll of thunder, the slow tolling of the church bell, set an ominous tone for the Act as a whole.

Compare, however, Stanislavski's notes for the play's opening with Chekhov's own stage directions: 'The sun has just set. Yakov and other workmen are busy on the stage behind the lowered curtain; sounds of hammering and coughing can be heard.' There is no suggestion of gloom in this very simple opening. Stanislavski deliberately 'thickened the atmosphere' in order to emphasise 'the sad, monotonous life of the

Plate 2 Act I of *The Seagull* at the Moscow Art Theatre (1898).

characters'.[16] Similarly, this is how the director conceived the ending of
Act I:

> Evening. The moon is rising. Two people, a man and a woman,
> exchange almost meaningless phrases, which show that they are
> not saying what they feel (Chekhov's characters often do that). In
> the distance, someone is playing the piano, a vulgar tavern waltz
> that evokes the spiritual poverty, philistinism and hollowness of
> the surrounding environment. Suddenly, an unexpected cry breaks
> from the innermost recesses of a loving girl's heart. And then –
> one short phrase, an exclamation: 'I can't ... I can't ... I can't ...'
> The whole scene does not say anything formally, but it arouses a
> mass of associations, memories, uneasy feelings.[17]

Stanislavski built the scene to a crescendo, with a polyphony of
sound. His notes read:

> Masha, sobbing, sinks to her knees and buries her head on Dorn's
> lap. A pause of fifteen seconds. Dorn strokes Masha's head. The
> frenzied waltz grows even louder; the tolling of the church-bell, a
> peasant's song, frogs, a corncrake, the knocking of the night-
> watchman, and all sorts of other nocturnal sound effects.
> Curtain.[18]

Lighting and sound effects, then, were used to reflect and amplify the
characters' inner feelings – to communicate the 'inner drama', the
'subtext'. The frenzy of the waltz reflected their emotional turmoil; the
doleful tolling of the church-bell sounded a note of impending doom.
These effects did not simply *complement* the dialogue, but played an
equal, if not greater part in creating the overall impact of the scene.
Clearly, the 'mood' of the scene struck powerful emotional chords in
the audience; at this point, Nemirovich recalled, a 'tremulous wave' of
emotion swept through the auditorium.[19]

Again, however, Stanislavski's directorial 'additions' actually 'thickened the atmosphere' in order to emphasise 'the sad, monotonous life
of the characters'. Chekhov's ending in the text is actually quite simple
and low-key:

MASHA: I'm in torment. No-one, no one knows the torment I'm in.
   (*Puts her head on his breast; quietly*) I love Konstantin.

DORN: They're all so agitated! So agitated! And there's so much love about ... Oh, this lake has cast its spell over everyone! (*Tenderly*) But what can I do, my child? What? What?

Working on *The Seagull*, Stanislavski said that the Art Theatre came upon an 'inner line of action':

> Once we found that inner line of the play, which we could not define in words at that time, everything became comprehensible of itself, not only to the actors and the stage directors, but to the artist and the electrician and the *costumier* and all the other co-creators of the production. Along this line of inner action, which Chekhov has in a greater degree than any other dramatist, although until this time only actors are aware of it, there was formed a natural force of gravity towards the play itself, which pulled us all in one direction.[20]

What was this 'inner line of action'? Stanislavski does not say. But in *The Seagull*, it might be argued, everything was directed towards showing the 'sad, monotonous life of the characters'. This 'ruling idea' may have helped to coordinate the elements of production and create an overall artistic unity. Crucially, however, the 'ruling idea' was *Stanislavski's*, not Chekhov's.

'The life of things and sounds ... '

Following the Art Theatre's productions, the notion of 'atmosphere' or 'mood' in Chekhov, *Chekhovskoe nastroenie*, became almost proverbial in Russia. However, it might be argued that this idea owed much more to Stanislavski, and Nemirovich, than to Chekhov.

Stanislavski wrote that Chekhov 'is a master of both external and internal truth on the stage'.

> No one can use lifeless, cardboard properties, scenery and lighting effects, as he does – and make them live. He has refined and deepened our knowledge of the life of things and sounds and lighting which, in the theatre as in life, exert a profound influence on the human soul. Twilight, sunrise and sunset, thunderstorm and rain, the first sounds of birds in the morning, the clatter of horses' hoofs on a bridge and the rumble of a departing carriage, the striking of a clock, the chirp of a cricket, the ring of alarm-bells – Chekhov needs all these, not for external stage effect, but in order

to reveal to us the human soul. How can you separate us, and our feelings, from the world of light, sound and things which surround us, and which human psychology depends so much upon? We were unjustly ridiculed for our crickets and other sound and lighting effects which we used in Chekhov's plays, when we were only following his numerous stage-directions.[21]

In other words, these external effects were seen as a means of reflecting and conveying the inner feelings of the characters. Stanislavski was being somewhat disingenuous, however, when he claimed that in his use of effects, he was simply following Chekhov's lead. It is true that Chekhov uses sound in his plays, but far more economically and selectively. Exasperated by the director's fondness for technical effects, he once jokingly remarked:

> Listen! ... I will write a new play, and it will begin like this: 'How wonderful, how quiet! No birds, no dogs, no cuckoos, no owl, no nightingale, no clock, no jingle of bells, not one cricket can be heard.'[22]

The stage, Chekhov said, 'reflects the quintessence of life, and there is no need to introduce anything superfluous onto it'.[23] His own battles with Stanislavski arose in part because he wished to curb the director's tendency to embellish and drown the plays in superfluous 'effects'. In Act III of *Three Sisters*, for example, Chekhov asks for 'the sound of the fire brigade going past the house'. Stanislavski wrote in his production plan: 'In the distance the fire brigade drives past: the noise of wheels, footsteps, the sound of empty barrels, chains, 2 or 3 bells with different tones. 2 or 3 voices all shout at once in the distance.'[24]

Later, where the text calls for 'the sound of firebells outside', Stanislavski suggested:

> The sound of a great alarm bell.
> The noise of the alarm bell, which had ceased, begins again, very much faster, agitatedly.[25]

Knipper wrote to tell him that Stanislavski was planning to create a sense of 'terrible commotion'. He replied:

> You write about the noise in Act III ... What noise? The noise is only in the distance, a vague muffled noise, but here on stage

everyone's exhausted, almost asleep ... If you spoil Act III the whole play will be ruined and in my old age I'll be hissed off the stage.

'Of course, the third Act must be played quietly, so you get the feeling that people are exhausted and want to sleep', he insisted in another letter. 'What noise is there? I have indicated where the bells should ring off-stage.'[26] Chekhov, then, was looking for a distant, background noise to underscore the scene faintly at certain points. Stanislavski, however, wanted to use sound much more emphatically to colour the tone of the whole scene, and intensify the dramatic impact. Instead of a feeling that the characters are exhausted, Stanislavski wanted to communicate a sense of intense internal agitation. A 'quiet' scene was turned into a scene of 'terrible commotion'.

Pauses

A significant innovation in the production of *The Seagull* consisted in the use of pauses. On the one hand, they made the dialogue 'nearer to life', Nemirovich claimed, because they diverted actors away from 'the even, uninterrupted "literary" flow, so characteristic of the old theatre'.[27] But pauses were also used to create the 'mood' and reveal the 'sad, monotonous life' of the characters. In Act IV, for example, when Polina is talking to Masha about Treplev, we can hear him playing the piano off-stage. Stanislavski noted:

> A pause. Ten seconds – they make the bed. The sounds of the piano can be heard very distantly. Slowly the two women stop their work, freeze in position, and stand like that for another ten seconds – only then does Polina speak.[28]

The 'pause' here – the silence, followed by stillness – makes it a moment charged with significance. It underlines the 'sadness' of these women's lives.

S. D. Balukhaty noted that a pause in Stanislavski's production 'never means a total absence of scenic action'. It was, rather, 'filled with other scenic elements: gesture, mime, movement, natural or musical sounds'.[29] Some of this was daring. In Act IV, for example, a brief pause indicated in the text became the pretext for an extended pantomime:

A pause. Dorn again paces up and down, humming. Treplev sits thoughtfully, leaning on Sorin's knees. Sorin strokes his head with one hand, and holds the newspaper with the other, and reads. Treplev sits and stares at one point. Masha looks thoughtfully at Treplev, and Polina at Dorn. Medvedenko stands by the stove. The sound of rain and gusts of the wind, and the rattling of the windows grow stronger. A long pause. Dorn crosses and sits in the rocking chair. After fifteen seconds Medvedenko takes out his cigarette case, goes to the writing desk and lights a cigarette.[30]

The action in the pause established a sense of a group of people, living through a quiet evening at home, at almost life-rate. It also signalled the feelings of the characters: Treplev's sadness and emptiness; Masha's longing as she watched him. But above all, perhaps, Stanislavski was preparing the audience for Treplev's speech, which followed almost immediately, describing Nina's life with Trigorin and her struggles to be an actress. He was establishing a note of melancholy and introspection. Treplev's speech was also broken up with several pauses, filled with sound effects:

A pause. Treplev props his head up with his hands, his elbows resting on his knees. He stares at one point. Dorn rocks himself in the chair and, as Treplev's story grows sadder and sadder, his rocking grows slower and slower, until at last, in the pause, he freezes. The whole scene proceeds like this. They are all motionless, as if frozen.[31]

Nemirovich argued that, in the use of pauses, there was an 'elementary closeness to Chekhov, who has two or three pauses on every page'.[32] However, it is clear that Stanislavski was going far beyond what Chekhov specified in his stage directions. Moreover, the pause was made to carry a weight and a 'significance' which Chekhov, arguably, had not intended.

In Act IV, Stanislavski aimed to create a mood of 'hopelessness and acceptance of the inevitable'.[33] He not only added numerous pauses but also a deluge of sound effects. This slowed the play down, and deflated the action. In the scene around the card table, half-way through the Act, Stanislavski used six pauses compared with Chekhov's one. For example: 'Masha deals the cards. *Pause*. (Wind, rattling of windows.) Dorn hums, and Arkadina smokes and hums along with him. Shamraev drums his fingers on the table. Sorin yawns sweetly.' And later: '*Pause*: wind, rain, rattling of windows, in the distance the sound of a piano (Treplev is playing). The pause lasts some ten seconds.'[34] The 'mood' of the scene was shaped by Stanislavski's use of pauses. Each of them was filled with sound – the wind and rain, the rattling of the window frames, etc. This created a sense of unease and foreboding.

The critic Aleksandr Kugel, when he saw the Aleksandrinski production of *The Seagull*, could not understand why, in Act IV, the characters 'play lotto and drink beer'.[35] In other words, the action seemed utterly trivial to him. Stanislavski's staging, however, seemed to make sense of the scene for audiences. The characters' words were banal – but the atmosphere was theatrically charged. Sergei Glagol described the scene:

> Evening. Outside an autumn wind is blustering and howling at the windows ... A little fire flickers in the fireplace. They play lotto and the calling out of the numbers is audible ... According to theatrical cliché the characters ought to rant and rave, but here their function is carried out by the elements: wind and fire.[36]

In other words, the impact of the scene was achieved, and the emotional subtext was conveyed, less through the acting, than through the combination of scenic effects.

David Richard Jones sees the lotto scene as the 'symbol', the 'most expressive format or setting' for Stanislavski's ruling idea: 'the sad, monotonous life of the characters':

> Things do not fall apart in this world, they just slow down. ... these people and their class in general can no longer convert spiritual energy into life-work; they increase their entropy by exchanges of spirit; their little universe, like the big one, tends toward a maximum of entropy, toward rigidification and death.[37]

There is no indication, however, that Chekhov intends the lotto scene to work in this way. Stanislavski had staged Act IV in accordance with his 'ruling idea'. But when Chekhov saw the production, he objected that, in this Act in particular, his play had been changed beyond recognition. He told the company, 'I suggest that my play should end with the third Act. I will not let you play the fourth.'[38]

Arguably, it was 'the mood that permeated that made *The Seagull* a hit'.[39] What audiences and critics applauded was the director's art, the skilful coordination of all the elements of production, the creation of an overall unity of impression.

> [T]he play has been staged excellently in every respect, with such a subtle understanding and masterly recreation of the play's spirit, its style and atmosphere, with such truth and beauty in the *mise-en-scène*, with such a harmonious *ensemble*, as we have not seen for a long time.
>
> (*Novosti dnya*) (*News of the Day*)

> The director was able to give the production that special atmosphere, which alone could serve as a true background for the melody of despair which escaped from Chekhov. … Soft, blurred half-tones in the background, and the foreground covered with a light haze, which did not allow any single colour to stand out. This was sustained from the beginning to the end, and the play made a greater impression as a result.
>
> (*Teatr i uskusstvo*) (*Theatre and Art*)[40]

Stanislavski made the play work on the stage. But in the process, he changed it. He *imposed* a mood on Chekhov's play. In his production notes, he created a second (meta-)text in parallel with Chekhov's original. It was like a 'musical score' of sounds and silence, a powerful piece of 'mood music' – a 'melody of despair'. But the composer was Stanislavski, not Chekhov.

Production notes

The Seagull, directed by Konstantin Stanislavski and Vladimir Nemirovich-Danchenko. The Moscow Art Theatre; first performance, 17 December 1898.

2 'Stanislavski has ruined my play … '

The first play that Chekhov wrote specially for the Art Theatre was *Three Sisters* (1901). The writer was present for the first read-through. Stanislavski recalled: 'After the reading, sharing our impressions of the play, some of us called it a drama, and others a tragedy, without noticing that these descriptions amazed Chekhov.' Irritated, even offended, Chekhov left the meeting. Stanislavski followed him home: 'I rarely saw him so angry.' The reason, it emerged, was that 'he had written a happy comedy, and at the reading we had all taken the play as a drama, and wept over it. This made Chekhov think that the play was not comprehensible and it was already a failure.'[1]

Jean Benedetti has argued that Chekhov's criticisms of Stanislavski's work can be attributed to his illness – he was dying from tuberculosis, and this made him 'a man of widely fluctuating moods': 'Gorky records that on a bad day Chekhov hated everyone. He therefore expressed various views in various ways to various people, depending on the moment. This has provided more than ample opportunity for selective quotation.'[2] However, to suggest that his arguments were simply the result of deteriorating health is to trivialise them, and marginalise the very real anger he clearly felt.

Chekhov was frequently labelled a 'pessimist' by critics, and dubbed 'a singer of twilight moods', 'a poet of superfluous people', 'a sick talent'.[3] This annoyed him intensely. Shortly before his death, he declared:

> I am describing life. It is a dull, average life. But it is not tedious whimpering. They either make me out to be a cry-baby, or simply a boring writer. I have written several volumes of humorous stories. And criticism puts me down as some kind of weeper. They invent something about me out of their heads, anything they like,

something I never thought of or dreamed about. This is beginning to make me angry.[4]

Chekhov's criticisms of Stanislavski's productions need to be seen in this context. On one occasion, he famously declared:

> You say you have cried at my plays. And you are not the only ones. But that is not why I wrote them, it was Alekseev [Stanislavski] who turned them into cry-babies. I wanted something else. I simply wanted to say to people honestly: 'Look at yourselves, look at how bad and boring your lives are!' The important thing is, that people should understand this, and when they understand it, they will, without fail, create for themselves another and better life. I will not see it, but I know – it will be completely different, and nothing like this life. And until it arrives, I will say to people again and again: 'Understand, how bad and boring your lives are!' What is there in this to cry about?[5]

Chekhov's objections to Stanislavski's productions, then, were not simply a question of genre ('are the plays comedies or tragedies?'). Beyond this, the productions seemed to confirm the image of Chekhov as a gloomy pessimist. Kugel, for example, thought that the 'essence of Chekhov's hopelessness, despondency and the meaningless of life', its 'elemental cruelty and aimlessness' had been effectively communicated by the Art Theatre.[6]

Kugel's favourite Chekhov production was *Uncle Vanya* (1899), which he loved for its quiet poetic charm. The play portrayed, he believed, a condition of tragic stasis; the characters cannot move, cannot escape from their 'self-enclosed circle of suffering'.[7] At the end of his production plan for the play, Stanislavski wrote: 'Finished 27 May 1899, K. Alekseev [Stanislavski]. And life itself is stupid, boring (a Chekhovian phrase – emphasise).'[8]

This can be seen as the leitmotif of the production. Kugel observed: 'All the acts begin with a pause. The pauses act like an introduction to the inner world of this stagnant life.'[9] Again, sound effects were used to reinforce an overall 'mood'. Here is Kugel's description of the opening of Act II:

> The professor sits at a table near his wife with his legs extended. The window is open onto the garden. The curtains flutter in the wind like sails. Then a soft rain begins to fall, then harder – a storm is brewing. A sound rings out on its own, incidentally, of a

breaking pane. The window is fastened and once again the measured sound of falling drops can be heard.[10]

Again, then, sound was used not simply for its naturalistic quality. Rather, it evoked a sense of these characters' inner lives. There was a sad monotony in the measured sound of falling rain. At the same time, there was a rumbling undertow of danger. The breaking pane, perhaps, anticipated the divisions that would erupt in violence at the climax of Act III.

The scene where Vanya tries to shoot Serebryakov should hit us halfway 'between wind and water, laughter and tears'.[11] But Stanislavski made the scene *tragic*, rather than comic. Vanya's entrance provoked chaos and confusion. Here are the notes from Stanislavski's production plan:

> *238.* Crowd scene. General clamour. Voinitski [Vanya] cries out, and leaps after Serebryakov. Elena screams, grasping Voinitski's hand. Telegin runs from the back, waving his hands and sobbing. Serebryakov has run in and flattened himself against the wall. Sonya tries to stop Serebryakov [?], and screams. Marina has thrown herself into a corner, afraid of the gunshots. Mariya Vasilevna is on the sofa; the dog has leapt from the arms of Mariya Vasilevna, and is running round the stage.
>
> *239.* Gunshot. General screaming, everyone has flinched.
>
> *240.* Voinitski presses the revolver against his own forehead, the women seize him and pull his hand away. Voinitski has dropped the revolver.[a]
>
> *241.* Elena begins to cry out in spasms, 'A! A! A!', clutching at her heart and sides; she falls to her knees, her face in the piano stool.
>
> *242.* Voinitski rubs his forehead hard, and sits near the stove.
>
> *243.* Sonya embraces Nanny in the corner. Telegin, from behind a pillar, clutching a handkerchief, has flattened himself against the wall, and cannot move.

---

a   This line is crossed out in the text in pencil.

244. Ten second pause. All freeze from exhaustion. General breathlessness, they breathe heavily, in motionless poses.[12]

The scene, as conceived by Stanislavski, presents an image of 'hopelessness, despondency and the meaningless of life'. It is, literally, an image of tragic stasis; the characters cannot move, cannot escape from their 'self-enclosed circle of suffering'. Stanislavski recalled how sound effects such as 'the clatter of horses' hoofs on a bridge and the rumble of a carriage' were used to reinforce the impact of the play's final scene:

> We were rehearsing ... the fourth Act of *Uncle Vanya*. All its meaning lies in the phrase, 'They've gone.' The director had to ensure that the spectator really felt they had gone – and everything in the house has become empty, as if the lid has been nailed down on the coffin, as if everything has died forever. Without this, there is no Act, without this the play has no ending. ... What would happen if the spectators did not feel 'they've gone', but simply that the actors had gone back to the dressing room to take off their make-up? Could an actor alone convey everything necessary, by his exit? They say there are actors who can do this. But I have not seen and I do not know any. During a tedious break in rehearsal, while we were trying to think of an answer, one of the crew who was tinkering with the set started banging with a stick. And we ... suddenly sensed in this tapping the clatter of horses' hoofs on a bridge. Why not use it, if it conveys the author's meaning truthfully and expressively, and gives us what we need, and helps to solve the problem?[13]

The sound, then, reinforced the *meaning* for the audience in an almost subliminal way. Other sound effects seemed to evoke the loneliness and desolation of the characters' lives:

> The banging of the night-watchman continues to the end of the scene. Guitar. Marina's snoring. Rain. ...

> [Sonya] faintly whispers some kind of prayer. Voinitski [Vanya] cries. The sound of a bell, rain on the window-pane. Telegin is now playing some kind of solemn/sad theme [on his guitar]. Marina's snoring. Mariya Vasilevna turns the pages [of her book] and reads in a monotone, Sonya whispers a prayer, Voinitski sobs. The sound of a cricket.[14]

'The ruling idea'

These effects, then, did not simply create 'mood'; they seemed to evoke a whole way of life. As Stanislavski said, the Art Theatre was mocked for its fondness for effects such as the chirping of crickets, but 'notice how Chekhov himself sedulously describes these "crickets". For him they are an integral symbol. All Russia is in these dreary crickets.'[15]

Stanislavski maintained that in every play there is a main theme, a 'ruling idea', the writer's 'superobjective' in writing the play. In his notes to *The Actor's Work on the Role*, he argued:

> In Dostoevsky's novel, *The Brothers Karamazov*, the superobjective is the author's search for God and the Devil in the human soul. In Shakespeare's tragedy of *Hamlet* the superobjective is '*the awareness (knowledge) of the secrets of life*'. In Chekhov it is the '*aspiration for a better life*' ('to Moscow, to Moscow').[16]

Rehearsing *Three Sisters*, Meyerhold jotted down in a notebook the basic themes of Stanislavski's interpretation:

> Longing for life.

> Call to work.

> Tragic quality against laughable [background] comedy.

> Happiness as future destiny.

> Work. Loneliness.[17]

In his settings, Viktor Simov sought to evoke an oppressive provincial milieu in which 'colours fade, thoughts become debased, energy gets smothered in a dressing-gown, ardour is stifled by a housecoat, talent dries up like a plant without water'.[18] He recalled:

> The director set me to embody the provincial spirit, its essence, its core, in one private residence on Dvoryanskaya Street. In it, we should see a reflection of Russia, in all its provincial banality. In the Chekhovian provinces they don't live, but suffocate, they don't work, but toil and strive (in their dreams) to go 'to Moscow, to Moscow'. It was necessary to show such a province, from which, indeed, all that remains is to escape without looking back.[19]

The design concept, then, reinforced the sisters' desire and need to escape this provincial life and go to Moscow. The set was almost an agent in the drama. It was not simply realistic; it created meaning, symbolically. Mariana Stroeva has argued that the banality of daily life became 'an active, aggressive force' in the production:

> It almost forcibly eats into people's lives, gradually enveloping everything, even the most intimate sides of their lives; it dogs all their actions, at every step it stifles their dreams; with indifferent contempt it takes away their energy, their aspirations.[20]

The company rehearsed the play, but for some reason it 'did not live, it seemed boring and long'.[21] They tried playing it fast, as if it was a vaudeville, but as a result it was hard even to understand what the characters were saying. Rehearsals came to a halt; 'the actors stopped in mid-sentence, ceased to act, seeing no sense in the work. They had no faith in the director or in each other.' It was at this moment, as they sat in silence, that Stanislavski heard a scratching sound, like a mouse, which for some reason 'reminded me of home; I felt warm inside, I saw truth, life, and my intuition began to work'. He suddenly realised what was missing in the production:

> Chekhov's characters came to life. They do not bathe in their own sorrow. Quite the opposite; they seek joy, laughter, courage; they want to live and not stagnate. I felt the truth in this view of Chekhov's heroes, this encouraged me, and I intuitively under-stood what had to be done.[22]

This, it seems, was a turning point in Stanislavski's approach to Chekhov. As we have seen, he had tended to emphasise the characters' suffering, and the sad monotony of their lives; but he now realised the danger in this approach. The actors must not 'bathe' in the characters' sorrow; rather the active striving of the characters must be stressed. When he was rehearsing a revival of *The Seagull* in 1917, Stanislavski reproached the cast for acting in some clichéd idea of a 'Chekhovian' style. He criticised them for 'Chekhovian whining'. Instead, he stressed the characters' cheerfulness, vitality and courage. He said that Treplev 'decides to commit suicide not because he does not want to live; he wants to live terribly, clutches at everything in order to become stronger in life, but everything falls through. ... His through-line of action is to live, to live beautifully, to long for Moscow, Moscow!' Chekhov, Stanislavski argued, 'was active, he wasn't a pessimist. Life in

Plate 3 Three Sisters at the Moscow Art Theatre (1901). Act IV: Stanislavski as Vershinin with Olga Knipper as Masha.

the 'eighties created Chekhov's heroes. Chekhov himself loved life, and longed for the best life, like all his heroes.'[23]

However much Stanislavski tried to emphasise this element of 'active striving' in the production of *Three Sisters*, he recognised that, for audiences, the play was filled with 'a desperate melancholy'.[24] When Aleksandr Blok saw the production, it left him 'completely shattered. … The final Act took place to the sound of hysterical cries. … Many wept, and I almost did so too.'[25] Critics attacked the play for its 'desperate pessimism'. It was said to infect you with 'a mood of hopelessness and gloomy despondency' and depict a 'grey, despondent life'.[26] Leonid Andreev, however, wrote:

> Don't believe that *Three Sisters* is a pessimistic thing, giving rise to despair and pointless pining. It is a light, lovely play. Go and see it, sympathise with the sisters, weep with them for their bitter lot and catch their invocatory cry on the wing: 'To Moscow! To Moscow! Towards the light! Towards life, freedom and happiness!'[27]

The Cherry Orchard

The common view of Stanislavski's production of *The Cherry Orchard* is summed up by Viktor Borovsky, who has described it as a 'wake for a defunct age' – suffused with nostalgia for a vanishing way of life.[28] Western and Russian critics have maintained that Stanislavski did not understand the play, and turned a comedy into a tragedy. Thus, Rolf-Dieter Kluge has written: 'Stanislavski reinforced the melancholic or even tragic subtext in *The Cherry Orchard* and reduced the element of comedy.'[29] This notion is based largely on a letter Stanislavski wrote to Chekhov after his first reading of the play. Chekhov had insisted the play was 'not a drama, but a comedy, in places even a farce'[30] – but Stanislavski's initial response was: 'It is not a comedy or a farce, as you wrote – it is a tragedy.'[31] But if we examine Stanislavski's production plan, we will find that the common view of the production is, in fact, a myth. In fact – perhaps in response to Chekhov's comments – the director treated the play as 'a comedy, in places even a farce'. In a later letter, Stanislavski wrote: 'It seems that the whole play will be in a different tone to its predecessors. Everything will be light, cheerful ... In short, we want to paint everything in watercolours.'[32]

The comedy element in the production plan is apparent from the first entrance of Epikhodov. He wipes a window with a cloth, and then immediately wipes his face with the same cloth. He gets his coat caught in the back of a chair, so that when he gets up, the chair immediately falls over. At the start of Act II, he is trying to impress both Dunyasha and Yasha – but unbeknown to him, he is standing on his own hat. Indeed, he has got his foot caught in it, so when he moves, he drags the hat along with him. The character makes a dramatic exit, declaring: 'Now I know what to do with my gun', but this is undermined in the production plan when we hear a crash off-stage: it seems he has tripped over a tree root, or run into a branch and fallen over.

Laurence Senelick has argued that by casting himself as Gaev and Knipper as Ranevskaya, and a lesser actor [Leonidov] as Lopakhin, Stanislavski changed the balance of forces in the play. The audience's sympathy was 'pegged to Ranevskaya and Gaev from the outset'; the play became a tragedy of dispossession and loss.[33] And yet, it is clear from the production plan that Stanislavski actually viewed the gentry with irony and gently mocking humour. He emphasised their refusal to face their problems. In Act I, as Lopakhin raises the issue of the sale of the orchard, the family are eating their supper:

The bread is buttered, the sausage and cheese are cut up. They eat chicken with their fingers, and break the bread by hand. ...

Lopakhin is determined, but very concerned about the fate of the inhabitants of the house. He tries to persuade them by the force of his words. The others are outraged and listen with disapproval. They are outraged by Lopakhin's barbaric idea, but they avoid addressing the real issue, for they know full well that none of them would allow such a thing.

They find wine in the basket and drink it. Lopakhin does not decline a glass.[34]

Stanislavski includes a child's table and children's chairs in the set for Act I, emphaising the theme of childhood – and also ironically commenting on the characters. The meal is set, for example, on the nursery table, and Gaev sits on one of the small chairs. (Comically, Simeonov-Pishchik also tries to sit on one of them, but it is clear that either the chair is too small, or Pishchik is too fat.) Meanwhile, Firs proceeds to attend at this little meal 'as if at a formal dinner'[35]; a comment, surely, on how low the family has now fallen from the wealth of its former days.

Stanislavski shows the ease with which Ranevskaya passes 'from tears to laughter, from light-heartedness to despair'.[36] 'Am I really here?' she cries in Act I – and leaps on to the sofa like a child, then immediately jumps off it and runs around the room. She kisses Gaev, the nursery table, the cupboard; then she suddenly freezes, nestled against the cupboard, and cries.[37] Throughout, Stanislavski emphasizes the 'Parisian' influence on her behaviour. (Nemirovich told Olga Knipper she must understand *above all* the two contrasting aspects of the role, or rather, of Ranevskaya's soul: *Paris and the cherry orchard*'.[38]) When the character enters in Act II, Stanislavski notes that she might be happy walking on a boulevard in Paris, but not among Russian villages. She 'has the Parisian habit of frequently getting out her powder-compact and mirror to powder herself and make herself beautiful'.[39] Thus, we can sense that she does not really belong in this world – and will not stay here long. In Act III, when she says to Trofimov, 'And I suppose I'm beneath love', Stanislavski notes:

Either from coquettishness or nervousness, she sinks her head on the table, and stands there in a coquettish pose. You can sense the French woman in her. (Anyway Olga Leonardovna [Knipper] must find the tone of a French woman.) Involuntarily you sense how she has spent her evenings in restaurants in Paris, sitting around a disorderly table till midnight. There is something in her of the Bohemian life, as it is lived on the Parisian boulevards. And now – her nerves are on edge, as they are after a tiring supper – she half-laughs, half-cries, or rather, she does both at the same time. This mood must be played with a nervous dissoluteness.[40]

Thus, even while showing her distress at the possible loss of the orchard, Stanislavski retained a certain critical distance towards the character, and ensured the audience did too.

Stanislavski as Gaev succeeded in creating 'a figure whose humour causes the heart to contract, like the humour in Gogol's *Overcoat'*.[41] He wrote:

I think Gaev must be lightweight, like his sister. He does not even notice the way he is talking. He understands when it's all been said. It seems I have found the tone for Gaev. With me, he comes across as something of an aristocrat, but a little eccentric.[42]

His critical view of the character is apparent in the production plan. After the 'bookcase' speech in Act I, he notes: 'A sad note can be detected. It is the sadness that he is an empty and irredeemable person.'[43] When Gaev later begs Anya's forgiveness for the things he has said about her mother, he seems 'pitiful, just like a child that has done something wrong'.[44]

Then, he tries to reassure them that the orchard will be saved. Stanislavski observed that he is so convincing and business-like that you could really believe he could be a bank director. But then he puts a sweet in his mouth. 'That is a wonderful touch, and instantly demolishes everything he has said. All trust in him is undermined.'[45] Thus, Stanislavski used irony and humour to point up the contradictions in the character's behaviour. Kugel in fact criticised Stanislavski for the element of irony he injected into Gaev. (The critic saw the character as a sad and despondent person, who makes others sad and despondent too.)

In Act IV, after Ranevskaya's final exit, Stanislavski's Gaev remained on stage. According to eye-witnesses to the American tour in 1923, his exit became the emotional climax of the production. The character turned to speak to his sister, but she had already left.

He is about to break into violent sobbing when suddenly he stuffs his handkerchief into his mouth like a schoolboy caught laughing. As he turns his back and goes out we see the twitch of the big

Plate 4   The Cherry Orchard at the Moscow Art Theatre (1904). Act II.

shoulders and it is almost more than an impressionable playgoer can bear.[46]

Sharon Carnicke has argued that leaving the character on stage in this way at the end turns the play into 'Gaev's personal tragedy'; this heartrending final moment moves the audience to tears and confirms Stanislavski's tragic reading of the play.[47] But this simply does not accord with the ironic treatment of Gaev in the rest of the play. In fact, it is clear that, in the final scene, Stanislavski was aiming for a tragi-comic effect. When he stuffed his handkerchief in his mouth like a schoolboy, the moment hit the audience half-way 'between wind and water, laughter and tears'. Stanislavski reported that he received praise from Chekhov himself for the staging of this scene.[48] It demonstrated, in fact, an awareness of Chekhov's humour, ambiguity and irony, which was so missing in the staging of the climactic scene in *Uncle Vanya*.

The treatment of Lopakhin in the production plan, while containing elements of irony, is less satirical than the portrayal of Gaev and Ranevskaya. In fact, he emerges as the most psychologically complex character – a man torn by internal contradictions. (This is most apparent in the scene when Lopakhin returns from the auction,

Plate 5 The Cherry Orchard at the Moscow Art Theatre (1904). Act IV.

and we see, in turn, the pride of a businessman; the 'hidden anger and bitterness he feels over the humiliations he suffered as a child'; and 'the honourable and good man, who tenderly loves Ranevskaya's whole family, and her especially'.[49]) Chekhov at first expressed some reservations about the decision to cast Leonid Leonidov in the role. Nevertheless, the actor was a leading member of the company; his other roles included Vershinin in *Three Sisters*. (He was, then, hardly a 'second-rater' as Senelick suggests.[50]) Leonidov once asked Chekhov how he should play the role. He replied: 'In yellow boots.' After one of the last rehearsals, Chekhov came to speak to him.

> I offered him a seat. He sat down. He was silent. But it was clear from his eyes that he was satisfied. And quietly, looking over his pince-nez, in a mellow bass voice, he said: 'Listen, it's very good now, and Olga [Knipper] is also good, only a little young.' I was very happy, hearing his approval, all the more so because Anton Pavlovich was generally sparing in his praise.[51]

Kugel found the character, on paper, 'completely lifeless and incomprehensible'; he simply did not fit into the critic's conception of the playwright's work: 'However much Chekhov would like to persuade us that this is supposedly a representative of the new, cheerful, conscious, active beginnings of life – it is not believable.'[52] Nevertheless, Kugel said the actor's performance was 'excellent' and gave the character some internal logic. His strongest objections were reserved for Vasili Kachalov's performance as Trofimov. He felt the actor damaged Chekhov even more than Stanislavski. He objected that the performance was too full of enthusiasm and *joie de vivre*. The scene at the end of Act II, when Trofimov persuades Anya that she should abandon the orchard, was full of life and youthful enthusiasm. But Kugel wanted to see the character portrayed in 'all his uselessness', as a 'good-for-nothing' (*nedotepa*), and all his idealism and efforts to understand the world exposed as futile. The critic objected that he could not discern, in the performance, any trace of 'Chekhovian melancholy' – and, indeed, this seemed to be missing from the whole production.[53]

Kugel's review in fact shows that Stanislavski's production was far from a tragic elegy for a vanishing past, as has been suggested. In fact, as Stroeva suggests, 'an optimistic call to the future could be clearly heard and felt, as well as an ironic mockery of the people of the past'.[54]

Stanislavski confessed that when the production opened it was far from ready; it 'enjoyed only an average success, and we blamed ourselves for not being able, from the very first, to portray the most important, beautiful and precious qualities of the play'. Nemirovich said that it was heavy and ponderous; only in time did it achieve a 'lace-like, graceful' quality.[55] A month later, the production was performed in St Petersburg. In advance, Kugel wrote a series of articles entitled 'The Melancholy of *The Cherry Orchard*'.[56] The play, he felt, captured the 'essence' of Chekhov. He saw it as a quasi-symbolic drama of hopelessness and despondency. 'They live, the inhabitants of *The Cherry Orchard*, as if half-asleep, shadowy, on the border between the real and the mystical. They bury life.' They are condemned (like the characters in Sartre's play, *Huis Clos*) to inhabit a house 'from which there is no exit and in which there is no light. Through the wall a ray of light scarcely breaks through – that is the limit of our horizon. From the outside can be heard the dull sound of an axe – that is our entire knowledge of the world lying beyond the limits of the boarded-up house.'[57]

Kugel was astonished when he saw the Art Theatre production, and the play emerged as 'light, funny, cheerful'.[58] Jokingly, he suggested he might now have to write a new series of articles, entitled 'Riotously Jolly Life in *The Cherry Orchard*'.[59] But he saw this as a *betrayal* of the author: the production lacked the pessimism, the sense of hopelessness and tragedy, which he had defined as the essence of Chekhov. Knipper reported his comments to Chekhov: 'He thinks that we are playing a vaudeville, when we should be playing a tragedy, and we haven't understood Chekhov. There, you see.'[60]

'Unnecessary' truth? Naturalism and the Art Theatre

The Chekhov productions established the reputation of the Art Theatre; the seagull became the theatre's emblem. Other theatres began to copy Stanislavski's productions. But in 1902 the company came under attack. The symbolist poet, Valeri Bryusov, wrote an article called 'Unnecessary Truth', in which he accused the theatre of propounding a form of crude naturalism.

> Contemporary theatres strive to reproduce life as truthfully as possible. They think they are fulfilling their function well if everything on stage is as it is in reality. The actors try to speak as they would in a drawing room, the set-designers paint landscapes from nature, the costume-designers cut their costumes to accord with archaeological data.[61]

It was time, Bryusov declared, 'for the theatre to stop imitating reality'.[62] He called for a *stylised* theatre. Stanislavski, however, maintained that the Art Theatre had *never* sought naturalism on the stage. The aim was always what he called 'spiritual realism', an *inner* rather than an 'outer' truth.

Unfortunately, Bryusov's article in many ways set the terms of the debate for years to come. He had labelled the Art Theatre 'naturalistic', and the label stuck. Stanislavski observed that this misunderstanding had taken root, and could not be dislodged, despite the fact that the theatre had passed through many different stages of experiment and development, and had explored a variety of theatrical styles.[63]

Others followed Bryusov's lead and attacked the Art Theatre. (Nemirovich observed: 'Everywhere people talk so much about the crisis in the theatre, symbolism, stylisation, realism, and so on. At all the big debates, they always start by cursing the Art Theatre.'[64]) Vsevolod Meyerhold – who played Treplev in *The Seagull* – became perhaps the company's most persistent and vocal opponent. He condemned what he saw as the excessive naturalism of some productions, the attempt to present '*an exact representation of life*'.[65] Our view of Stanislavski's production of *The Cherry Orchard* has been heavily influenced by an article Meyerhold wrote, 'The Naturalistic Theatre and the Theatre of Mood' (published 1908). He criticised, for example, the attempt in the production to create a 'real' environment in Act II, with 'real' bridges and a 'real' chapel (and yet the 'sky' was made from two big pieces of blue canvas with tulle frills). It is true that Stanislavski's description of the setting (in a letter to Chekhov) appears naturalistic:

> A little chapel, a ravine, a neglected cemetery in the middle of a small oasis of trees in the steppe. ... In the distance, you can see the sparkle of a stream, and a farmstead on a slight rise. Telegraph poles, and a railway bridge. ... Before sunset the town will be briefly visible. Towards the end of the Act, mist; it will rise especially thickly from a ditch downstage. A concert of frogs, and a corncrake at the very end.

However, it is clear from the production plan for Act II that Stanislavski was aiming less for a 'naturalistic' interpretation than a lyrical evocation of nature, a genre painting 'in the style of Levitan' (a Russian landscape artist).[66] Naturalistic elements were combined in a way that was, ultimately, *non-naturalistic*.

The 'pastoral' element in the production actually began at the end of Act I. Stanislavski reinforced the lyrical quality in Trofimov's words: 'Anya. My sun. My spring', through sound and lighting effects: 'The shepherd plays on his pipe; we hear the sounds of horses snorting, the lowing of cows, the bleating of sheep, the bellowing of a herd. Birds twitter. The sun rises and dazzles the spectators.'[67]

This is the opening of Act II in the production plan:

> It is nearly evening. Sunset. Summer. Hay-making. Heat. The steppe. The town cannot yet be seen in the mist. Some kind of small bird calls persistently, monotonously. Now and again a gust of wind brushes the leaves and causes a rustling. In the distance a field of rye sways, like waves (the reflection of a spotlight on a metal sheet). Occasionally a withered branch falls to the ground. There are people walking through the wood, and we hear the crack of snapping twigs.
>
> A corncrake, frogs, songs, mist from the trap-door.
>
> Dunyasha and Yasha sit on the steps and Epikhodov on a grave-stone. There are many mosquitoes and flies. Dunyasha and Yasha swat mosquitoes on each others' hands and faces. It's their way of flirting.

The sounds of nature are drowned out by the discordant sound of the characters' singing:

> As the curtain rises, Yasha and Dunyasha sing a duet, and Epikhodov tries to join in, but he doesn't succeed. They sing very badly, as none of them has an ear for music.[68]

The lyricism of the setting forms a majestic backdrop to the comic fooling of the characters in the foreground. This, in fact, might be seen as the dominant note in Stanislavski's staging of the Act. Comic scenes are punctuated by moments of stillness and reflection in the heat of the late afternoon. For example, when Anya and Varya enter, they join Ranevskaya, who is sitting on a haystack. They embrace and kiss and even slobber over each other. 'They grunt and make inarticulate noises, because they can't breathe, and laugh when a kiss lands on a ticklish spot, for example the ear. ... The whole thing ends, of course, in a crescendo of tickling and noise.' They are covered in hay, and there is 'general laughter and tender affection'.[69] Shortly after this, however, the mood becomes dreamy and lethargic. Lopakhin's line, which follows, might be seen as the leitmotif of Stanislavski's interpretation of the scene: 'Sometimes, when I can't sleep, I think: "Lord, you gave us enormous forests, immense fields, the broadest horizons. Living here, we should really be giants".' Immediately after this, Stanislavski interposes the following, extraordinary scene: 'The air is still, only the bird sings. They are all silent.' A new swarm of mosquitoes descends: 'From time to time you hear the slap of hand on forehead, cheeks, hands. They all sit thinking, and swat mosquitoes.'[70]

Act III

The director's overall conception of Act II is certainly not naturalistic; it moves the play towards a form of pastoral comedy. The lyrical, pastoral elements in the production plan seem, in fact, excessive at times; Stanislavski intended, for example, to bring on a choir of peasant women at one point, singing as they return from hay-making; their colourful sarafans, their rakes and shining scythes, would be glimpsed on the horizon.[71]

Meyerhold argued that in Act III, the leitmotif is 'Ranevskaya's premonition of an approaching storm'.

> Everybody around is behaving stupidly: there they are, so self-satisfied, dancing to the monotonous tinkling of the Jewish band, spinning round, as if in a nightmarish vortex, in a tedious modern dance devoid of enthusiasm, passion, grace, even lust. They do not know that the ground on which they are dancing is vanishing under their feet. Ranevskaya alone foresees Disaster, and waits for it; she rushes around, then stops the revolving carousel for a moment, this nightmare dance of marionettes in a puppet show.

A 'counterpoint' is established between, on the one hand, 'the lamentations of Ranevskaya with her presentiment of approaching Disaster (a crucial element in the new mystical drama of Chekhov); on the other hand, the puppet show'. (Not for nothing, Meyerhold suggests, 'does Chekhov make Charlotta dance amongst the "philistines" in a costume favoured in the puppet theatre – a black tail-coat and checked trousers'.[72])

Meyerhold saw the play in quasi-mystical terms, as an image of horror in the face of approaching death. He wrote to Chekhov:

Your play is abstract, like a Tchaikovsky symphony. Above all, a director must capture its sound. In the third Act, against a background of the stupid stamping of feet – this stamping must be heard – enters Horror, completely unobserved by anyone. 'The cherry orchard is sold.' They dance on. 'Sold.' They dance on. And so on to the end. When you read the play, the third Act produces the same effect as the ringing in the ears of the sick man in your story *Typhus*. Like an itch. General mirth, in which can be heard the sounds of death. In this Act there is something terrible, something Maeterlinckian.[73]

Meyerhold opposed this 'symbolic' reading to the Art Theatre's supposedly 'naturalistic' interpretation of the play. But in fact, as we will see, these 'symbolic' overtones *were already present in Stanislavski's production*.

Meyerhold specifically criticised Stanislavski's staging of the scene in which Charlotta performs conjuring tricks. This, he said, should emerge from the background of dancing only for a moment before merging with it once more. But the Art Theatre turned the conjuring into a major sequence; meanwhile, the spectator lost sight of the leit-motif, 'Ranevskaya's premonition of an approaching storm'.

Let us again examine Stanislavski's production plan. Here is the description of the ball:

> The ball is a complete failure. There are few people. Despite all efforts, it has not been possible to get more people to come. They have barely managed to drag out the Station-master and the Post Office Clerk. A soldier (the son of one of the servants) in a coarse military uniform (ordinary, not ceremonial),[b] a steward in a jacket and red tie, a young boy (the old woman's son) who is dancing with the tall and thin daughter of the priest's wife, and even Dunyasha – all are allowed to come to the ball. Half of the dancers do not know the figures for the quadrilles, never mind the *grand rond*.[74]

The characters in the scene are given a realistic base. (For the non-speaking roles, Stanislavski created individual character biographies to help the actors.) However, the staging is clearly intended to go beyond realism. The dance is comic, absurd, even grotesque: a young boy

---

b   The note about the soldier is crossed out in pencil.

dances with a tall and thin woman; half of the dancers do not know the steps, and so on. There is a sense that the characters are almost 'puppet-like' grotesques.

Despite the music and dancing, Stanislavski notes that a kind of 'stillness' reigns throughout the scene. As soon as each dance finishes, the guests do not know what to do; they sit frozen, bored. 'You might think they had all got together for a funeral.'[75] Ranevskaya enters, and Stanislavski notes that she is nervous. In fact, he stresses her nervousness throughout. This *is* the leitmotif, or the 'through-line' in the Act; the ball forms a grotesque background to it. Charlotta is described as the only person who is genuinely enjoying the occasion. Stanislavski emphasises her role as clown, a kind of macabre court-jester at this crazy feast. (There is a photograph of the actor, E.P. Muratova, dressed as Charlotta in a black tail-coat, bow-tie and top hat, a monocle in her eye; she looks almost puppet-like.) It is true that Stanislavski elaborates her magic tricks into a major sequence (his notes last for several pages). But it is emphasised that her conjuring is only a temporary distraction. Ranevskaya forgets her anxieties for a time and is excited like a child. In fact the sequence only highlights, by contrast, the ghastliness of the rest of the ball. As soon as it is finished, suddenly 'all life has been extinguished'.[76] The guests sit a long time in their places and do not know what to do. Ranevskaya becomes agitated again, and Varya is downcast.

When Ranevskaya hears a rumour that the orchard has been sold, she is distraught. The guests continue dancing in the inner room – a counterpoint to her feelings. She dances with Pishchik, but she is so preoccupied that 'she does not even know what she is doing'. She has a worried and nervous expression. Finally she sits down, distracted, and drinks tea; then she freezes again; 'her face is full of anxiety and she stares continuously at a single point. She is motionless for some time, then suddenly she drinks her tea again energetically.'[77]

Shortly after this, Charlotta enters, dressed in men's clothes – actually Gaev's. She runs through the room, Stanislavski notes, like a clown across the circus arena. Her actions seem particularly bizarre at this moment: she performs unusual *entrechats* and then a cancan with a police officer. Ranevskaya has been awaiting Gaev's return; now, Charlotta's entrance in his clothes prefigures in a grotesque way Gaev's own entrance, from the sale, which follows shortly.

After Lopakhin knocks down the chandelier and says, 'I can pay for everything', the doors to the inner salon are closed, and dancing resumes in there. We hear the heavy stamping of feet, and the vulgar cries of the dancers. In the billiard room, the game is played wildly; the

clacking of billiard balls can be heard. Anya and Trofimov lead
Ranevskaya away, so the stage is empty. The stamping of feet is so
loud that glasses on the table rattle, and a piece of plaster falls down
from the ceiling and lies broken on the ground. We might recall
Meyerhold's words here:

> In the third Act, against a background of the stupid stamping of
> feet – this stamping must be heard – enters Horror, completely
> unobserved by anyone. 'The cherry orchard is sold.' They dance
> on. 'Sold.' They dance on. And so on to the end.

We can now see that this terrifying sound of stamping, an omen of
destruction, was in fact *Stanislavski's* invention.

The director, then, was clearly very aware of the 'symbolic' dimension in the play. He suggested to Chekhov that Act IV should be set in
the nursery, now stripped of possessions. As Vera Gottlieb suggests:
'The visual image here provides a very strong sense of reality – of the
passage of time and of the characters' ownership and relationship to
the house.'[78] But it is also *symbolic* – suggesting desolation and emptiness. The setting – like the play itself – could be read both realistically
and symbolically. The old furniture was covered in shrould-like wraps.
The shutters were closed, which meant the room was 'shut off from the
trees, the light and the world outside'.[79] It was a kind of waiting room
or limbo 'on the border between the real and the mystical' (Kugel); a
fragile and crumbling shell awaiting destruction and obliteration.

We have been wrong, then, to follow Meyerhold's lead, and label
Stanislavski's production 'naturalistic'. Rather, it hovered 'between
realism and symbolism'.[80]

'Conspicuous' details

Chekhov once insisted that the author 'is the owner of a play and not
the actors'. His friend, Nikolai Leikin, had argued that if an author is
present during rehearsals, he or she only disturbs the production and
hampers the actors. But Chekhov replied: 'If you reduce the author's
participation to nothing, then God knows what will happen.'[81] He told
Knipper it was essential for him to attend rehearsals for *Three
Sisters*;[82] but in the event, he could only attend some early sessions
before the cold weather, which affected his health, drove him out of
Moscow. However, it seems he decided to ignore the cold when it came
to *The Cherry Orchard*. He arrived in Moscow early December, 1903.
In a letter he wrote that he was at rehearsals from 12 o'clock until 5

o'clock, 'and when there are no rehearsals, I cough, and my wife doesn't let me out of the house'.[83] However, the records seem to suggest that he in fact only attended four or five rehearsals in all. Tensions soon emerged between the writer and the director. Simov recalled that on one occasion, Stanislavski,

> dissatisfied with a scene, slated it and, as was his custom, rose from the director's table and showed the actors how to do it; not content with the result, he again demonstrated the method of acting he wanted. And after this, Anton Pavlovich, in his turn not approving of the suggested style, made an observation from his seat (he always sat somewhere further off, out of sight). Carried away by his own plan, the director did not comment on the author's remark. Then Chekhov got up and left. This produced an extraordinarily painful impression on everyone; there was a pause, the rehearsal was broken off, and we began to discuss how to repair the situation, all the more so since we sincerely loved Anton Pavlovich.[84]

Stanislavski felt that the play was 'not yet blooming' in rehearsal. 'The blossoms had only just begun to appear when the author arrived and messed everything up for us.'[85] Nemirovich took his side; they both seemed to feel that the problem was that 'authors don't understand the theatre'. Finally, Nemirovich told Chekhov: 'Go home, because you are only disturbing everyone.'[86]

Subsequently, Nemirovich reflected that, in rehearsal, Chekhov had perhaps encountered 'the crossing of those two trends, which were always strong in the Art Theatre – both strong, both complimenting each other, and both impeding each other'. Olga Radishcheva suggests he meant the clash between 'external vividness' and 'internal essence'.[87] Nemirovich himself felt that, in staging Chekhov, Stanislavski tended to get carried away by his excessive love of details and vivid 'external' effects – and this sometimes obscured the 'essence' of Chekhov's work. For example, Stanislavski wanted the character of Astrov in Act I of *Uncle Vanya* to have a handkerchief on his head to keep off mosquitoes. Nemirovich objected:

> I am unable to accept this detail. I can tell you for certain that it cannot possibly please Chekhov, a man whose taste and work I know well. I can tell you for certain that this detail does not introduce anything new. I wager that it will merely be numbered among those 'excesses' which only irritate, and have no benefit either for the cause or the task you are undertaking. This is one of those

details that simply 'upsets the geese'. Finally, even from the point of view of real life it is – forced. In a word, I cannot find one serious argument in favour of this *conspicuous* detail.[88]

When Nemirovich saw rehearsals for *Three Sisters*, he felt the production was

> overloaded with ideas, well-conceived and executed with talent, but embellished with an excess of detail. I realised that the actors were not yet used to them, but all the same they seemed too much to me. I am talking about all the moves, the noises, the exclamations, the external effects, etc., etc. It seemed to me almost impossible to create a harmonious, complete whole out of the fragments of separate episodes, thoughts, moods, the characteristics and developments in every character, without damaging the stage-worthiness of the play, or the clear expression of each of these details.

In other words, the abundance of details was obscuring the writer's work. 'But little by little, after eliminating a very small number of details, a sense of the whole started to become clear'.[89]

But it was clearly the excess of details in the productions that so irritated Chekhov. When he heard that Stanislavski was planning to add a concert of frogs and corncrakes in Act II of *The Cherry Orchard*, he wrote pointing out that 'hay-making normally takes place from 20–25 June. By that time, the corncrake is no longer heard, the frogs are also silent. Only the oriole is heard.'[90] Stanislavski also wanted to introduce a train in the distance: 'Let us have a train go by with little puffs of smoke in one of the pauses. That might work splendidly.'[91] Chekhov wrote to Knipper: 'Konst. Serg. [Stanislavski] wants to bring in a train on stage in Act II but I think we must stop him doing it.'[92] He told Stanislavski: 'If you can show the train without noise, without a single sound, then go ahead.'[93]

When Chekhov saw the production, he declared that Stanislavski had ruined his play.[94] 'I can't understand it', he told a friend, 'either the play is no good, or the actors don't understand me. ... The way they are doing the play now, it is impossible to put *The Cherry Orchard* on.'[95] In the days that followed, he tried to correct several details that he felt were inaccurate or simply wrong. S.G. Skitalets found him at home conducting a 'rather business-like' conversation with Nemirovich and other members of the theatre. Chekhov, Skitalets recalled, pointed out 'several small, minor faults' – where

Dunyasha should powder herself, for example, and what the sound of the snapping string in the second and fourth Acts must be like.[96] These points might have seemed 'minor', and yet they clearly mattered a great deal to Chekhov. He was angered by the fact that the theatre seemed unable to follow his stage directions closely. Shortly afterwards, he wrote in irritation:

> Tell Nemirovich that the sound in Acts II and IV of *The Cherry Orchard* must be shorter, much shorter, and seem far away. How petty, they simply cannot cope with a trifle, with a sound, although everything is written down so clearly in the play.[97]

Chekhov's anger, then, was not simply caused by the 'final ravages' of his illness, as Benedetti suggests.[98] He was infuriated by the way Stanislavski seemed unable to stage his plays as he had written them, but continued to remake them in his own image. On 24 April 1904, the writer met Evtikhi Karpov – the same Karpov who was responsible for the first production of *The Seagull* at the Aleksandrinksi Theatre. Karpov had recently seen in Yalta a production of *The Cherry Orchard*, by a company from Sevastapol. His memories of the production make amusing reading:

> On the poster it said in large print that the play would be performed in the style of the Art Theatre production, under the supervision of the author himself. I bought a ticket and at eight o'clock set off for the theatre.
>
> An hour passed, an hour and a half, and the production still hadn't started. The audience was grumbling. Some backstage gossips spread the rumour that they were waiting for the author. The audience was agitated.
>
> At last at about ten o'clock, the curtain went up. Wretched, torn scenery. A pitiful set. Several Viennese chairs. A brand new and cheap cupboard, evidently on hire. In the window, a branch, sprinkled with large pieces of paper, had to stand for the cherry orchard. The set was typical for a provincial theatre from the sticks.
>
> The whole 'production in the style of the Art Theatre' manifested itself in the way that, from behind the scenes, the assistant director whistled, cawed, cuckooed, rattled, croaked and squeaked throughout the entire play, drowning out the words of the actors with the sounds of birds and frogs. Only he could not, however much he tried, drown out the prompter, who literally crawled out of the prompt-box to give the actors the text of the play. The

prompter drowned the voices of the actors and the singing of the birds and the croaking of the frogs with his hoarse bass.

The result was something incredibly chaotic. The actors, unable to hear the prompter, rushed around the stage, muddled and deafened by the sounds of 'nature as it awakens'. Not knowing their roles, they garbled the text mercilessly, got confused, and made nonsensical pauses, as if 'living through the mood'.

The actor playing Gaev resembled in his appearance and costume an assistant in a chemist's shop. Two actors, playing Ranevskaya and Anya, spoke with a burr, and pronounced their 'r's' in the French manner, lisped, swallowed whole phrases, charging and scurrying around the stage, like mad cats.

The audience, filling the theatre from top to bottom, was evidently at a loss. From the back voices were heard from time to time: 'Louder! What? I can't hear! Prompter, don't yell! Birds, shush!' and so on. I felt hurt and ashamed for Chekhov. After the third Act I left the theatre with a headache, vexed and indignant.

Soon after this momentous production I went to Autka [where Chekhov lived] to see Anton Pavlovich, determined not to say a word about this *Cherry Orchard*.

Chekhov, it was clear, was unwell. He shrugged his shoulders, rubbed his hands nervously, and coughed frequently. We had not spoken two words when Anton Pavlovich began to talk about the production.

'They tell me you saw *The Cherry Orchard*?' Anton Pavlovich asked, not looking at me.

'Yes ... '

'How they've ruined it! It's an outrage! It still says on the poster that they are acting under my supervision. And I've never set eyes on them. It's scandalous! They all want to ape the Art Theatre. And all in vain. There, the whole complex production is achieved by incredible work, by the expenditure of a colossal amount of time, by loving attention to every detail. They can do it ... This lot have put in so many noises, they say, that the whole text disappeared. Half of the words were inaudible ... And in the Art Theatre, all these theatrical details distract the spectator, stop him listening, overshadow the author. And here ... I can imagine what it was like ... You know, I would like them to perform my work quite simply, primitively. As in the old days – a room; on the forestage, a sofa, chairs ... And with good actors. And that's all. No birds, no theatrical mood. I would really like to see my play performed like that. I'd like to know, would my play collapse? That is very interesting! Perhaps it would collapse. And perhaps not. Who knows ... '[99]

Some weeks later, on 2 July 1904, Chekhov died.

Production notes

Uncle Vanya, directed by Stanislavski and Nemirovich-Danchenko. The Moscow Art Theatre; first performance, 26 October 1899.

Three Sisters, directed by Stanislavski, Nemirovich-Danchenko and V.V. Luzhski. The Moscow Art Theatre; first performance, 31 January 1901.

The Cherry Orchard, directed by Stanislavski and Nemirovich-Danchenko. The Moscow Art Theatre; first performance, 17 January 1904.

3 'The line of intuition and feeling'

Chekhov and the Stanislavski 'system'

When Stanislavski staged his Chekhov productions, he had not even begun to develop his 'system' of acting; but he actually saw the writer's work as an important influence on his thinking, helping to pave the way for the 'system'. He declared:

> Chekhov gave that inner truth to the art of the stage which served as the foundation for what was later called the Stanislavski System, which must be approached through Chekhov, or which serves as a bridge to the approach to Chekhov.[1]

It is wrong, Stanislavski argued, to act Chekhov superficially, 'to play the external form of a role, without creating the inner form and inner life'. It is wrong 'to try to *act*, to "*present*" the characters. You must *be* – that is, *you must live, exist*, following the deep, inner, spiritual line of development.' Stanislavski called this 'the line of intuition and feeling'.[2]

Staging *The Seagull*, he discovered ways to help the actors to 'live' on the stage. The 'external' elements of the production influenced the actors, and helped them to find 'inner truth'. For example, Stanislavski argued that the 'mood' of the production was intended less to impress the audience, than to affect the *actors*. Surroundings 'have an influence on our feelings', he wrote.

> And this happens on the stage as well as in real life. ... In the hands of a talented director, all these scenic means and effects are not used to make a coarse imitation of life, but are transformed into artistic and creative devices. When the external production of a play is inwardly tied up with the spiritual life of the characters, it often acquires even more significance on the stage than in real life. The mood which is produced, if it meets the needs of the play, is a

wonderful help to the actor in finding the inner life of a role. It influences his feelings and his whole state of mind.[3]

Without the various lighting and sound effects, 'it would have been difficult to create inner truth on the stage, to create true feelings and emotions among the external, coarse, obtrusive falsehoods of the theatre'. In other words, the 'mood' of the production helped the actors to become absorbed in the 'world' of the play. The 'atmospheric' elements of light and sound acted as a kind of trigger, touching subconscious emotional chords:

> They felt external truth, and intimate memories of their own lives rose again in their souls, enticing from them those feelings which Chekhov was talking about. Then the actor ceased to act, and began to live the life of the play, became the character. ... *It was a creative miracle*.[4]

The sets, designed by Viktor Simov, were on the surface very realistic – but they were also very atmospheric. ('Simov understood my plans and purpose of stage direction, and began to help me marvellously towards the creation of the mood.'[5]) The set for Act I, for example, was so 'realistic' that a 5 year-old boy, at one performance, turned to his mother and said: 'Mama, let's go for a walk in that garden.' But the dense network of trees and bushes also helped to create a sense of gloom: 'it was often so dark on stage, that not only the actors' faces, but even their figures could not be seen'.[6]

Stanislavski rejected conventional theatrical sets, which were often simply taken from stock. He deplored the way, in other theatres, actors were often left exposed, standing on an empty stage, 'among the external, coarse, obtrusive falsehoods of the theatre':

> You know from experience what the smooth, bare, empty floor of the stage feels like to an actor; how difficult it is to concentrate on it, and how hard it is to play even a short exercise or a simple etude.
>
> Try to stand up in such a space, as if on a concert platform, go onto the forestage, and convey the whole 'life of the human spirit' in the role of Hamlet, Othello or Macbeth. How difficult it is to do without the help of a director, a *mise-en-scène*, without objects and furniture that you can rest on, lean against, sit on, or group yourselves around! Because each of these positions helps you to live on stage and to give physical expression to your inner mood.

... We need that third dimension, that is, an arrangement of the stage in which we can move, live, and act.[7]

Simov's settings created a 'real' environment in which the actors could 'move, live, and act'. In Stanislavski's production plan, at the start of the play, Masha and Medvedenko walked through trees and bushes. The audience heard a snatch of their conversation, and then they disappeared into the trees. They crossed and exited once more, on a different topic of conversation. This was a bold device, breaking up the formality of conventional stage duologues (where actors stood and spouted at each other, or even stood facing the audience). The staging created a sense of a natural conversation. For the actors, too, this must have fostered a sense of simply strolling through a park, rather than being 'on stage'.

Across the footlights, Simov placed a bench. Here, actors sat at different moments with their backs to the audience. Most famously, during the performance of Treplev's 'play', the 'audience' on stage sat in a line on the bench. This was a bold and even *theatrical* gesture on Stanislavski's part, 'in direct opposition to all the accepted laws and customs of the theatre of that time'.[8] Turning the actors' backs to the audience established a sense of a 'fourth wall' between the auditorium and stage. This, in turn, must have helped the actors to concentrate on the action unfolding on the stage, and increased their sense of 'living through' their roles.

The designs for subsequent acts were also 'realistically based'. Nemirovich argued: 'the search was for harmony between the experiences of the characters and the entire setting.'[9] The set for Act III, inside the house, 'seemed so lived-in that it extracted a gasp from the spectators'; and Knipper remarked that the set for the last Act felt so cold and dusty that 'you wanted to wrap yourself in a shawl'.[10] It seems in fact that the settings both helped the actors to *believe* in the drama – they were 'realistic' and three-dimensional – and also provoked a feeling reaction, a 'mood' in them ('you wanted to wrap yourself in a shawl').

At the beginning of his career, Stanislavski's method of rehearsing was dictatorial. In his production plan, he outlined all the actors' moves in advance, prescribing every gesture and intonation. In *My Life in Art* he explained:

At that time, our actors were as yet inexperienced, and so a despotic method of work was almost inevitable. I shut myself in my study and wrote a detailed *mise-en-scène*, as I felt, saw and heard it in my imagination. In these moments I thought little about the emotions of the actor. I sincerely thought at that time that it was possible to order others to live and feel at someone else's behest.[11]

In some ways, then, Stanislavski's production plan fixed 'the external form of a role, without creating the inner form and inner life'. He later rejected this way of working; when S.D. Balukhaty began to prepare *The Seagull* notes for publication, Stanislavski warned him that the *mise-en-scène* 'was based on the old methods, which have long been rejected, of forcefully imposing our personal feelings on the actor'.[12]

Stanislavski's notes are, in a sense, like a novelisation of the plays, filling in the details of behaviour that are missing in the text. In Act I of *The Seagull*, for example, Treplev is talking to Sorin.

TREPLEV: (*straightens his uncle's tie*) Your hair and beard are a mess. You need a trim or something.
SORIN: (*combing out his beard*) It's the tragedy of my life. When I was young it was the same, I always looked drunk.

Stanislavski wrote: 'Sorin takes out a small comb unhurriedly and during the whole of the next scene (sitting with his back to the audience) he combs his beard, then he takes off his hat, combs his hair, adjusts and redoes his tie.' Treplev, meanwhile, who is lying next to Sorin on the bench, shows his agitation by puffing away at his cigarette and shaking off the ash, or 'he bends down, picks a flower or a blade of grass and begins to tear it up nervously. Perhaps he sits up with a start, then lies down again abruptly, lights his cigarette nervously and throws away the matches.'[13] The actions suggested by Chekhov's stage directions are extended by Stanislavski into a continuous stream of activity.

In *Drama in Performance* Raymond Williams distinguished two kinds of 'detail' in Stanislavski's production notes. He analysed the scene between Treplev and Sorin thus:

> There is action like the tearing of the blades of grass, which is probable if you conceive the character to be agitated, and there is action like Sorin's untying his cravat, which is probable in the sense that he has to listen to a long speech by Konstantin [Treplev] and must presumably be doing something meanwhile. In neither case does the particular action necessarily follow from the speech; but there is an evident difference of degree of relevance. The grass-

tearing is relevant, given the assumption of agitation; but sitting
on the bench, smoking, and so on, are merely 'something for the
characters to do while they talk'.[14]

It might be argued that Stanislavski includes too much activity that
is simply 'something for the characters to do' – in other words, there
are too many 'naturalistic' actions. However, the 'score' helped to
create a sense of a continuous 'life' on stage. The actors continued with
their actions, continued to 'live through' their roles, even as another
actor was speaking. Thus, there was no sense of 'turn-taking', of a
character only moving when it was his or her turn to speak.

Many of the actions in Stanislavski's score focused on the use of
objects. Nemirovich suggested that they

> not only occupied the attention of the spectator, helping to give
> the stage a mood of reality, but to an even greater degree they
> were useful to the actor, whose greatest misfortune, perhaps, in the
> old theatre, was the fact that he found himself, in his very being, as
> if he was outside time and space.

The actions aided the actors' belief and concentration, and helped to
make their performances more 'truthful':

> the match and the lighted cigarette in the darkness, the powder in
> Arkadina's pocket, Sorin's rug, a comb, cufflinks, the washing of
> hands, drinking water in gulps, and so on, *ad infinitum*. The actor's
> attention must be trained to focus on these things, then his speech
> will be simpler. Later, within perhaps not more than seven or eight
> years, there was a reaction, a battle over precisely these things. At
> this time, however, Stanislavski proposed to utilize them in large
> measure; he was even extravagant in the use of everyday colours.
> And so he fell into extremes, but as the plan passed through my
> hands, I was able to cast aside anything that seemed superfluous
> or simply too risky.[15]

Merely by performing the actions they had been given, it seems, the
actors found a certain authenticity. They became absorbed in the task.
We may speculate that they felt that they were acting 'with the fourth
wall down'. Working on *Three Sisters*, Meyerhold was struggling with
the role of Tusenbach. One day in rehearsal, Stanislavski suddenly
threw him a piece of paper and said:

You go to the piano, say your first three words and, suddenly seeing this piece of paper, you pick it up, and as you cross to where you are supposed to be sitting, you tear the paper up into little pieces, as you carry on talking.

Meyerhold concluded: 'It helped a lot. I got what I needed for the scene.'[16]

A similar moment from the same production was recorded by Miroslav Krleza:

I think that never, so long as I live, shall I forget that moment [in the scene between Masha and Vershinin in Act II] when Knipper-Chekhova in her nervousness went on striking matches and blowing them out, laughing and crying, a wonderful woman, laughing and snapping matchsticks while that officer was speaking to her of love.[17]

When Michel Saint-Denis saw Stanislavski's production of *The Cherry Orchard* he was struck by a moment in Act III when Ranevskaya 'takes a cup of tea from the old servant while she is engaged in talking to someone else. Her hand shakes, she's burnt by the tea, drops the cup which falls on the ground and breaks.' The moment was greeted with applause because 'the reality of this action was so complete, so untheatrically managed as to be striking even from a distance'.

I had the opportunity of asking Stanislavski how he had achieved such balanced and convincing reality. He replied, 'Oh, it's very stupid. She [Knipper] couldn't get it. We rehearsed for seven months but she still couldn't get it; so one day I told the stage-manager to put boiling water in the cup. And he did.' And I couldn't help saying – I was twenty-five at the time, (but that man was wonderful) – 'Yes, that was stupid.' He laughed. 'It was absolutely stupid. But you have to do everything, anything, even stupid things, to get what you need in the theatre.'[18]

In rehearsal, then, it seems Stanislavski concentrated on making the actor perform the action, and perform it accurately. But the aim was not simply to achieve an external verisimilitude or 'truth'; rather, it was to awaken in the actors an 'inner' sense of 'truth'. For example, simply by performing the actions Stanislavski prescribed for Treplev in Act I of *The Seagull* (tearing the blade of grass, etc.) the actor (Meyerhold) may have begun to experience a sense of the character's nervousness. In other words, the *external* action helped the actor find 'the inner form and inner life' of the role. Here is another example, from Meyerhold's account of his work with Stanislavski on *Three Sisters* (told to members of his own theatre company in 1936):

> Another time this happened. I wanted to make the words sound anxious, but I didn't feel the slightest bit anxious. It wasn't working. Then he gave me a bottle of wine and a corkscrew and said: 'Do your speech, and at the same time open the bottle.' And really, when I started doing it, I found that what little anxiety I did feel began to grow. And I got it from the difficulty I was having opening the bottle of wine. I did it rather expertly, after all I know how to open a bottle (*laughter*). I hated Stanislavski, hated the bottle, hated everything – obstacles arose in my path, and then in my speech I found the intonation of truth.[19]

At this stage, it seems, Stanislavski's approach to acting began with the *external* as a 'way-in' to the 'inner life' of a role. The physical actions established an external 'score' for the actor. Referring to Treplev's actions, Dieter Hoffmeier has argued: 'There is not a single word of analysis or explanation by Stanislavski of the complexity of the psychological process, the emotional changes' in the character. Instead 'we find little external tasks which never once or barely produce a unified action'.[20] But there *is*, in fact, a clearly unified action and 'through-line' in Treplev's behaviour: his nervous anticipation of the performance of his play. Stanislavski conveys the 'complexity of the psychological process, the emotional changes', not through analysis, but through concrete actions.

Interestingly, when members of the Art Theatre asked Chekhov for pointers on how to play his characters, he always answered them, not with an explanation of motivation or psychology, but in terms of minute details of behaviour, and physical actions. For example, when Kachalov was rehearsing the role of Trigorin, Chekhov advised him that the character's fishing rods should be 'home-made' – 'he makes them himself with a pen-knife' – and he smokes a good cigar – 'perhaps not very good, but certainly wrapped in silver paper'.

> Then he was silent and thoughtful for a while, and said: 'The main thing is, the fishing rods … '
> Then he fell silent.

But Kachalov was dissatisfied and persisted with questions. So Chekhov added:

> 'You know, when he, Trigorin, drinks vodka with Masha, I would certainly do this, certainly.' And at this he got up, adjusted his waistcoat, and cleared his throat awkwardly a couple of times.
>   'You know, I would certainly do that. When you've been sitting for a long time, you always want to do that ... '
>   'But how can you play such a difficult role', I continued. Then he even got a little angry.
>   'There's nothing more, it is all written down', he said.[21]

When Chekhov watched rehearsals for *The Cherry Orchard*, he felt that the performances of the actors were at times 'theatrical' rather than real. 'Why are you doing that?' he told them. 'It is really just like life.' But, as Nemirovich observed, 'that was the most difficult thing – to make it "just like life"'. Chekhov's advice focused on the execution of simple physical tasks: when, for example, Stanislavski was at a loss on stage, and said, 'I can't do anything ... ', Chekhov told him: 'Pour some milk in a wine-glass and drink it.' ('He gave good advice', Nemirovich observed.)[22] It seems, then, that Chekhov wanted actors to 'anchor' their performances in the precise execution of simple, physical actions, based on a close observation of 'real life', on the way people actually behave.

Towards the end of his life, Stanislavski developed the 'Method of Physical Actions'. Rehearsing Molière's *Tartuffe* (1936–8), he told actors he wanted them to learn to act 'above all *physically*'.[23] He began rehearsals by establishing a physical line or sequence of actions, demanding that every one, even the most insignificant, must be executed with 'control, clarity and completeness'.[24] He recognised that even the simplest actions, which we carry out without thinking in real life, are very difficult to perform on stage. The actor needs to recall the 'exact method and order' in which actions are performed. The aim of this work, however, was not to create a 'naturalistic' performance. Rather, it was intended to help the actor to *believe* in their actions, and find a sense of 'inner truth'. ('Now do you see', Stanislavski wrote in *The Actor's Work on the Role*, 'how many realistic details and minute truths you must find, in order to make yourself believe, physically, in what you are doing on stage?'[25])

The method was a way of going from the 'external' to the 'internal'. Every physical action, Stanislavski saw, contains a psychological element – 'an inner psychological action' which gives rise to it;

conversely, 'every psychological inner action' is always expressed *physically* in some way.[26] Thus, by beginning with simple physical actions, the actor could start to penetrate 'the deepest and most complicated feelings and experiences'.[27] In the 1930s, Stanislavski made the 'Method of Physical Actions' the centre of his 'system' of acting. It has been seen by some as a complete break, a complete change in his approach – but, in fact, we can trace its source right back to his work on Chekhov, where he discovered ways the actor can go from the external to the internal, from physical action to inner feeling.

Communicating the subtext

Stanislavski said that the appeal of Chekhov's plays 'does not lie in the dialogue, but it is hidden behind the lines, in the pauses, in the looks of the actors, in the emanation of their inner feelings'.[28] The production plan for *The Seagull* can, in fact, be seen as an attempt to communicate or 'emanate' the characters' inner feelings through physical actions. When the play was first staged at the Aleksandrinski Theatre, Kugel wrote that he could not understand why Nina falls in love with Trigorin.[29] In his notes, Stanislavski was careful to establish the attraction between the characters from the start. As she is about to take her leave, in Act I, Nina passes Trigorin, 'who looks intently at her', and she 'significantly gives him her hand a second time, is embarrassed and runs off. Trigorin follows her with his eyes.'[30] This perhaps makes the attraction rather obvious, but it ensures that the actors are playing the subtext underneath and between the lines, and the relationship between the characters continues even when there is no dialogue.

We will recall that Efros feared an 'inattentive reader' might be puzzled by the apparent suddenness of Treplev's suicide – having overlooked the significance of Chekhov's stage direction: 'Over the next two minutes he silently tears up all his manuscripts and throws them under the desk, then opens the righthand door and goes out.' However, Efros said that at the Art Theatre, the actor (Meyerhold) understood the significance of the action, and as a result 'the whole auditorium was paralysed with terror'. It was only necessary 'to understand deeply and live through' the drama according to Chekhov's hints for the spectator to be 'shaken'.[31] But Stanislavski also had a hand in creating this sense of 'terror'. In his production plan, he expanded on Chekhov's laconic stage direction, and created an extended scene of pantomime.

Treplev gazes for a moment on the pile of manuscripts on his desk, and then slowly starts to tear them up. He collects all the scraps of paper and goes to the stove (noise of opening the stove door). He throws the paper into the stove, leans against it with his hand, and watches his writings burn for a long time. Then he turns round, thinks, rubs his forehead, then quickly goes over to his desk and opens a drawer. He takes out a bundle of letters and throws it in the fire. He walks away, stops, thinks, looks round the whole room once more – and exits thoughtfully, slowly.[32]

The dramatic burning of the manuscripts emphasizes Treplev's anguish, and helps prepare the audience for his suicide. The action is both physical and psychological, and reveals the internal drama taking place in the character's soul.

Frequently, Stanislavski asked the actors to bring out the subtext and to 'display' the emotions of the characters, externally, in a more overt way than Chekhov, perhaps, intended. In the play, for example, towards the end of Act I, Masha goes to take a pinch of snuff, but Dorn takes the snuff-box away from her and throws it away. In Stanislavski's plan, this simple action becomes much more highly charged and demonstrative: 'Dorn lets her have her snuff, then quickly runs up to her, snatches the snuff-box out of her hands and throws it into the bushes.'[33] In Act IV, Polina and Masha are making up Sorin's bed when they hear the sound of someone playing the piano in the next room.

POLINA: Kostya [Treplev] is playing. That means he's sad.
MASHA: (*silently takes a few waltz steps*) The important thing, mama, is not to see him.

This is how Stanislavski envisaged the scene:

Masha sighs again, waltzes to the window, stops by it, and looks out into the darkness. She takes out a handkerchief, in such a way that her mother can't see, and wipes two or three tears that roll down her cheeks.[34]

Efros described this moment in the Art Theatre production:

Once you'd seen it, you never forgot the deep grief, the eerie, almost horrible feeling that echoed in your soul from those wordless, almost automatic waltz-turns that Masha made, and indeed all its hopelessness, accompanied by Kostya's music drifting in from the next room. She simply went and spun round a few times at a waltz tempo. That's all ... And never had her maimed life been so painful as in those seconds of no dialogue.[35]

In other words: the emotion, the subtext, was communicated, not through the lines, but through a simple physical action: the silent, almost mechanical waltz-turns. Today, however, Stanislavski's staging seems rather sentimental. In the text, the character's emotion is hinted at; in Stanislavski's version, she wears her heart on her sleeve.

In Act III, Treplev begs Arkadina to replace the bandage on his head. But then the scene turns into a bitter altercation. Stanislavski noted: 'To make the play more vital and comprehensible to the audience, I would very much advise the actors not to be afraid of the *sharpest* realism in this scene.'

> Arkadina, beside herself, flings the end of the rolled-up bandage she was holding in her hand in Treplev's face. She walks away from her son. Treplev, beside himself with fury, tears the bandage off his head, and almost screams at his mother.[36]

Stanislavski, then, used the bandage as a focus for the actors, and a way for them to express their internal agitation. (Similarly, later, Treplev tugs at a handkerchief nervously, and Arkadina drinks a glass of water, her hands shaking.) But again, it can be argued that Stanislavski was making the emotion too dramatic and demonstrative. It may be that he felt he *had* to spell-out the subtext in this way if the point, the 'meaning', was not to be lost on his audiences. But he was also, arguably, intensifying the 'drama' in certain scenes to make them more 'exciting' theatrically. In Act IV of *Uncle Vanya*, Astrov takes his leave from Elena. Stanislavski felt the character should act like the most passionate lover, 'snatching at his own feelings like a drowning man clutching at straws'. But Chekhov told Knipper:

> that's not right, not right at all! Astrov likes Elena, she charms him with her beauty, but in the last Act he already knows that nothing will come of it, that Elena is vanishing from his life forever – and he talks to her in this scene in exactly the same tone as he talks about the heat in Africa, and he kisses her simply for something to do. If Astrov plays this scene forcefully, it will ruin the whole mood of Act IV, which is quiet and languid.[37]

This is how Stanislavski planned the encounter between Sonya and her father, Professor Serebryakov, at the climax of Act III:

> Serebryakov drinks water in gulps. Sonya approaches him from behind, strokes his back. She tries to kiss him, kisses his hand. Terribly nervous, shivering, as if in a fever.[38]

When he saw the Art Theatre production, Chekhov objected to the staging of this scene, which he found false and theatrical. It prompted his famous observation: 'All the meaning and all the drama of a person lies internally, not in external manifestations.'[39] It seems, however, that Stanislavski, at this stage in his directing career, sometimes tried to convey the 'meaning' and 'inner drama' through rather crude 'external manifestations'.

Psychological action

Stanislavski's production plan for *The Cherry Orchard*, written in 1903, differs in significant ways from the plan for *The Seagull*. He continued to work from physical actions, but also, for the first time, the score 'contained notes on the motivations of the characters' and 'explanations of the psychological and social mechanisms at work'.[40] Observe, for example, his notes on the moment when Ranevskaya looks out on the orchard in Act I:

RANEVSKAYA: (*125*) If only I could lift this heavy weight from my shoulders, if only I could forget my past. (*126*)

125. Standing at the window.
126. She covers her eyes with a handkerchief. Leans on the window frame. Pause.

GAEV: (*127*) Yes, and now the orchard's going to be sold to pay our debts. Strange as it seems ... (*128*)

127. Sadly. Motionless.

128. Pause. Both stand motionless. Sounds of morning.
129. A sudden commotion.

RANEVSKAYA: (*129*) Look, mama is walking in the orchard – our own dead mama – in a white dress! (*Laughs happily*) It is her. (*130*)

130. Enraptured. God knows why she suddenly sees her mother. Probably she has put herself so vividly back into the past, that she has forgotten that she is no longer a child.

Then, Trofimov enters. Ranevskaya remembers the death of her son, Grisha; she embraces Trofimov and cries quietly.

RANEVSKAYA: (*quietly weeping*)
My boy was lost –
drowned... Why? Why, my
friend? (*Quieter*) (*137*) Anya's
sleeping in there, and here I
am talking loudly ... making
a noise ...

*137. She stands up. She embraces
Trofimov as if he was her Grisha.
Now she thinks about Anya again.
Up until this point she has been
crying loudly and did not think of
her, but now, as she remembers her
son, it makes her care all the more
for her daughter.*[41]

Stanislavski is here carefully plotting a course through the character's *internal* thought processes – creating the character's 'inner form and inner life'. He offers a series of logical steps which takes the actor from one thought to another. Looking at the orchard, for example, takes her back to her childhood and she almost feels she is a child again. She sinks so deeply back into these memories of the past that she almost 'hallucinates' as she thinks she sees her mother again. Then seeing Trofimov makes her thinks about Grisha, and she embraces Trofimov as if he is her son, as a kind of substitute. Aware of herself as a 'mother' again, she thinks of Anya. Much of this thought process is invisible to the audience. It is as if Stanislavski realises now the need to plot, alongside the external 'score' of the role, a continuous *inner life*, an *inner* score.

A similar series of 'steps' guides the actor playing Lopakhin through the scene in Act III when the character returns from the auction. Stanislavski observed that Lopakhin 'buys the cherry orchard almost by accident and then is actually embarrassed about it. That's why he gets drunk, perhaps.'[42] In his production plan he outlined the way he felt the scene should be played:

RANEVSKAYA: Has the cherry
orchard been sold?
LOPAKHIN: (*202*) Yes, it has.
RANEVSKAYA: (*203*) Who bought
it?

*202. Guiltily, running his handker-
chief through his hands. He is
looking at the floor and does not
answer at once.*
203. Pause. Barely audible.

LOPAKHIN: *(204)* I did.
(*Ranevskaya is overwhelmed; if she was not standing near the [armchair and] table she would fall. Varya takes the keys from her belt, throws them on the floor in the middle of the room, and goes out.*)
(205) I did!

204. *Pause. Even quieter and more embarrassed.*

205. *An agonizing pause. Lopakhin feels terrible, and this stirs the beast in him. The awkwardness of his position begins to make him angry. Nervously he tugs at his handkerchief. … Varya breaks the pause. She steps into the centre of the room, throws the keys to the ground and goes downstairs. This makes Lopakhin lose patience. He flies into a rage. He almost shouts with bitterness and insolence: 'I did.'*

He calms down for a moment. Sitting at a distance from Ranevskaya, his embarrassment gives way to a sense of pleasure and commercial pride. As he tells the story of the auction, he begins to boast, 'as a businessman does when faced with a fellow trader or landowner'. He declares, 'Now the cherry orchard is mine! Mine!' He orders the band to play, and then dances backwards, bumping into Ranevskaya. At the sight of her tears, Lopakhin's mood changes suddenly: we see again 'the honourable and good man, who tenderly loves Ranevskaya's whole family, and her especially'.

LOPAKHIN: *(reproachfully)* *(220)* Why, why didn't you listen to me?

220. *He goes up to her, kneels before her, kisses her hands, her skirt like a little dog (the drink also plays a part here). He cries. The more sincerely and tenderly the better. Why then, if he has such a tender soul, didn't he save Ranevskaya? Because he is a slave to the prejudices of merchants, because the other businessmen would have laughed at him. 'Les affaires sont les affaires.'*[43]

Ranevskaya embraces him, and they cry together.

Stanislavski plots a course through the complexities and contradictions of Lopakhin's feelings. He is asking the actor to play extremes of behaviour, reflecting the contradictions in Lopakhin. He marks the turning points – the moments when a new impulse makes Lopakhin change direction. To assist the actor in making the transition from one extreme to another, the director offers certain physical 'triggers' which spark a change in the character. Thus, when Varya throws down the keys, it is the trigger which makes him lose patience and fly into a rage. Later, he boasts about the auction like a businessman; but then, when he sees Ranevskaya's tears, he changes again in an instant, and kneels before her pleadingly.

Stanislavski also looks for physical actions which at each stage express the character's feelings. First, he gives Lopakhin an object – the handkerchief – which he tugs at – a 'psychophysical' action reflecting his anxiety and guilt. Then, a series of actions express, by their force and violence, his feelings of rage and ecstasy: he beats his breast, strikes the table, etc. Later, he kisses Ranevskaya's hands and her skirt 'like a little dog' – an action which very graphically conveys his shame and self-abasement.

Applying the 'system'

The production plan for *The Cherry Orchard* may have been more sophisticated than for *The Seagull*; but Stanislavski was still prescribing the actors' moves, *dictating* their performances – trying to 'order others to live and feel' at his own behest. In rehearsal, he was something of a despot. Nemirovich thought he was inhumane when at one rehearsal he forced Leonidov to repeat the same phrase some hundred times in different ways. He felt it was senseless and degrading to try to drive actors in this way.[44]

Stanislavski began to develop his 'system' of acting after 1906. It is interesting to see how this changed his method of working on Chekhov. The evidence we have is not substantial but still illuminating. In 1917, he began work on a new production of *The Seagull*. It was to feature Mikhail [Michael] Chekhov as Treplev and Alla Tarasova as Nina. Olga Knipper continued in the role of Arkadina.[45] An early rehearsal – on 10 September 1917 – turned out to be a disaster. Stanislavski – as noted earlier – felt the actors were offering some generalised idea of a 'Chekhovian' style. There was too much 'Chekhovian whining'. He said: 'It's terrible. They are turning the production into a funeral.'[46] He did not want the actors to 'demonstrate' the emotion, to 'show' the grief or sadness of the characters. In subsequent rehearsals, he emphasized the 'action' – both internal and external. He insisted: 'Don't look for the results of every scene; look for a series of living steps. When a result is shown, it is not interesting.'[47]

14 September 1917: Working with Mikhail Chekhov and Tarasova, on the scene between Nina and Treplev in Act I, Stanislavski tried to help the actors to find the 'living steps'. He advised them to apply the 'system', and break each scene down into units and objectives – defining the characters' *internal* 'action'.

> Let us take the largest unit of Act I – the meeting of Treplev and Nina. The most immediate through line of action for Nina is to go on the stage, be successful and so on. In connection with this through line at the very beginning Nina wants to know the truth: is she late or not. That means that here she has a moment of looking around and orienting herself. You need to try to find the keys to this scene. To enter, to look round, to calm down, to pause for breath.

Thus, Stanislavski established a through line, a 'superobjective' for the character: she wants to go on the stage, to be successful. But he was then concerned with the *concrete actions* that she performs. He broke these down into a series of logical steps which had to be executed clearly and accurately. This created a 'score' of the role.

Stanislavski urged the actors to look for 'keys' to the characters in every episode. He defined these 'keys' in terms of certain psychophysical actions. For example: the 'keys' to Nina in this scene are to 'enter, to look round, to calm down, to pause for breath'. The 'keys' to Treplev at this moment are: 'to listen to her steps, infect Sorin with his attention, convince him. Nina is arriving.' When she enters, his actions are 'to welcome her, to express to her his feelings, his joy'. All of these actions are driven by one thing: Treplev's love for Nina: 'What is important for Treplev at this moment – the play, or Nina? Nina. He loves her, she disturbs his inner equilibrium. What is the *key* to Treplev? Even the sound of her footsteps is dear to him!'[48]

Stanislavski was thus breaking down the scene, and working with the actors to create a 'score' of 'living steps' or actions. There were no actions which were simply 'something for the actor to do'; they were all 'psychophysical', and motivated by an overall purpose or objective.

17 September 1917: Stanislavski worked with Knipper and Chekhov on the scene between Arkadina and Treplev in Act III. He had already told Chekhov that his role 'must attain a high level of temperament'. However, to achieve this here, he argued, required a *restraint* in the use of gestures. 'The more restrained the gestures, the stronger the temperament.'[49] He emphasized the need to look for 'minute truths'.

He suggested that when Treplev broaches the subject of Trigorin with his mother, he does so 'very carefully'. There is a mutual desire to preserve a peaceful relationship. In the 1898 production, we will recall, Stanislavski called for the 'sharpest realism' in this scene, the most overt expression of the characters' feelings. But now, the approach was quite different. He told them to *hold back* the emotion: 'The more restrained this scene is, the more powerful and nervous it will be.'

Again, Stanislavski broke the scene down into stages. Discussing his suicide attempt, 'Treplev examines his feelings' and 'convinces himself not to do it again'. Then, he kisses his mother's hand. 'This kiss physically links him with life. It's a straw he clings to. Hence his tenderness to his mother.'[50]

Stanislavski recognised that complex psychological states are often expressed in simple physical actions; for example: 'What is Lady Macbeth occupied with, at the culminating moment of the tragedy? A simple physical action: washing the bloodstain from her hands.'[51] In this instance, Treplev's desperation was expressed in a concrete action: the kiss. The actor was told not to 'show' the character's feelings, but to play the *action*.

> 'If only you knew! I have lost everything.' This is again a straw. But Treplev here already does not love his mother but simply physically clings to her. In him there is again the despair of the second Act. But it is necessary to be active, to look for a way out of his condition, otherwise the actor will play despair.

Stanislavski next invited Knipper and Chekhov to do a series of exercises, or improvisations, on the theme of the argument and reconciliation between the characters, 'physically verifying the truth'. Afterwards, the director (always extremely exacting) criticised them both for mechanically forcing the emotion. He saw theatrical clichés in their work, especially in Chekhov (in trying to 'show' Treplev's love for his mother). 'It is best to try to find physical truth without words', he suggested. 'It is necessary to think, not *how* to do something, but *what* to do. Then you get the completeness, the seal of physical truth.'[52]

In his production plan for the 1898 *Seagull*, Stanislavski defined exactly *how* the actors should execute their actions. In 1917, he was much more concerned with *what* the characters are trying to do, and *why* – the 'living steps'. He did not prescribe *how* the actors should carry the actions out.

In rehearsal, he explored the 'inner life and inner form' of the characters. But this 'inner life' was inextricably linked with the character's physical life. When, for example, Treplev greeted Nina, in Act I, his actions – 'to welcome her, to express to her his feelings, his joy' – were both *physical* and *psychological*. Stanislavski was aiming for the *unity* of the internal and external, the physical and psychological. This unity he termed 'organic action on the stage'.[53]

We cannot know how this production, staged using Stanislavski's 'system', would have worked. It was aborted because of the illnesses of Tarasova and Chekhov.[54]

Revolution

On 25 October 1917 the Russian Revolution began in St. Petersburg. The following day, in Moscow, the Art Theatre was scheduled to present *The Cherry Orchard*. There was an air of tension in the city, and soldiers were massing outside the Kremlin. Yet, at this revolutionary time, the theatre was performing a play which sympathetically portrayed the life of the landed gentry – 'the very class the Revolution was directed against'. The actors backstage were worried they would not be able to finish the performance. 'They'll drive us off the stage', they said. But in fact the audience sat spellbound. 'It seemed they wanted to wrap themselves in the atmosphere of poetry, and to say goodbye forever to the old life, that now demanded purifying sacrifices.' Trofimov and Anya's final lines in the play before they exit – 'Goodbye, house! Goodbye, old life!' 'Hello, new life!' – must have seemed particularly resonant at the time, and strangely prescient. 'The performance ended with a tremendous ovation', Stanislavski recalled, 'and the spectators left the theatre in silence – and who knows, some of them may have been getting ready to fight for the new life.'[55]

The Revolution had 'drawn a red line' between the 'old' world and the 'new' – dividing the world into 'before' and 'after'.[56] There would soon be calls for both the Moscow Art Theatre, and Chekhov, to be consigned forever to the scrap heap of history.

II Chekhov in Russia
After Stanislavski

4   Vakhtangov and Meyerhold

Evgeni Vakhtangov was talking one day to his student, Nikolai Gorchakov, who was urging him to form a theatre of his own. He replied:

> 'A theatre ... Chekhov had *his own* theatre.'
> 'The Art Theatre?'
> 'No, his own. The one he created in his heart, whose performances he alone saw.'
> '??!'
> 'In his imagination ... '
> 'And in the Art Theatre?'
> 'That was where his plays were *interpreted* – by Stanislavski and Nemirovich-Danchenko.'
> 'Have you never staged Chekhov, Evgeni?'
> 'Some of his stories. Not his big plays. We planned to stage *The Wedding* in the Studio a few years ago.'
> 'We did it at school.'
> 'Was it good?'
> 'The rehearsals were fun.'
> 'So you think a wedding is a happy event in life?'
> 'Maybe ... '
> 'Did Chekhov think so?'
> 'Not much!'
> 'Then who's right? Chekhov? Or you?'[1]

Vakhtangov was a student of Stanislavski's. He joined the Art Theatre in 1911. Stanislavski was quickly impressed by his grasp of the 'system'; in fact, he once declared Vakhtangov could 'teach my system better than I can'.[2] In 1912, Stanislavski opened the Art Theatre's First Studio. It was designed as a centre for learning and experiment, where the 'system' could be taught. Vakhtangov acted in several productions, and directed *The Festival of Peace* (1913). Perhaps the Studio's most celebrated production was *The Cricket on the Hearth* (1914). Based on a story by Dickens, it was directed by Boris Sushkevich and featured Vakhtangov as the toy manufacturer, Tackleton, and Mikhail Chekhov as Caleb Plummer. The Studio's theatre space was small and intimate. The term 'emotional realism' was used to describe the company's productions;

> truth of feeling took on a confessional aspect. The proximity of the public necessitated an absolutely life-like tone, movement and gaze. It turned out to be possible to achieve such naturalness in the studio conditions largely because here the actor was freed from the many demands of outward expression indispensable in a large theatre.[3]

Partly because of this, Stanislavski thought that in the production of *The Cricket on the Hearth*, 'perhaps for the first time, those deep and heartfelt notes of subconscious feeling could be heard, in the measure and form I dreamed of then'.[4] Critics wrote: 'For several minutes, you forget you are sitting in a theatre, that this is only a performance, and not life' (*Vremya*); and: 'no other theatre has created such a close intimacy and cosiness' (*Russkie vedomosti*).[5] Meyerhold, however, criticised the production, and the Studio's work in general, for appealing to the voyeurism of the audience. It was as if the spectators were gazing at life through a keyhole. It was comparable to the desire to eavesdrop on the conversations of strangers, or join the crowd watching an argument on the street. The theatre was called 'intimate' because 'the first row of the audience is only some two meters from the stage. What happiness, to be so near to the keyhole!'

> When spectators forget they are in a theatre, when they forget it is only a performance, when it seems to them that this is life itself, oh, then … ! See how the spectators behave in such a theatre, according to the account in one newspaper: 'The spectators no longer cough, blow their noses, talk; this intimacy is not broken by any external causes or outside interference' (*Russkie vedomosti*). 'Everyone came and relaxed.' Well, so what! It is all so cosy: a soft armchair is moved close to the keyhole, 'the auditorium is plunged into darkness', and you can watch without blushing as someone gets dressed.[6]

This has to be seen in the context of Meyerhold's continuing campaign against the Art Theatre for its supposed 'naturalism'. In a talk given in 1907, 'On the History and Technique of the Theatre', he had declared himself in favour above all of dispensing with theatrical illusion, and celebrating the 'theatricality' of theatre. The spectators, he argued, should not forget they are in a theatre, watching actors; the actors should never forget they are performing before an audience. Following Bryusov's lead, he rejected naturalism, and called for a 'stylised' theatre.[7]

The Russian theatre seemed to be split along a historic fault-line, between two alternatives, two contrasting trends: 'realism' and 'stylisation'. Realistic theatre, Ruben Simonov saw, 'was in danger of becoming naturalistic', and neglecting the demands of external theatrical form; while 'conventional' (or 'stylised') theatre 'was in danger of becoming formalistic' – i.e., interested in external form at the expense of inner life or reality. It seemed 'as if one had to choose between art that was true to life but uncertain in its mastery of form, and art rich in form but poor in content'.[8]

Stanislavski and Meyerhold seemed to symbolise these two trends. They were seen as opposites: one concerned with inner 'content', the other with external 'form'; one celebrating 'truth of feeling', the other 'theatricality'. But this was simplistic. Meyerhold himself declared:

> The assertion that Meyerhold and Stanislavski are antipodes is wrong. This notion is meaningless in such an ossified and static form. Neither Stanislavski nor Meyerhold represents something completed. Both are in a constant process of change.[9]

Stanislavski had been labelled a 'naturalistic' director, but he had, in fact, worked in a range of theatrical styles – staging symbolist dramas by Andreev and Hamsun, for example, and fairy-tale fantasies by Maeterlinck and Ostrovsky. He had always maintained that the theatre must present the 'life of the human spirit' in an 'artistic form'.[10] In other words, there must be both inner content *and* external form.

It seems true, however, that the work of the First Studio, in its early years, focused more on the actor's *internal* rather than external technique. It was an intimate, psychological theatre, exploring the inner life of the 'human spirit' rather than the external demands of 'artistic scenic form'.[11] In 1917, the Studio was working on a production of *Twelfth Night* (with Mikhail Chekhov as Malvolio). When Stanislavski saw the work-in-progress, he felt it was in a lamentable state. 'He descended on us with fire and brimstone', one actor recalled, 'and tore our so-called work to shreds, as they say. He rebuilt everything in his own way.'[12] The production in many ways signalled a decisive shift in the Studio's work. It was a celebration of theatricality. Stanislavski imposed a rapid pace on whole performance, 'removing everything that might have impeded the action, the episodic development of the comedy'.[13] S.V. Giatsintova, who played Maria, said that this was 'not intimate chamber theatre, but one which drew the entire auditorium into the performance. This was something new.'[14] But Vakhtangov was shocked: he could not understand this new emphasis on theatricality and 'external form'. 'I believe the production will externally be very interesting', he wrote. 'It will be a success, but it will not be a step forward, in an internal sense. The "system" will not gain by it. And the face of the Studio will be obscured. Not changed, but obscured.'[15] As Stroeva has commented, Vakhtangov only came to an understanding of this new step later, in his own way.[16]

'Truth' and theatricality

The years following the 1917 Revolution saw an explosion of theatrical activity in Russia, and experiments in new forms such as futurism and constructivism. The Moscow Art Theatre, however, seemed to be stagnating. Stanislavski feared it had lost its purpose and direction. There were rumours that it would be forced to close. Between 1917 and 1922 the theatre staged only one new production (Byron's *Cain*). The repertoire, then, was stuck in the past, and the company was increasingly attacked as outmoded and even 'counter-revolutionary'. The critic Vladimir Blyum said that it represented the best in Russian bourgeois culture, but it had died a natural death on the night of the October Revolution, when the bourgeois class was overthrown.[17]

Vakhtangov declared that the Revolution had 'drawn a red line' between the 'old' world and the 'new' – and so, 'how can it not touch the heart of the artist?'[18] Perhaps influenced by the Art Theatre's critics, Vakhtangov now began to distance himself from Stanislavski – to see him as part of the 'old' world. He wrote in his notebook: 'Stanislavski's theatre is already dead and will never be resurrected. I am happy at this. Strange, but I now find it unpleasant to recall even *Three Sisters* and *The Cherry Orchard*.'[19] He now attacked Stanislavski for emphasising the truth of inner feelings over the demands of theatrical form: 'Carried away by his enthusiasm for truth in general, Stanislavski brought the truth of life to the stage'; he demanded 'genuine, natural feelings on the stage, forgetting that the actor's feelings must be conveyed to the audience by theatrical means'.[20] Nick

Worrall has characterised Vakhtangov's career as a 'journey away from Stanislavski towards Meyerhold'.[21] 'Of all Russian directors', Vakhtangov declared, 'there is only one who has a sense of theatricality – and that is Meyerhold.' However, he also argued that, 'carried away by his enthusiasm for theatrical truth, Meyerhold did away with the truth of feelings'. He used theatrical means – but the means were dead, there was no real 'flesh and blood', no real emotion. Vakhtangov summed up the difference between Meyerhold and Stanislavski, as he saw it, thus:

> Emotion in theatre and in life is the same, but the ways or means of conveying this emotion are different. A partridge is exactly the same, whether it is cooked at home or in a restaurant. But in a restaurant it is prepared and served up in a theatrical way – while at home it is something domestic, not theatrical. Stanislavski served up truth as truth, water as water, and a partridge was simply a partridge, while Meyerhold did away with truth altogether; that is, he retained the dish, and the way of preparing it, but he served up paper, not a partridge. And the emotion was cardboard, too. Meyerhold was a master, and served things up in a masterful way, as in a restaurant, but you couldn't eat it.[22]

To some extent, Vakhtangov's criticisms of Stanislavski simply reflected a desire to escape his influence, and establish his own artistic identity. One of Vakhtangov's students, Boris Zakhava, has argued, with justification, that the Stanislavski 'system' remained 'the lasting and firm *foundation*, on which Vakhtangov erected his own building'.[23] The director wanted to explore new theatrical forms – but he continued to place great value on the 'truth of feeling'. In fact, Zakhava has argued that Vakhtangov attempted to reconcile the two trends represented by Stanislavski and Meyerhold.

> Stanislavski and Meyerhold! The beginning of a synthesis in the art of theatre. Vakhtangov's theatre stands for both, and everything they symbolize. Stanislavski and Meyerhold, content and form, the truth of feeling and the theatrical representation of events, that is what Vakhtangov wanted to unite in his theatre.[24]

Vakhtangov sought a vivid and theatrical style of performance – or, as he termed it, 'imaginative realism':

There should be no naturalism or realism in the theatre, but there should be imaginative realism. The appropriate theatrical means give the author a real life on stage. Means can be learned, but form must be created, it must be a product of the imagination. That is why I call this imaginative realism. Imaginative realism exists, it should be in every art form now.[25]

The phrase, 'imaginative realism', suggests a need to combine the *internal* and *external* – an inner 'emotional realism', and an external theatrical *form*. When he staged Strindberg's *Erik XIV* in 1921, Vakhtangov described it as an experiment in 'searching for theatrical forms for stage content (the art of feeling)'. He wrote:

Until now, the Studio, true to Stanislavski's teachings, has doggedly aimed for the mastery of inner experience. Now the Studio is entering a period of search for new forms – remaining true to Stanislavski's teachings, which search for expressive forms, and indicate the means to be used to achieve them (breathing, sound, words, phrases, thoughts, gestures, the body, plasticity of movement, rhythm – all these in a special, theatrical sense founded on an internal, natural basis).[26]

In the search for 'new forms', Vakhtangov became interested in the concept of the 'grotesque'. This term did not imply a form of 'coarse exaggeration or vulgar, primitive caricature'. Rather, Vakhtangov defined it as acting which achieved the 'maximum *expressiveness of scenic form*'.[27] In the production of Strindberg's *Erik XIV*, he used non-naturalistic make-up to create a sense of the 'grotesque'.

Stanislavski debated the concept with Vakhtangov. Later he recorded their conversation. He argued he had seen few real 'grotesque' performances in his time. The 'grotesque' should not mean *external* exaggeration with no *internal* justification:

No, a real grotesque is the external, the most vivid and bold justification of a tremendous inner content, exhaustive to the point of exaggeration. An actor must not only feel and live through human passions in all their component elements – they must be condensed and made visible, irresistible in their expressiveness, audacious and bold, bordering on caricature.

Simply sticking a crooked eyebrow on an actor's face (as Vakhtangov did in *Erik XIV*) does not create the 'grotesque': 'To inflate something which is not there, to inflate emptiness – that makes me think of blowing soap bubbles.'[28] This, then, did not imply a rejection of 'theatricality', but only of a *false* theatricality. New 'forms' cannot be simply imposed on the actor.

Vakhtangov's *The Wedding*

In 1921, Vakhatangov wrote in his notebook: 'Let naturalism in the theatre die. Oh, how you could stage Ostrovsky, Gogol, Chekhov! I have an impulse to get up' – he was ill in a hospital sanatorium – 'and run to tell them about my new ideas. I would like to direct *The Seagull* theatrically, as Chekhov wrote it.'[29] Presumably, he meant that the play was not simply a 'slice-of-life'; he wanted to find its theatrical *form*.

According to Zakhava, Vakhtangov taught that 'every play demands its own form of presentation'. The form 'must be organically bound up with the content of the work'. But this did not simply imply being faithful to the 'form' created by the author. Vaktangov believed a production must also 'satisfy the demands of the present time'. The theatre company must determine its *attitude* to the material. 'It follows that the new theatre does not fuse with the author. It separates itself from him. It creates on stage not only the life that the author of the play shows, it *discovers its own standpoint*, from which it considers life.' Thirdly and finally, 'the form of the production must belong organically, naturally to the respective theatre. It must show the artistic face of the theatre collective at the respective stage of its artistic development. So three elements determine the form of a production: the author, the present time, and the theatre collective.'[30]

In 1920–1, Vakhtangov directed *The Wedding* at his own Studio.[31] To some extent, the 'form' of the production was determined by the time. Chekhov's work, he argued, had been sentimentalised; the average person thought that the plays 'console us with the idea that life will get better – and meanwhile ... "let's have a cup of tea and dream"'.

> Vakhtangov said this deliberately in an exaggerated 'Chekhovian' tone. He sighed, raised his eyes to the sky, and imitated with startling accuracy the excessively sentimental tones of someone playing Anya in *The Cherry Orchard*: 'Don't cry, dear mama, don't cry! We will plant a new orchard, more beautiful than the old one ... We will see a sky of diamonds!'

(These are not Chekhov's lines – Vakhtangov was improvising.) The director continued: 'No, I would stage Chekhov's plays as very cruel works, whose living reality is not softened by any "moods" or by the melodious intonations of the actors, but shown exactly as it is.'[32]

Ruben Simonov (an actor and student at Vakhtangov's studio) observed that theatre-goers now reacted differently to Chekhov's work:

> If, in the past, Chekhov's plays were heard in intense silence and, in fact, both men and women in the audience had often used handkerchiefs to wipe away their tears, now during the performances the audiences more often laughed. The merry reaction in the auditorium seemed to highlight the comic scenes in Chekhov's plays.

After the Revolution, directors 'could not approach Chekhov's work with a "compassionate", sentimental attitude to humanity. It was necessary to express a more active denunciation of Philistinism, of narrow-mindedness and the all-consuming vulgarity, so characteristic of the old petty bourgeois society.'[33] Chekhov had to be reinterpreted, even appropriated, to make him seem relevant to a new age.

Simonov declared that Vakhtangov 'in his new interpretation of Chekhov was ridiculing the Philistine way of life, as if to banish it forever from the new, revolutionary reality'.[34] It would be a mistake, however, to see the production of *The Wedding* simply as a Marxist critique of 'the old petty bourgeois society'. In fact, what Vakhtangov created was closer to a dark, cruel, nightmarish image of human absurdity. In a conversation with Nikolai Gorchakov, he said:

> Perhaps it isn't life at all, the way they live in Chekhov's plays. Everybody dances, as if they are enjoying themselves, celebrating the wedding; everything is 'as it should be', even a 'general' has been 'hired', but that's not life! They think they live, but in fact someone is pulling the strings and telling them: 'That's how it should be.' They dance, quarrel, make up, drink, eat, love, hate, buy, sell …

In other words, this was life seen as a 'puppet show' – recalling Meyerhold's description of *The Cherry Orchard*. Gorchakov realised that this interpretation could be seen as 'mystical' – and viewed with suspicion in a society now dedicated to a Marxist, 'materialist' view of reality. But Vakhtangov responded that this was 'one possible interpretation of the theatrical essence of Chekhov's plays'.[35] In the production, he

Plate 6 Vakhtangov's production of *The Wedding* (1921). Design by Isaak Rabinovich.

used a technique, which had long interested him and which he had already recommended for work on *The Infanta's Doll* by P.G. Antokolski [directed at the Studio by Yuri Zavadski]. He suggested to the actors that they move like puppets. There was a fundamental difference, however. In the *Infanta's Doll* he wanted you to show a living toy. Here he wanted to reveal the dead essence in a living human being. There, a marionette acted like a person; here a human being like a marionette.

As a result, in the production of Chekhov's comedy, everything became strange and unusual. A funny incident turned into its opposite and showed its senseless and unnatural, and so tragic essence. The spectator laughed, but in time became frightened by his own laughter. Laughter stuck in his throat. The comic turned into the tragic. The funny became horrible. If, on stage, dead dolls become living, that is not horrible. It is comic and funny. They move the spectator, and the spectator begins to love them. But when the spectator senses that a clockwork, mechanical heart lies inside a living human being, that is frightening for him. In Chekhov's *The Wedding*, Vakhtangov showed, not the living in something dead, but death in something living.[36]

Simonov recalled work on the production.

A noisy quadrille opened the play. A group of people, strangers to each other, whirled around, meeting and parting again, to the commands of the master of ceremonies, accompanied by the rapid, but doleful, tinkling sounds of an out-of-tune piano. Colliding and then scattering in different directions, they were noisy and jolly; but in their noise and merriment you felt the emptiness and heartlessness of this marital feast.

We may see parallels here with both Stanislavski's staging of Act III of *The Cherry Orchard*, and Meyerhold's reading of the same scene. There was again a sense of a 'puppet show'. The dancers were comic, even absurd: a sailor, Mozgovoi (played by Zakhava) 'runs at top speed, squatting rather than dancing the quadrille'; a Greek confectioner, Dymba (Simonov) 'is dancing God knows what'.[37] There was a gap between the surface gaiety, and the hollowness within. Rehearsing the dances, Vakhtangov asked the dancers to pause at moments, to freeze, and exchange wary glances, as if suddenly sensing the emptiness of the occasion. He thought it would be interesting to see 'what these jumping jackasses would look like, as they dance, and then come to their senses for a few seconds, after the crazy, but necessary wedding ritual'.[38] Thus, the dancing represented a kind of crazy merry-go-round, which stopped briefly, leaving the participants dazed – but unable to get off.

One member of the Studio, watching the rehearsal, observed: 'It looks wonderful when everybody stops. Something like a frozen symbol, like the tableau in Gogol's *Inspector General*. Grotesque!' But he was reprimanded by Vakhtangov. He did not want the actors to aim for some purely formal or external sense of a theatrical 'style'. It is vital, he insisted, 'to live in this pause and not to hold it mechanically. To live, to think, to act.' The work must be based, not on external form, but on inner content. 'Each performer must find a reason why he has to dance so much and why everything around stops.' In other words, the pause had to be justified internally. Someone suggested: 'The pianist's fingers grow stiff. You always need a couple of seconds now and then to give your hands a shake.'[39]

Here, then, was an example of Vakhtangov's desire to marry the internal and the external; to ensure that external actions and gestures were never executed mechanically, but had an inner justification. 'During the rehearsals of *A Wedding*', Simonov recalled, 'we learned from our teacher the art of creating characters both truthful and grotesque; we learned the art of acting which is both inwardly inspired and outwardly expressive'.[40] The actors had to combine the psychological and physical, the internal and external; both *living* the role, and presenting it in a vivid theatrical form.

The ugly and 'grotesque' aspects of the characters' behaviour were emphasised. Thus, the groom, Aplombov, 'had a big long nose, angry eyes, a tuft of hair that fell carelessly on his forehead. A thin, long figure, dressed in a tail-coat (clearly bought cheaply, second-hand), he wandered around the stage with an eternally dissatisfied look on his face, depressing the guests around him.' His bride, Dashenka – fat and lazy – was indifferent to everything, including her husband: 'The food on the table interested her much more than the guests.'[41]

The grotesque, Vakhtangov declared, is both 'tragic and comic'.[42] There was a certain desperation to the characters in *The Wedding*. Their behaviour was comic, but this concealed an inner unhappiness. For example, Zmeyukina, the midwife, arrayed in a bright crimson dress, clearly saw herself as 'the *tsarina* of the ball, a charming, irresistible woman surrounded by a crowd of admirers. In truth, there was only one admirer, the telegraphist Yat, but that was enough for Zmeyukina: she wants to give the impression of an unusual, outstanding woman and Yat was an entirely suitable audience for her.'[43] The character had a strong 'superobjective': to be the centre of attention, to be attractive to men. But this drove her into slightly eccentric behaviour. The audience could see the gap between her aspirations, and the tawdry reality. She was, at once, both comic, tragic – and 'grotesque'.

In the play, the guests are anticipating the arrival of a general to honour their feast. When he appears, it is 'to some extent the realization of a dream of a more beautiful life'.[44] However, he turns out to be only a captain from the navy. When the truth emerges, the guests turn on him angrily; they shout and argue, while the band strikes up a march. The captain, angry and humiliated, staggers out, crying: '*Chelovek! Chelovek!*' The word in Russian means both 'human being' and 'waiter'. In Vakhtangov's production, this 'hopeless lament of the insulted old man suddenly received a symbolic meaning'; it seemed like a cry for humanity, and 'resonated with a melancholy echo in the heart of the spectator'. [45] Simonov described the staging of this scene:

> The characters of the play stand motionless, their backs to the audience. ... The dream is no more! In this world, it is impossible to attract a genuine general, even with money. Softer and softer sounds the sad quadrille. The feast is over. Daily routine begins.[46]

Chekhov's play ends in a scene of farcical confusion. Vakhtangov's ending was much more downbeat. Arguably, the director was darkening the play, in a way which perhaps Chekhov did not intend. The form he found for *The Wedding* reflected his own attitude to the material. It was 'one possible interpretation of the theatrical essence' of the play.

The ending became a 'concluding chord' which allowed the audience to sum up its impressions 'and once more realise the basic idea, the theme of the production'.[47] The 'dream' was torn away, leaving only a sense of emptiness and absurdity. The comic turned into the tragic, and laughter froze on the audience's lips. When Mikhail Chekhov saw the production, he was bathed in tears, and cried, 'What a horror! What a horror!'[48]

*   *   *

Meyerhold: *Thirty-three Swoons*

> Two things are essential for a play's production, as I have often told you. First, we must find the thought of the author; then we must reveal that thought in a theatrical form. This form I call a *jeu de théâtre* and around it I shall build the performance.[49]

On 25 March 1935, to mark the seventy-fifth anniversary of Chekhov's birth, Meyerhold staged three one-act farces: *The Anniversary*, *The Bear* and *The Proposal* under the collective title, *Thirty-three Swoons*. He calculated that there are thirty-three occasions in the course of the plays when a character swoons, or says they are about to faint, clutches their heart, or calls for a glass of water. He claimed the swoons were 'the manifestation of the neurasthenia which was highly prevalent in Chekhov's day. Neurasthenia is a clear indication of the lethargy and loss of will-power which is typical of Chekhov's characters.'[50]

> In the course of studying the time and milieu depicted by Chekhov, we assembled a large variety of material which confirms the unusually high incidence of neurasthenia amongst the intelligentsia; in the 'eighties and 'nineties, it became a kind of epidemic. (In the theatre, there even appeared a special role, the 'neurasthenic'.) We know well enough what the social basis for this phenomenon is.[51]

This, then, was the 'ruling idea' of the production – or the 'thought of the author' – as Meyerhold saw it. But also – and perhaps more importantly – the swoons gave him the 'form' for the production. He saw them as a formal device, which would become the linking motif between the three vaudevilles.

At the first rehearsal, Meyerhold noted that a characteristic of vaudeville is their *lazzi*, or 'jokes, peculiar to the theatre': 'Without this, vaudeville is inconceivable.'[52] In his work in this genre, Chekhov 'took one trait, also characteristic of vaudeville – the frequent collapse in a swoon'. Meyerhold speculated he chose this because he was a doctor, and suggested the actors needed to approach the swoons with a certain clinical observation, 'so that while vaudeville remains vaudeville, and a joke remains a joke', nevertheless the action would assume a certain verisimilitude.[53]

The fainting swoons became self-contained pantomimes punctuating the action (and dividing it into episodes). Each swoon was accompanied by special music – a fanfare of brass for the men, a theme on stringed instruments for the women. All these fainting fits 'were extremely varied, with a wide range of tints and characters'.[54] Norris Houghton, who observed rehearsals, recalled that in *The Proposal*,

> the simple direction, 'He drinks a glass of water', becomes a small scene. Ilinski [who played Lomov] breaks off his speech, clutches

his heart with one hand, his coat lapel with the other. The father rises, steps back a pace and holds out both his arms, as though Ilinski were about to swim to him. The maid in the background raises her broom and holds it poised in mid-air over her head. There is a pause. The Chopin music begins to play. Ilinski, still holding his lapel, reaches out with the other hand for the glass on the table. He holds it at arm's length from his mouth; his eyes grow bigger; the music plays louder. The father and the maid stand motionless. With a quick jerk Ilinski draws the glass to him and downs the water. The music stops, the maid returns to her sweeping, Ilinski carefully smooths his lapel and returns the glass to the table. The father continues with the next line.[55]

Meyerhold had talked about the characters' lethargy and loss of will-power; but in performance they actually seemed driven by a kind of manic energy, an extraordinary volatility and nervous excitement. As the above example demonstrates, the director sought to physicalise the characters' extreme emotional states. He used objects as focal points for the action. In *The Proposal*, for example, Natasha and Lomov become embroiled in a row about who owns a strip of land called Ox Meadows; in Meyerhold's production, this was physicalised through a 'play with objects'.[56] The characters fought over a silver tray and a napkin, tearing it away from each other. Again, then, this was a way of physicalising or externalising the characters' emotions. But the 'play with objects' also became another kind of theatrical 'joke', an opportunity for an elaborate pantomime.

Some critics accused Meyerhold of exaggeration or 'hyperbole'. However, he pointed out that, in Chekhov, the characters' actions are even more extreme. The climactic scene from *The Anniversary*, for example, 'shows that I have not exaggerated, but rather underplayed Chekhov'. A clerk, Khirin, becomes enraged, and starts to drive another character, Tatyana, out of the room. 'Clear out!' he declares, and stamps his foot. 'When Chekhov writes "stamps"', Meyerhold argued, 'that is a particular action, which he wants to single out from the text.' In the play, Tatyana then jumps on a chair, and falls on the sofa as if she has fainted. 'I must say', Meyerhold concluded, 'that my exaggeration is very cautious and very delicate in comparison with this!'[57]

Meyerhold attempted to offer an alternative model and method of acting to Stanislavski. Rejecting the 'psychological' approach, he emphasised instead the *physical*. He declared that the actor's art is the art of gesture and movement, or 'plastic forms in space'. He wrote:

Plate 7 Scene from *The Proposal*, in Meyerhold's *Thirty-three Swoons* (1935). Igor Ilinski as Lomov and E.V. Loginova as Natasha.

> All psychological states are determined by certain physiological processes. By finding the correct solution for his physical state, the actor reaches the point where he experiences the *'excitation'*, which affects the spectators, involving them (or, as we used to say, 'gripping' them) in the actor's performance. This excitation is the essence of the actor's art. From a whole series of physical positions and states, there arise these *'points of excitation'* which are coloured with some particular feeling.[58]

Emotion, in other words, is the result of physical action. The 'external' leads to the 'internal'. If you perform an action – for example, if you raise your hand – this generates a physiological response. The 'correct' physical action or gesture does not simply *express* the feeling; it *creates* it.

Meyerhold's position, however, was somewhat mechanistic. He was effectively treating the human body as a machine, in which emotion is purely a by-product of physiological processes.

Meyerhold believed that Stanislavski's emphasis on the Method of Physical Actions in his later years brought the two men closer, in both theory and practice. Aleksandr Gladkov records that after several long conversations with Stanislavski, 'Meyerhold repeated with great pride that now, nothing divided them'.[59] However, crucial differences in fact remained. Stanislavski believed that working from physical actions would stimulate the actor to explore the character's *inner* life. A simple action such as entering a room, for example, would immediately make the actor ask: 'What is my "objective"? *Why* do I want to enter the room? What is the situation (or the "given circumstances")?' In other words, 'external' action would lead the actor to discover the 'internal' action. The score of 'physical actions' was only the 'bare bones' of a role; it was only the beginning of the actor's work.

Meyerhold, however, saw physical action almost as an end in itself. He based his productions around patterns of physical movement, which were carefully choreographed. In rehearsal, his method of working was to demonstrate what he wanted, and ask the actors to repeat it. In a rehearsal for *The Proposal*, the actor playing Chubukov read the opening four words: 'Why, it's Ivan Lomov.'

> 'Wait!' said Meyerhold. 'You must read the line this way', and he illustrated. Chubukov read the line again.
>
> 'Stop!' said Meyerhold. 'You are not giving it quite the same reading as I did. I wonder if you know why you are saying those words? To read it the way I just did, you must understand what sort of character I want Chubukov to appear.'
>
> Then Meyerhold started in on a brilliant dissection of the line, of the juxtaposition of words and sounds that made up the line, of the meaning of it, of the characterization, of the style of the play as it would be set by that opening speech. 'The sort of character *I* want Chubukov to appear.' Not the sort of character which the actor visualized nor his interpretation of the part at all. Instead, 'Watch me! This is the expression Chubukov must wear to point his absurdity. My expression now ... Do you see? Now you try it.'

Houghton reported that the rehearsal continued for three hours in this painstaking way, and only some dozen pages of the script were finished.

> But when finally the play had been read through, it seemed to me that it was already set. All this was so different from the Art Theatre. Here there was no seeking the underlying meaning, no discussion of the real thought of emotions which some speech conveyed, no feeling the way. Meyerhold had analyzed it all out in advance. He was leading his actors along a brilliantly lighted path,

pointing out all the curves and pitfalls and bringing the cast swiftly around them all. They had only to follow. Once they reached the end, they were through; they must memorize the route they had taken and then they could present the performance.[60]

The 'path' through the performance, then, consisted only of physical actions, which were executed technically, without any reference to motivation. The style of the performance was created by the director, and *imposed* on the actors.

Each piece of interpolated action, such as the fainting fits, threatened to become simply a technical effect, a theatrical 'joke' for its own sake. The fainting fits, the 'play with objects', etc., were elaborate routines, executed with great skill and invention; they were dazzling, but left audiences cold. The production in some ways demonstrated the limitations of Meyerhold's approach to acting. The problem (as Vakhtangov saw) was that, 'in his enthusiasm for theatrical truth, Meyerhold did away with emotional truth'. He used theatrical means – but the means were dead, there was no real 'flesh and blood'.

Meyerhold's devices proved somewhat laboured, and slowed the pace of the production down. He told Gladkov:

> We were too clever by half, and consequently lost sight of the humour. We must look the truth in the face: the audience at any amateur production of *The Proposal* would laugh more than they did at our theatre, even though Ilinsky was acting and Meyerhold was the director. Chekhov's light, transparent humour could not bear the weight of our ideas, and the result was a failure.[61]

'Socialist Realism'

In 1934, all Russian writers were united in a single union and were forced to adopt a single style: 'Socialist Realism'. It was decreed that all art should be accessible, and 'realistic', but also offer a positive picture of life in Soviet society, and advance the building of Socialism. According to Anatoli Lunacharski, the 'socialist realist' must be 'convinced of mankind's Communist future and believe in the power of the proletariat, with its Party and its leaders'.[62] 'Realistic' art was seen as healthy, and contrasted with 'formalism'. This was the ultimate term of abuse at the time, implying a concern with style over substance, with the 'tricks and affectations' of external form over inner content. An editorial in the magazine, *Teatr*, declared: 'Formalism is one of the most hostile and harmful manifestations of bourgeois influence on our art'.[63] Much of the most innovative theatre work in recent years, including Meyerhold's, was now castigated in this way. (Indeed, the term 'Meyerholdism' was virtually synonymous with 'formalism' in the theatre.) The Soviet authorities had intervened in the artistic battle between the 'realistic' and 'formal' trends in the theatre – and forcefully imposed its own bureaucratic solution.

All theatres were now standardised on the model of the Moscow Art Theatre. As Yuri Lyubimov saw, this was tantamount to the 'destruction of theatre as a form of expression'.[64] It was fatal even for the Art Theatre itself. Stanislavski, meanwhile, was turned into an icon. He was portrayed as the great progenitor of 'Socialist Realism'. Soviet newspapers heralded him as 'Our Pride', 'The Genius of Theatre', 'The Creator of Realistic Theatre', and on the frontlines in 'The Battle for Realism'.[65] His experiments in a range of different theatrical styles (such as symbolism) were marginalised. The 'system' became the approved curriculum in all theatrical institutes. His ideas, then, which he always saw as exploratory and developmental, were fossilised and turned into official dogma, 'caricatured and canonised'. Lyubimov commented: 'The whole world had forgotten what he said constantly: every five years, an actor must learn everything again, and develop a new theory of the art of the stage.'[66]

Stanislavski seemed to welcome the campaign against 'formalism', evidently believing it proceeded from a concern for 'true art'. In 1937, on the 20th Anniversary of the Revolution, he declared:

> Since the beginning of the Great Socialist October Revolution, the Party and Government has taken over all care for the Soviet Theatre – not only material, but also spiritual. They have kept watch over the truth and popular appeal of art and protected us from every false tendency. It was the Party and Government which raised their voice against formalism and for a genuine art. All that obliges us to be genuine artists and make sure that nothing false and alien slips in to our art.[67]

We cannot be sure Stanislavski was being sincere here, or if he was simply saying what he thought his political masters wanted to hear. We know that he was suspicious of some 'formalist' trends in the theatre. The 'external', he insisted, 'however beautiful and sharp in form, cannot live on the stage by itself'. It 'must be justified from within, and only then does it engage the spectator'. He recognised significant advances had been made in the actor's *external* technique – in the flexibility of movement, in diction, and 'the whole expressive apparatus' – but *internal* technique had been neglected.

> So long as the physical culture of the body assists the main creative tasks of art, i.e. *to convey the life of the human spirit in an artistic form*, I welcome wholeheartedly the new external achievements of the contemporary actor. But the moment that physical culture becomes an end in itself in art, the moment it begins to constrain the creative process, and creates a split between spiritual aspiration and the conventions of external acting, the moment it stifles feelings and experiences, I become an ardent opponent of these fine new achievements.[68]

Stanislavski criticised some of Meyerhold's productions, and admired others. For example, he praised the staging of Nikolai Erdman's play, *The Warrant* (1925): indeed, in the third Act, 'Meyerhold realised Stanislavski's dream', in creating a sense of the 'genuine grotesque'.[69]

Anatoli Efros has suggested that, when Stanislavski played Trigorin and Meyerhold played Treplev in *The Seagull* in 1898, 'this already carried the seeds of a great conflict. Two such different artistic types, taking such different directions.'[70] And yet it is clear that the two men continued to respect each other's work. Meyerhold described himself as Stanislavski's pupil, and Stanislavski called him his 'prodigal son'.[71] On 8 January 1938 the Meyerhold Theatre was closed. The Committee for Artistic Affairs declared that over the entire period of its existence, the theatre 'had been unable to free itself from thoroughly bourgeois formalistic positions alien to Soviet art'.[72] Stanislavski then surprised everyone by inviting Meyerhold to work with him, first as a teacher in the new Opera–Drama Studio and then as director at the Stanislavski Opera Theatre. When people objected, he told them Meyerhold was needed in the theatre. He accepted full responsibility for the decision. It was a bold move – offering protection to someone in Stalin's disfavour. It seemed, in fact, as if the two men, who had polarised the Russian theatre, might be coming together to achieve a 'synthesis' in their methods. Indeed, Meyerhold himself concluded that they were, ultimately, working towards the same goal: combining the actor's freedom and creativity with the demands of theatrical form. They were 'like the builders of a tunnel under the Alps: he is coming from one side, and I from the other, but somewhere in the middle, inevitably, we must meet'.[73] A few weeks before his death, Stanislavski said to the Opera Theatre's production manager, Yuri Bakhrushin: 'Take care of

Meyerhold. He is my only heir in the theatre – not only in our theatre, but in general.'[74]

Stanislavski died on 7 August 1938, and was buried in the Novodevichi Cemetery, next to Chekhov and Simov.

In June 1939 Meyerhold was arrested. He was shot in prison on 2 February 1940.

Production notes

The Wedding, directed by Evgeni Vakhtangov. Vakhtangov Studio; first version, September 1920. Moscow Art Theatre Third Studio; second version, September 1921.

Thirty-three Swoons, directed by Vsevolod Meyerhold. The Meyerhold State Theatre; first performance, 25 March 1933.

5 Efros and Lyubimov

In 1940, Nemirovich-Danchenko staged a new production of *Three Sisters*.

At the first rehearsal, he declared that 'life has not only changed completely' since the play's premiere in 1901, 'but it has filled us – as artists – with new matter, guided us along a path where one must and can look at Chekhov differently, in a new way, and experience Chekhov afresh'.[1] He 'firmly warned the performers away from "Chekhovianism", from dismal whinings, protracted rhythms, elegiac intonations – in short, from everything begotten by the MKhAT [Moscow Art Theatre], which had already degenerated into cliché'.[2] He defined the ruling idea of the play – as Stanislavski did – as 'the yearning for a better life'. But in Russia, under Stalin, the phrase seemed to take on new meanings.

The success of the production may partly have been due to a sense of nostalgia for a vanished world. 'The mere evoking of the old way of life in the present day was bound to have a dramatic impact in a Moscow which had so recently been through the terror of Yezhov's secret police.'[3] At a time of fear and repression, here was a world in which everything seemed 'beautiful and light – the souls, the thoughts and faces of the heroes, the quiet beauty of nature, and the peaceful cosiness of the house'. As one spectator recalled: 'We cried over the sad fate of the three sisters, and waited, like them, with faith and hope, for the arrival of a beautiful, bright future.'[4]

Soviet critics, however, also gave a particular slant to the production. V. Komissarjevsky wrote that the theme of 'yearning for a better life' gave the play 'a deep-rooted touch of optimism in the eyes of the Soviet people, who had achieved this better life'.[5] One reviewer described the production's final moments:

The sisters take each other by the hand. Their faces are stern and solemn. They speak little about what is in their hearts. Their eyes talk. Their eyes sparkle, not with tears, but with a stubborn belief in the future. And the three sisters here begin to show that they are great and strong, a magnificent type of Russian womanhood, with its suffering, self-renunciation and moral strength.[6]

The production 'had set a new standard and begot a new tradition. In opposition to the notion of Chekhov as pessimist, another extreme attitude arose: interpreters began to look for traits of the fighting revolutionary in Chekhov's heroes. His protagonists were credited with a strong will and much energy, with courage and optimism.'[7] When *Uncle Vanya* was revived at the Art Theatre in 1947, the director, Mikhail Kedrov, sought to rid the characters of 'dreamy passiveness'; rather, they were seen as struggling against banality, and for 'the future liberation of their country's creative powers'.[8]

This 'positive' reading of Chekhov's work was clearly an ideological reduction and distortion. Chekhov was being turned, in his way, into a classic of Socialist Realism.[9] In part, this was an attempt to rescue Chekhov from the 'negative' image he had been given, as the 'singer of twilight moods', the 'poet of superfluous people'[10] – and reinvent him, as 'a robust realistic poet passionately driven towards the future, devoted to and deeply fond of his country'.[11] B.I. Aleksandrov declared that the main content of Chekhov's art lay in the 'active and destructive element (in respect to the old world). Therefore, Chekhov belongs to us, to the people of the revolution, and not to the old bourgeois society overthrown by its forces.'[12] Chekhov's hopes for a 'better future' were portrayed as a humanitarian ideal – which was being realised in the Communist utopia. It was now expected that, in any Chekhov production, 'the future must shine through; the heroes must have strength and perspective, so that Chekhov's beliefs can be fully communicated'.[13]

Efros' *Three Sisters*: An 'elegy of doom'?

Anatoli Efros' production of *Three Sisters* at the Theatre on the Malaya Bronnaya in Moscow (1967) challenged the dominant ideological view of the play and characters. *Three Sisters* emerged as an 'elegy of doom'.[14] A 'harsh atmosphere supplanted Chekhov's fragile lyricism'.[15] 'For the first time', one critic wrote, 'we understood how profoundly pessimistic Chekhov is: the beautiful human soul is perishing and dying, and the expected bright future will not come for his characters.'[16]

The first shock, perhaps, was the set. The space was dominated, centre-stage, by a tree with gilt iron leaves. Black trees were painted on the back wall. In this Beckettian limbo, the souls of Chekhov's characters seemed to wither and perish 'in loneliness, in agonising and joyless thoughts about the future, like the dead, metallic autumn leaves, hanging feebly on black trees'.[17] There was an unusual energy in the performances – but a kind of deranged energy, seen most clearly in Chebutykin's Act III monologue: the actor Lev Durov rushed on stage, wound up a gramophone, and performed a disturbing and macabre dance of despair to the anachronistic tune of 'If You Knew Susie'.

The production was attacked principally because the characters' positive speeches about work and the future were evidently treated with irony. For example, when Tusenbach discoursed on the future, Chebutykin derisively thumped the piano, and the others characters looked on in amusement. Efros, however, later denied any satirical intent:

> I once heard the opinion that in *Three Sisters* we are ridiculing work. Tusenbach has a monologue – 'The yearning for work, O my God, how I understand it!' And it was said that in our production, Tusenbach spoke this monologue ironically. Of course, this was never our intention. What nonsense! I myself, and all the actors engaged in the production, work from morning to night, and in fact, we find both meaning and joy in it – why should we speak ironically about work?!

Efros suggested that, in these lines, Tusenbach is perhaps sending himself up a little because he is aware his words are very high-flown – but he still believes deeply in them.

> Moreover, Tusenbach's wonderful monologue is like a poem, a beautiful and familiar poem. And I suggested the actor read the monologue in a slightly sing-song voice, as if reminding the others of some poetic idea, known and loved by all. But because this was unusual, someone saw it as mockery.[18]

The controversy persisted, however. After six months, the production was banned.

The Taganka *Cherry Orchard*

I love *my own* Stanislavski. (Efros)[19]

The Taganka Theatre in Moscow was founded by Yuri Lyubimov in 1964. The first production, Brecht's *Good Person of Szechwan*, signalled a break from the dominant 'realistic' mode of acting and production. The company became known for its 'presentational' acting style; so when Efros was invited to direct *The Cherry Orchard* at the Taganka in 1975, it raised some eyebrows. But Efros reflected: 'What a good idea, after all – to stage Chekhov at the Taganka. In a theatre where Chekhov seems unthinkable. Where there are always bare brick walls, and the actors *show* their characters, in a Brechtian way.'

> Perhaps, indeed, one should search for the truth only in contrasts. A comedy by Gogol should be staged tragically, then it will be *funny*. Brecht should be staged in a 'Chekhovian' style, without the mocking Brechtian tone. ... And *The Cherry Orchard* should be staged in a theatre where they are least of all 'experts' in the 'Chekhovian tone'.[20]

It seems Efros hoped that the actors at the theatre would be able to combine the internal and external; both *living* the role, and presenting it to the audience.

The director was once asked if he thought he was closer to Stanislavski or Meyerhold. He replied that he did not want to be the 'slave' of any one method.

> In human terms, Stanislavski is closer to me. He is more intelligent, warmer ... But Meyerhold drove the art of the theatre forward, compared with so-called 'conventional realism', that is conventional psychological realism. I think that art today cannot follow only the line of Meyerhold, or the line of Stanislavski. There must be a miraculous combination of both.[21]

Vakhtangov, of course, also sought a 'miraculous combination' of Stanislavski and Meyerhold. Like Vakhtangov, Efros rejected naturalism or 'domestic truth' in the theatre. ('This domestic truth was always boring and uninteresting to me. It is not interesting when people sit on the stage, wearing their jackets.'[22]) The stage, he insisted,

Plate 8 Design by Valeri Levental for *The Cherry Orchard*, directed by Anatoli Efros (Taganka Theatre, 1975).

Plate 9 The Cherry Orchard, directed by Efros (Taganka, 1975). Vladimir Vystotski, right, as Lopakhin, and Alla Demidova, centre, as Ranevskaya.

'does not simply reproduce everyday reality, but instead offers us a condensed, heightened and almost symbolic picture'.[23]

> It always seemed to me, and I still believe, that the contemporary theatre must not be based on such a ... how shall I put it ... *literary* psychology, perhaps. Stanislavski introduced into our profession such words as 'action', 'inner action' – and through this, he achieved a revolution. Of course, it's not a matter of words, but terms are also important. We ... have been educated in these ideas, they are the bases of our professional outlook. ... Personally, with time it became clear to me that it is necessary to take inner action to its limit, almost to absurdity.

Efros drew a comparison with painting: you can stay within the limits of realism – or you can go beyond it.

> It is possible to apprehend and depict that life of the hyperbolic, the grotesque, the exaggerated. That is the question: how to find exaggerated tasks, exaggerated action, exaggerated activity – not breaking living truth, but subordinating it to some greater, you could say sharper, goal.[24]

Here again, then, we see a desire to combine inner 'truth' with a 'heightened' performance style. The acting in Efros' productions was based on an inner, 'psychological' realism, but it was also 'highly kinaesthetic': 'He believes that, whatever is going on inside a character must come out in the flesh.' The stage, he said, 'should always be highly active, outwardly expressive. However, it should also be psychologically subtle.'[25]

This was evident in *Three Sisters*. The final scene between Irina and Tusenbach in Act IV is usually played with a surface calm; the characters' 'pain, yearning and suffering' remain in the subtext (or, as Nemirovich might have said, on the 'secondary level'). In Efros' production, however, the characters suddenly cried out, the lines torn from them 'like the last words before death':

TUSENBACH: Say something! Say something!
IRINA: What? What?
TUSENBACH: Something!

The 'subtext' was not buried; it was physicalised. As Alla Demidova observed:

The 'secondary level' was played as the 'first', the principal level. It was like an explosion. For me this was, at the time, one of the most powerful theatrical impressions.
  Efros subsequently often used this method in his productions. It became almost customary. 'Efrosian'.[26]

Efros argued that in *The Cherry Orchard*, Chekhov presents us not with 'a simple realistic, living picture, but a grotesque, sometimes farcical, sometimes utterly tragic picture'.[27] In the Taganka production, there was a permanent set for all four acts – a mound of earth, like a flower-bed, or a graveyard. On this mound, a table, an antique armchair, a garden bench and some children's chairs stood among gravestones and crosses. Again, there was a tree, centre-stage: a cherry tree. On the backdrop hung large, sepia-tinted photographs – old family portraits, *momenti mori*. At the sides of the stage hung lace curtains which billowed in drafts from the windows. One spectator saw the set and commented, 'The Moscow Art Theatre lies buried there.'[28]
  The characters wore white – like ghosts in this graveyard. At the opening of the play, they all entered, and sang a jolly song (Epikhodov's ballad from Act II: 'What do I care for the noisy world … ') – but they sang it in a *tragic* manner. It was like a bizarre requiem for the dead. The song acted as a framing device; at the end, the characters returned and sang it again. This encapsulated Efros' desire to seek the 'truth' in contrasts; the tragic and the comic were juxtaposed to achieve the 'grotesque'.
  Alla Demidova's Ranevskaya was no 'grand dame exuding old world charm and given to melodramatic handkerchief clenches'. Instead, here was 'a contemporary woman of fashion whose gowns are low-cut and who stalks about the stage with the grace and beauty of a thoroughbred. Slouching one moment, a cigarette dangling carelessly from her hand, she is seized the next by a blast of neurotic energy which leaves her breathless.'[29] Efros once said: 'When we look at a medical cardiogram and see a straight line without waves, it means that there is no life. The waves mean life.'[30] The inner life of a character, then, should be represented as an oscillating line. The image suggests that actors should look for, and explore, strong emotional contrasts rather than pursuing a single, straight emotional 'line'. These contrasts were visible in Demidova's performance: 'The sharpness of passing from one state to another became the main pattern of her acting.'[31] When she recalled the death of her son, in Act I, she threw herself on the mound, and made her way almost on her knees through the gravestones and crosses, crying out (where the text specifies that she '*cries*

quietly'): 'My Grisha! … My boy! … Grisha, son … Drowned … Why? Why, my friend?' It was, again, a moment when the subtext, or 'secondary level' of the scene, was transformed into the 'first'. The 'inner action' was taken to its limit, 'almost to absurdity'. A moment later, however, she changed to another 'extreme': she was flirting and coquettish with Trofimov.

When Lopakhin and Gaev returned from the auction, she sat down on the bench, and suddenly became absolutely quiet. Smiling, she asked about the sale of the orchard, 'as if about something unimportant'. It was like 'the last smile before death'.[32] This disturbing calm was suddenly followed by an outburst of hysteria.

Lopakhin was played by Vladimir Vysotski. He was 'quiet, concentrated, sad' as he tried to save the estate – 'like a doctor trying to teach his stupid patients that there is an illness and it is time to do something about it'. Returning from the auction, however, he was 'angry and destroyed by what he has been forced to become – a part of the axe himself', about to cut down the orchard.[33] He poured out his anger in a 'high-stepping victory dance which borders on hysteria. Lopakhin continually falls to the ground, only to come up kicking once more until he is totally spent and must be helped from the stage.' Such hysteria, Spencer Golub observed, 'waits in the wings at every Efros production, ready to spring forth at a moment's notice. His actors seem to be performing at the edge of their own existence. The sense of danger that is implicit in such a performance never completely subsides.'[34]

'The most topical political theatre in Moscow'

Yuri Lyubimov came to the first run-through of *The Cherry Orchard*. Demidova recalled: 'Before he saw anything, he was already sitting almost sideways, and he watched with a scowl on his face. Everything irritated him.' Members of the theatre's Artistic Council sensed Lyubimov's disapproval, and, 'hoping to flatter him, began to criticise the production strongly. Or perhaps they really understood nothing. And it was so aggressive … The main argument was: it isn't the "Taganka"! To this day they can't explain what *is* the "Taganka" and what isn't.'[35] Lyubimov in fact felt: 'it is not our production, it is too refined, there is none of the Taganka's conventionality, impertinence, immediate connection with the present time, it is all too "psychological" and "elusive"'.[36] He edged it out of the theatre's repertoire.

Lyubimov was removed from his post as Artistic Director of the

Taganka in 1984. Efros took his place, and revived *The Cherry Orchard* (now without Vysotski, who died in 1980). He once said that the theme, the fundamental problem in the play, is 'that life is like a whirlwind':

> People are left trailing in the wake of this whirlwind. The whirlwind throws people down and carries them away. The whirlwind is always over us. We are the footprints of this whirlwind called *time*. Time is ruthless, swift, relentless. It changes itself and changes us, as a volcano changes the shape of the earth. And people in general are always helpless in the face of a volcano. A volcano reforms the shape of the earth. Chekhov felt in those years that the shape of the earth was changing. And wrote the play about it. This play contains the past, the present and the future of Russia of the day. And everything is connected.[37]

Unexpectedly, when the production was revived, it became 'almost the most topical political theatre in Moscow'.[38] In 1990, as the Soviet parliament was debating the issue of private property, the *Moskovskie novosti* (Moscow News) published an article (together with photographs of the Taganka production) about Russia's new 'Lopakhins', under the title, 'The class which does not exist but will':

> The situation is recognisable: our contemporary country estates have fallen into decline, they are overrun with debts, and the haggling over them has already been announced ... What will happen to the cherry orchard? Before us ... we again face the same questions as Chekhov's heroes faced at the beginning of the century.[39]

In the sound of breaking string could be heard 'the beginning and end of Russian history of the twentieth century, its old pains and its new hopes'.[40]

Sadly, Efros himself did not live to see the whirlwind of time blowing through his own country. He died in 1987.

Yuri Lyubimov: The art of 'plastic forms in space'

On the wall in the foyer of the Taganka Theatre there are four portraits: Brecht, Meyerhold, Vakhtangov and Stanislavski. Lyubimov recalled that at first, there were only three portraits: Brecht, Meyerhold and Vakhtangov. But the authorities said that without a fourth portrait, these three could not hang there. I always had great respect for Konstantin Sergeevich [Stanislavski]. But all the same, for some reason, these three portraits appeared first. Then they said: 'You put Meyerhold up; now take him down.' I replied: 'I'm sorry, I didn't put him up there. And so I won't take him down. Take him down yourself.' And then they said: 'Then add Stanislavski.' That's how there came to be a portrait of Stanislavski at the Taganka Theatre.[41]

Asked which of the portraits he felt closest to, Lyubimov answered: 'Probably Meyerhold.'[42] He had seen several of Meyerhold's productions.

I have drawn on this legacy in a very pragmatic way. Many of my friends, many men of the theatre who knew Meyerhold well, have often told me that my productions are very different from his. If I have recreated something of that period, it is not by choice, or after theoretical analysis, but by intuition. [43]

'We usually like to oppose Stanislavski and Meyerhold', Lyubimov has observed, 'and it is true that the two men are very different, as irreconcilable as snow and fire.'[44] Like Meyerhold, Lyubimov has reacted against 'the exclusive monopoly of the psychological realistic school in the theatre'.[45] He also sees acting as the art of gesture and movement, or 'plastic forms in space'. He wrote:

Amongst us, there is still a tendency to regard bold plastic solutions with suspicion: we are accustomed to strive for verisimilitude and everyday reality. Yet the important thing in art is not to reproduce reality, but to give an artistic image of it. Despite this, there is a strange but very widespread tendency to underestimate form in the creation of imagery. The psychological mood of the actor cannot be conveyed clearly and convincingly to the audience unless it is expressed in precise dramatic form.[46]

Theatrical form 'is the more expressive way of saying the truth', Lyubimov maintains; 'it is the maximum sharpness of an idea'.[47] This attitude has left him open, like Meyerhold, to the charge of 'formalism'. Like Meyerhold, he has been accused of reducing actors to puppets, mechanically repeating the actions they are given.[48] In fact, he has described the actor as 'an executive artist', who should master and execute an external 'score' of movement. Productions 'must be staged like a ballet, with the same attention to plastic and spatial problems. For there are occasions when the turn of a head can change the whole tableau.'[49]

Despite the portrait of Stanislavski hanging in the foyer of the Taganka, Lyubimov is actually opposed to the Stanislavskian principle of 'living through' a role. Directing *Boris Godunov*, for example, he advised an actor: 'you must not live it through internally in that way'.[50] In rehearsal, he asks the actors to focus not on the psychology of the characters, but rather to concentrate on conveying the *idea*. 'Speak simply, just express the idea. Think about the idea', he tells them.[51] What does this mean? In part, it means expressing the sense of the line, at any given moment – embodying it in words and movement. But it also implies 'an understanding of the role of this idea in the overall conception of the production'.[52] In rehearsing *Boris Godunov*, he told the actors not to worry about feelings: 'They will come of themselves. When you begin to colour your words with emotion, then meaning departs from the stage.' 'Find the courage to play freely, don't worry about feeling. ... It might not always come to you in a given rehearsal or performance. But you can play truthfully, if you focus on the idea.'[53] Anatoli Smelyanski has suggested that, where Efros is interested in 'complications and psychological contradictions', Lyubimov prefers clarity and directness – a *straight* rather than oscillating line.[54]

Lyubimov's *Three Sisters*: Making connections with the present

In 1981, Lyubimov staged *Three Sisters*. In many ways, the production was almost anti-Stanislavskian; it was Chekhov stripped of psychological realism.[55] The backdrop to the set was a high metallic icon-wall, weather-beaten and rusting. The faded faces of a fresco could be dimly perceived – like faces from a Russian icon painting. At the back stood three iron bedsteads – army bunks, perhaps. It was as if this was an old monastery, which had been turned into a military barracks. There was a sense, too, that it was a gulag prison-camp, and the officers were prison guards. It was a bleak environment, stripped of all Chekhovian 'atmosphere'. The typical elements of a traditional production – armchairs covered in dust-sheets, a piano with candles and flowers – were confined to small corners of the stage, like so much detritus.

In the centre stood a small trestle platform, a stage-within-a-stage. Two rows of chairs were arranged for an 'audience' in front of the platform. Characters sat here when not involved in the action. At times they turned to stare at the audience – as if *we* were the 'stage', and they were watching *us*. They looked 'so searchingly and insistently, we begin to feel uncomfortable'.[56]

Stage-left, there was a large wall of panelled mirrors, giving a slightly blurred reflection of the audience. At the start of the performance, the sound of a military band could be heard, faintly, playing an old wartime march. Then, the mirrored wall slowly opened to reveal the band, in uniform, standing and playing in the open air on the street outside the theatre. Behind them could be glimpsed the traffic on the main road outside; and in the distance, on the skyline, the towers of a church. It was an ingenious *coup de théâtre*, and immediately made a 'connection with the present time'. There it stood: Moscow, the great hope, the dream of the sisters – slightly tatty and tawdry now, under the neon street lights. Involuntarily, the audience was made to compare the dream with the present-day reality – to ask itself what had become of the sisters' hopes for a better future, in all the years since the play's premiere in 1901.

> The theatre is saying: 'Look around: the "future" is here already.' … The theatre does not want to comfort the audience, does not want us to accept harsh reality as a necessity. And so it is sounding the alarm.
> The wall goes down and the fresh wind of Moscow blows in our faces.[57]

Then the wall closed, and the audience stared again at its own reflection in the mirror. Masha, looking into the audience, spoke what might be seen as an epigraph for the whole production: 'It seems to me one must believe in something … Either you know what you're living for or else it's all empty, empty.'

Audiences at the Taganka were accustomed to reading 'subversive' meanings encoded in Lyubimov's productions. In *Three Sisters*, he undermined the 'positive' reading of the play. The characters' dreams and hopes were seen as hollow and even absurd. When Irina in Act I spoke about the need to work, she stood on the platform stage and delivered her lines with a gauche and naïve enthusiasm, like a school girl reciting lines learnt by heart from an approved Soviet textbook. She received the ironic applause of the 'audience' on stage. When Tusenbach began philosophising in Act II, he goose-stepped, like one of the guards in front of Lenin's tomb. At certain points, all the characters stood facing the audience, marching on the spot –

Plate 10 'The wall goes down and the fresh wind of Moscow blows in our faces ...' (Scene from Lyubimov's *Three Sisters*, Taganka, 1981.)

mocking, it seemed, the socialist dream of a forward march to a brighter future.

The production eschewed the usual 'lyricism' associated with Chekhov. (As Gershkovich saw, 'the theatre built a cold, heartless, deliberately intellectual action' to illustrate Lyubimov's stark interpretation of the play.[58]) In these barracks, there were 'no living people': 'everything here is dead, life is empty'.[59] The characters moved at times like automata. Olga was often seen sitting marking books – swiftly, mechanically making ticks in the margin – drilled, it seemed, to execute the task with military precision. At one point in Act I, Tusenbach and Soleny stood facing each other on the platform stage, as if lining up for a duel. Then Tusenbach recoiled, as if shot; he hit the back wall of the platform stage, his whole body jerking erratically, mechanically, in a puppet-like dance – a macabre dance of death, in time to military music. This mechanical movement suggested a world in which bodies without souls repeated 'meaningless, empty words' and gestures.[60]

The production, which ran for some two and a half hours, without interval, was staged almost like a 'speed-run' of the play.[61] There was no sense of real people actually 'living through' the events of the drama. Lines were spoken rapidly, in a plain, deadpan voice, deliberately at odds with the emotion in the words. At certain points, Lyubimov incorporated tape recordings of past productions. Before Tusenbach's monologue about work in Act I, for example, we heard the first lines spoken by Kachalov (who played the role at the Art Theatre). His soft, velvety voice made a sharp contrast with the blunt and matter-of-fact delivery of Lyubimov's actors. Here, then, was a deliberate, even nostalgic echo of a quite different acting style – and a reminder of 'how Chekhov used to be played'.[62] At the same time, the device emphasised how old-fashioned this more lyrical style now seemed.

One performance in the production, however, seemed distinct from the rest. Alla Demidova's Masha also reminded some critics of 'how Chekhov used to be played'. It seemed that Lyubimov had released Masha from the 'rigidity, the militarily drilled, formal intonations, movement and gestures, which he imposes to a greater or lesser degree on the other characters'.[63] In fact, this was the only performance which appeared to have been imbued with a realistic inner psychology. Announcing Vershinin's arrival in Act I, Anfisa brought in an army coat which Masha took and put on over her shoulders, emphasising her love of the military. Subsequently she kept the coat on – wrapping herself in it, sensuously. She seemed in fact to have a military fixation, perhaps the influence of her father. There was a touch of Hedda Gabler in this Masha. In Act IV, as Vershinin stood centre-stage, waiting to say goodbye to her, we saw Masha, at the side of the stage, leaning her head on an army coat, and gently touching it, caressing it – as if Vershinin had already gone, and this was all that reminded her of him. This was a *psychological* action, suggesting the character's inner feelings.

It has been suggested that Lyubimov treated Masha differently because he sees positive and redeeming qualities in her. (Marina Litavrina, for example, said that this Masha stood out as the only sister who continued to 'dream, to think, to yearn, to try to break free'.[64]) However, it is also possible that this, the most 'non-Lyubimovan'[65] of Lyubimov's actors, was in fact – consciously or not – choosing to play *against* the dominant style of the production. Her acting followed an 'oscillating' rather than a straight line.

Some critics called the production 'arbitrary' and 'coarse', a reduction of the play. Lyubimov was criticised for a lack of psychological depth in the characters and of using a purely formal approach incapable of revealing the layers of Chekhov's subtext.[66] G. Zamkovets, for example, said the production denied the spectator the possibility of empathy and understanding the characters' pain. But, behind these arguments, there were also *ideological* objections to Lyubimov's reading of the play. The same critic, for example, objected to the 'evident sneer' in the speeches about work and the future, which cancelled 'the essence of Chekhov's world-view' – his love for humanity, and his hopes for a better future.[67]

Lyubimov's next productions – *Vladimir Vysotski, Boris Godunov, The Possessed* – were all banned before they reached public performance. Then in 1983–4, while he was working abroad (directing productions in London and Bologna), he made a number of comments criticising the Soviet regime. In March 1984, he was dismissed from his post as Artistic Director of the Taganka, and in July, he was stripped of Soviet citizenship.

Lyubimov's work was fuelled by his opposition to the Soviet regime. When he returned to Moscow and the Taganka in 1989, it seemed in some ways as if the 'whirlwinds of time' had swept past both the director and the theatre. He became almost a forgotten man. His work, shorn of its 'pertinency' and 'immediate connection with the present time', now seemed little more than a series of theatrical devices – clever, but cold. In his 'enthusiasm for theatrical truth', Lyubimov, like Meyerhold, 'did away with the truth of feelings'.

In the work of Efros and Lyubimov, we can see a continuation of the 'historic split' in the Russian theatre, between two trends: the 'psychological' and the 'conventional'. Smelyanski has observed that 'there is a continual interpenetration and enrichment of the two methods' – but a synthesis has proved difficult and elusive.[68] Stanislavski himself concluded, in *My Life in Art*, that it is vitally necessary to develop the actor's 'inner' technique, and raise it to the level of external, physical technique.

> Only then will a new form receive the necessary inner basis and justification, without which it remains lifeless and loses its right to existence.
>
> This work, of course, is far more complicated and takes much longer. It is far more difficult to heighten feelings and experiences than to heighten the external form of embodiment. But theatre must be a spiritual art form, and it is therefore necessary to tackle the job without delay.[69]

Production notes

Three Sisters, directed by Vladimir Nemirovich-Danchenko (with N.N. Litovtseva and I.M. Raevski). The Moscow Art Theatre; first performance, 24 April 1940.

Three Sisters, directed by Anatoli Efros. Theatre on Malaya Bronnaya; first performance, Autumn, 1967.

The Cherry Orchard, directed by Anatoli Efros. The Theatre on the Taganka; first performance, 30 June 1975.

Three Sisters, directed by Yuri Lyubimov. The Theatre on the Taganka; first performance, 16 May 1981.

III Chekhov in America

6   Lee Strasberg
Truth in acting

The visits of the Moscow Art Theatre to the States in the 1920s left a lasting influence on American acting. *Tsar Fedor Ioannovich* by Aleksei Tolstoy opened in New York, at the 59th Street Theater, on 8 January 1923. 'The emotions of the audience rose to match the emotions on the stage', it was reported. 'At the close there were cheers and shouts as New York had never heard.'[1] This was followed by Gorky's *Lower Depths*; but it was perhaps the productions of *The Cherry Orchard* and *Three Sisters* which made the greatest impact.

As part of the advance publicity for the visit, Oliver Sayler had published a series of articles and books on the company. Translations of the plays performed were published, with introductions by Sayler. This helped to prepare audiences to appreciate Chekhov's work. Sayler wrote:

> I think the master key to the Art Theatre's interpretation of Chekhov and to its use of realism is a certain repression, a holding-back, a minimization, – the utter pole of the exaggeration which characterized the old florid rhetorical theatre and now once more the theatre of the impressionists and the futurists. The impression came to me vividly, with an inherent poignancy regardless of the matter of the scene, that this was life, not merely copied but interpreted or brought to the point where there seems to be no interpretation. And this impression came to me somehow from inside, not as if the actors were shrewdly and successfully copying life but as if they were driven by some unseen influence to live their lives in front of me in such a way that their joys and sorrows became clear to me even if they themselves did not understand.[2]

What American critics and audiences most admired in the acting was its 'truthfulness'. But what exactly *was* this quality of 'truth'?

Kenneth MacGowan was not alone in praising 'the welding of all the various performers of a play into an ensemble of fluid, varied, yet concerted and pointed quality'.[3] This was explicitly contrasted with the 'star' system which dominated the American theatre, and which encouraged a spirit of competitive individualism and exhibitionism. 'Our actors smirk and ogle and are quite at home with the gathering before them', wrote Alan Dale. But these Russian actors 'evinced complete oblivion to an audience'. They 'concentrated on their work' and had been taught 'to sink their personalities' into their roles.[4]

'Truth', then, was seen in part as an absence of conventional theatricality. Thus, Percy Hammond observed with astonishment that the 'most important' of the actors 'can come into a room or leave it without theatrical emphasis. You suddenly discover that they are present or that they are absent.'[5]

Reviewing *Three Sisters*, Maida Castellun wrote that

> the acting of the Russian actors makes a responsive spectator feel that he is committing the indiscretion of looking through the open window and listening to the private affairs of the Prozorov family and their friends. From their shabby rooms to their unassuming, appropriate clothes they are children of life, not of the stage.[6]

There was a sense, moreover, that the actors were 'living through' their roles as if for the first time. Hammond described Stanislavski as Vershinin,

> in that hopeful soliloquy which he delivered as a reverie, reclining, eyes closed, in his chair and seeming to improvise it to its ultimate dissonance. And Mme. Chekhova [Olga Knipper as Masha] when she listened and listened, as if she had not been hearing it for twenty-five years. And, in fact, all the others when we chanced to set our eyes, if not our ears, on them.[7]

Sayler described the final scene between Vershinin and Masha as 'the most unaffected, most deeply moving farewell of the modern theatre. To see it is to feel a knife cut clean through the heart.'[8] Years later, Lee Strasberg recalled how

> they looked at each other, and then they grabbed each other. I'll never forget that grabbing. I remember literally holding onto the seat. The simple reality of that good-by, of two people clinging to each other, will stay with me always.[9]

Actors and directors now wanted to know more about Stanislavski's methods. They wanted to know the secret of this 'truth'. Richard Boleslavsky had been a member of the Moscow Art Theatre; he played the tutor in Stanislavski's production of Turgenev's *A Month in the Country* (1909) and directed *The Wreck of the 'Hope'* at the First Studio (1913). He emigrated after the Revolution, and he was in New York to greet his former colleagues when they arrived in 1923. He presented a series of lectures on the Stanislavski 'system'; a member of the audience later described these talks as being 'like the coming of a new religion which could liberate and awaken American culture'.[10] A subsequent series of articles in magazines were later assembled in the book, *Acting: The First Six Lessons* (1933). For a number of years these articles (and the sketchy outline in *My Life in Art*) were the only published guides to the Stanislavski 'system'. (*An Actor Prepares* was not published until 1936.) In his talks, Boleslavsky stressed the importance of 'living the part': 'An actor who "lives his part" is a creative actor; the one who simply imitates different human emotions without feeling them each time is a "mechanical" one.'[11]

In 1924, Boleslavsky founded the American Laboratory Theatre. The aim was to create both a school and a theatre 'in which each actor strives to act his part, however humble, as if it were a major part of the play, but harmonized toward a perfect ensemble'.[12] Actors who joined the Lab were looking for answers to that elusive quality of 'truth' in acting. Among its early members were Stella Adler, Harold Clurman and Lee Strasberg. 'It was marvellous training', Adler recalled. 'It was thorough and complete, well-rounded and systematic, at an unmatchable level. And remember, we all had the recent model of the Moscow Art Theatre players to goad us, and to inspire us.'[13]

The programme included work in affective and sense memory. Clurman said that affective memory was 'the element that most excited many of the Lab's actors' – it was so novel.[14] Stanislavski developed exercises in 'affective memory' at the First Studio. He was inspired by reading the works of the French psychologist, Théodule-Armand Ribot (for example, *The Psychology of Attention* and *Diseases of the Will*). Here, he found the idea that experiences and emotions, like sights and sounds, leave traces in the memory. Sometimes these memories are revived in us quite spontaneously, and something of the original feeling returns; but they can also be consciously evoked. Exercises were devised to help the actor to tap into his or her store of affective memories, and release feelings analogous to his or her character's. In the First Studio's production of *The Cricket on the Hearth*, for example, Vera Soloveva as Bertha had problems in crying on command, so she used the affective memory of her own mother's death. It worked; after several performances, however, the power of this memory waned, and she had to seek other memories to create the same effect. Mikhail Chekhov was a member of the Studio. One day, as a class exercise, Chekhov 'relived' the memory of his own father's funeral. Stanislavski was very moved, and embraced Chekhov, thinking the exercise again proved the power of affective memory. However, Stanislavski later discovered that Chekhov's father was in fact still very much alive. The young actor had simply used the power of his own imagination.[15] The concept of affective memory has, in fact, proved very controversial. In later years, Stanislavski himself came to recognise that forcing emotions from memory could be dangerous, producing a kind of inner hysteria in actors.

It has been suggested that Boleslavsky's understanding of the Stanislavski 'system' was limited to the early experiments at the First Studio, and he knew nothing of later developments, such as the Method of Physical Actions; hence his emphasis on affective memory. In fact, it seems that Boleslavsky himself was somewhat bemused and exasperated by the way students at the Lab seemed to seize on the notion of 'affective memory', and neglect other aspects of the 'system' – especially the importance of 'action'.[16]

The Group Theater

In 1931, Clurman, Strasberg and Cheryl Crawford founded the Group Theater. This move was based, in part, on the desire to form a permanent ensemble, on the model of the Moscow Art Theatre. The link with Stanislavski can be seen in a letter the Group wrote to him in 1933. They described the Stanislavski 'system' as their guiding star.[17] From the beginning, Strasberg hoped to develop a shared approach to acting in the company through improvisation and through exercises in affective memory. Clurman recalled: 'The first effect on the actors was that of a miracle. ... Here at last was a key to that elusive ingredient of the stage, true emotion. And Strasberg was a fanatic on the subject of true emotion. Everything was secondary to it.'[18] Strasberg later described affective memory (together with sense memory) as 'the cornerstone of the modern method of training the actor'.[19] He said that memory was 'essential to understanding the entire process that goes into acting'; otherwise, 'experiencing on stage cannot be done night after night'.[20] The 'most difficult thing to do in acting' is to produce a truthful emotional reaction, for example to a moment of 'shock' – and to be able to do it, on cue, night after night: 'The only way of doing it, if you want a guarantee, is by means of affective memory.'[21]

More than one actor with the Group Theater, however, came to resist the emphasis on affective memory. Phoebe Brand said:

> I lent myself to it for a while – it is valuable for a young actor to go through it, but it is too subjective. It makes for a moody, personal, self-indulgent acting style. It assumes an actor is an emotional mechanism that can just be turned on. Emotion can't be worked for in that way – it is rather a result of truthful action in given circumstances. Lee insisted on working each little moment of affective memory; we were always going backwards into our lives. It was painful to dig back. ... Lee crippled a lot of people ... [22]

Elia Kazan, who joined the Group in 1932, notes that it was 'recommended, even insisted upon, that before entering a scene, an actor of our company was to "take a minute" to recall what would arouse him emotionally to the pitch Lee believed was proper for the scene, and only then to play it. Did it work? Yes. In good ways and in bad.' The problem was that the actor on stage 'was more concentrated – not on whoever else happened to be on stage with him but on his memories'. This created a very internalised form of acting. Increasingly, Kazan argued, the actors in Strasberg's productions 'would perform on stage as if they were moving in a miasma of self-devotion. When we see a person on the street behaving in that way, we call it "sleepwalking". When we see it on stage, we may say, "That's Method acting." '[23] In 1934, Stella Adler met Stanislavski in Paris and told him that since using his 'system', she had stopped enjoying her acting. She did not like affective memory at all. He replied: 'If my system doesn't help you, don't use it ... but perhaps you're not using it correctly.'[24] He told her that he now only used affective memory when all else failed. It was wrong to try to force feelings too directly; instead, the actor should concentrate on the *action* and the *given circumstances*.[25] Stanislavski believed that if the actor pursues an action, in the 'given circumstances' of the play, then the feeling should follow. The Russian actor and director, Iosif Rapoport (who appeared in Vakhtangov's production of *Princess Turandot*), offered the following example. You cannot act 'sorrow'. But you might, say, be acting a scene in which someone you are close to is seriously ill. 'You want to help him, ease his suffering, but you are unable to do so. Here is your task, fulfil it, fight for the person's health, do this in all sincerity – and you will evoke the authentic stage feeling which corresponds to the feeling we call sorrow.'[26] In other words, the actor should concentrate on the 'action' – the steps needed to fulfil the 'task'. The 'action' will create the feeling.

Adler returned to the States and shared what she had learnt from Stanislavski with the Group. 'Stanislavski said we're doing it wrong', she said. Strasberg's response was unequivocal. 'Stanislavski doesn't know', he declared. '*I* know.'[27] He subsequently claimed that he was, in any case, not teaching the Stanislavski 'system', but rather his own development of it. (Hence, he called it the 'Method', to distinguish it from the 'system'.) He thought Stanislavski was wrong now to place so much stress on 'action', and reject the notion of 'affective memory'. 'Action we have always used', he later said, 'but the emphasis on action as the main thrust, no. If you are unable to bring in emotion, then what is the point of action?'[28] Simply pursuing an action does not necessarily generate the 'feeling' – it 'doesn't always happen'. 'We can differ theoretically, but the point is that affective memory worked, that's all I can tell you.'[29]

The debate in the Group Theater led to a historic split. Adler continued to oppose affective memory, which she maintained induced hysteria.

It's polluted water, and yet Americans, typically, continue to drink it. Stanislavski himself went beyond it. He was like a scientist conducting experiments in a lab; and his new research superseded his earlier ideas: the affective memory belonged to the older, worn-out ideas. But Lee always thought it was the cornerstone of the Method, and in this way he became a laughing stock.[30]

Strasberg's influence on a generation of actors, however, through his work at the Actors Studio, has been profound. The stars who attended the Studio, such as James Dean and Marilyn Monroe, helped to build his reputation as the guru of the American Method.

A 'subjective' approach to performance?

The Studio was formed in 1947 by Cheryl Crawford, Robert Lewis and Elia Kazan. The aim was 'to provide a place where the talented young actor could continue to work on problems of craft, correct errors and defects of approach or ability and receive fresh stimuli toward new creativity'.[31] Strasberg joined in 1949, and became the artistic director in 1951. Twice a week he would observe scenes and exercises performed by actors, and then comment. The sessions were closed to the public, and this helped to foster a certain mystique about the Method. The Studio's success, in fact, bred notoriety. It was accused of emphasising the actor's internal work at the expense of external technique. As Strasberg himself wrote:

> An entire mythology of Actors Studio methods has been created. Supposedly, in the temple of 'the Method' actors are taught and encouraged to mumble, grumble, slouch, spit, bite, scratch, ride motorcycles, wear sweatshirts and blue jeans, be so carried away by their emotions that they forget themselves and do each other physical harm, jeer at the audience, sneer at Shakespeare and the classics and raise the banner of a violent realism.

In response to this, Strasberg pointed out the 'first problem set for one of our recent new members, Geraldine Page':

> Miss Page does not need studio recognition as proof of her talent. But what we did demand from her ... is to get rid of her personal mannerisms of speech and behavior, to differentiate between her real talent and the banalities of personal habit, to speak clearly and precisely, to erase the peculiar voice habits.[32]

Nevertheless, Strasberg himself recognised that the Studio's work had tended to focus on the 'internal' and had not sufficiently encompassed 'the actor's sense of the external as part of the creative process, wherein the external elements themselves become heightened, and the human being thereby becomes a more wonderful instrument of expression and therefore responds, like a rare violin, more deeply and truly to the dictates of the inner technique'.[33]

The Studio was accused of encouraging a 'subjective, autobiographical approach to performance'.[34] Robert Lewis (who left the Studio in 1948) objected to what he saw as the cult of 'real feeling' at the expense of the *play*:

> Are those 100 per cent 'living the part' folks really living the part, or are they living themselves and adding the author's words to that life? When they speak of 'psychological truth' do they mean their psychology, or the truth of art which includes, in addition to true feeling, all the circumstances of the character, the situation, the style of the play, etc.?[35]

Similarly, Harold Clurman argued:

'The Method' has a particular appeal to the young American actor ... because while *not the whole of the Stanislavski System*, it emphasizes the inner nature of the actor's self, the truth of his private emotion as the prime source of artistic creativity. This disclosure of self strikes the actor as a veritable revelation – in both the personal and professional sense. Too frequently he tends to make a cult of it, a sort of therapy akin to the benefits of psychoanalysis. When this occurs – and a lack of cultural background conspires to make it occur – it becomes a distortion of art in general and of Stanislavski's teachings in particular.[36]

The Method, then, seemed to emphasise the actor's subjectivity, and the 'truth' of his or her own feelings – without reference to the larger 'truth' of the play. It was claimed it scaled drama down to what the actors could handle rather than encouraging them to rise up to meet the demands of the play. 'Whatever the actor felt was "right" became the starting point for the performance.'[37] But this was not Strasberg's intention. In fact, he rebuked actors if he thought they were letting their own subjective feelings get in the way of the character. Once, for example, after seeing Ellen Burstyn working on a scene at the Studio, he told her: 'you went so much with the personal thing, that you lost some of the things that she has. I lost – in the way in which you cried, I lost the character.'[38]

Strasberg made an important distinction between his own work, and Stanislavski's. Stanislavski urged the actor, in working on a role, to try to put him/herself in the character's shoes, and imagine: 'What would *I* do if *I* was in this situation?' Thus, in working with an actor on the role of Lady Macbeth, Stanislavski might have asked: 'Now, if you were Lady Macbeth, how would you do this? How would you behave?' Strasberg argued that in doing this, Stanislavski 'often made the aesthetic mistake of taking the role down to the actor'.[39]

The Stanislavski formulation often does not lead the actor to seek the kind of reality which the author conceived and which underlies the lines he wrote. It becomes almost a way of bringing every dramatic thing down to a naturalistic level which cannot support the drama. Stanislavski's formulation will then only help the actor by accident.[40]

Strasberg preferred Vakhtangov's revision of Stanislavski's formula. Instead of imagining 'what would I do if I was in this situation?', the actor asks him/herself: 'What would make me feel and behave as the character does?' So, for example, Vakhtangov might have asked the actor playing Lady Macbeth: 'If you had to do such and such a thing, as Lady Macbeth does, what would have to happen to you, what would motivate you to do that?' In other words, Vakhtangov 'places the aesthetic intention first and then uses the technique as a way of carrying out the aesthetic intention'. The aim is to help the actor to 'ascend to the level of the character'. 'You see, work on a part helps create the reality and so we must be careful to bring the actor to the reality of the play by motivating him to act as the character acts.'[41]

On one occasion, Strasberg told the Studio members that, in playing Shakespeare, 'we must never permit ourselves to fall into simply bringing these people down to the ordinary level of reality in order to make them human'.

> Don't forget that even in ordinary plays I bemoan that approach. The purpose of this work is not to make everything casual and ordinary. On the contrary, our purpose is to fill everything with the utmost significance, to bring out the most important and fullest and most dramatic responses of the human being.[42]

Applying the 'Method': Strasberg's *Three Sisters*

In 1962 a decision was made to form the Actors Studio Theatre. The first season began in March 1963 with Eugene O'Neill's *Strange Interlude*. The sixth, and final, production of the company's short life was *Three Sisters*, which opened on 22 June 1964 (Morosco Theatre, New York). Strasberg claimed he had been planning the production in his mind for years. Susie Mee recalled that 'among his students and disciples, expectations ran high. It seemed to us as if the Great Lee ... had received the creative torch direct from Stanislavski himself. This, we thought, would be the authoritative, the quintessential *Three Sisters*.'[43] The production was in fact 'long talked of as the great American attempt to immortalize Method acting, to conquer Stanislavski on his own ground'.[44] Moreover, it was *judged* in these terms as a representation of the Method in practice – even though Clurman objected that it was not 'obliged or intended to demonstrate anything in particular. It is (or should be) done to reveal Chekhov's play on the stage.'[45] It became the occasion for the continuation of the debate about the Method. The production, as we will see, finally turned into a disaster for the Actors Studio Theatre, and for Strasberg himself; but it is time, perhaps, to re-evaluate it.

The principle behind the theatre was not to form a permanent ensemble, but to use actors for each production. However, because the actors were all supposed to be Studio members, a shared approach, a shared 'Method', would hopefully inform the work. As Geraldine Page observed: 'We all know each other – we've worked at the Studio, watched each other struggle with problems. The kind of work we do there is so agonizing and soul-baring, it welds a family feeling.'[46]

Strasberg's last production on Broadway had been in 1951; since then, he had concentrated on teaching, in the Studio, and in his own private classes. The question now was: could he apply the work of the classroom to the theatre? It has been suggested, in fact, that when it came to *Three Sisters*, Strasberg largely abandoned his own theories, and seemed to fall back into quite old-fashioned methods of directing, giving moves and even line readings.[47] But in fact this is a myth. The evidence suggests that Strasberg, in the limited time available for rehearsals, tried to turn classroom theory into actual practice.

Drawing on Chekhov's reported comments on the theatre, Strasberg believed that the writer 'was insistently opposed to fake dramatic vision. He didn't like sentiment. He didn't like the actors to be too aware of acting. He didn't like points to be made too emphatically on the stage.' Strasberg felt that, even in Stanislavski's productions, the acting was too 'emphatic': 'The emotional power of their acting was so great that watching them was like being bathed in emotional life. ... The Moscow Art Theatre productions were rich and full, but Chekhov never quite liked that kind of thing.' Strasberg wanted a 'lighter touch'. 'It is possible', he concluded, 'that the technical work we do here, which strips the actor of obvious theatricalities, can lead to the fulfilment of Chekhov's intention.'[48] Gerald Hiken, who played Andrei, recalled:

> ... Lee talked to us frankly about doing something that had not been done on the stage for a long time, a feeling for the poetic truth of a play, of living vocal tones rather than acting tones, people rather than characters. [It's] the difference, for example, between what we were doing and Olivier's *Uncle Vanya* which, when you listen to it, sounds like a group of eccentrics. [Strasberg] didn't want eccentrics. He wanted people. He didn't want 'characterization', he wanted living. And he didn't care if people were blocked at times or hidden or inaudible. He said, 'And you will have a lot of people who won't like it.'[49]

At the first rehearsal, Strasberg gave a preliminary talk. He discussed the life of the characters in a small provincial Russian town –

the 'given circumstances' of the play: the sense of isolation, the need to generate your own entertainment, and so on. Hiken:

> Strasberg talked a great deal about his own memories of Russia as a child, the difficulties of travelling, the hardness of life, which meant that when you did enjoy something you threw yourself into it, because it was a rare opportunity. The masquers became very important for that reason. It wasn't just another party. It was one of the few out of the whole year, and the most important of those. Everything was then intensified emotionally from that point of view. ... And you grabbed at every bright, new face like Vershinin. You reached out to anyone with any qualities at all. Friendship was not a casual thing. There weren't many friends to choose from.[50]

In rehearsal, Strasberg continued to stress the importance of 'the atmosphere that would surround us and how it might affect us'. For Act I, for example, the given circumstances were defined as follows: 'The sunshine, the bright day, what it's like the first day of Spring when you've had a very hard Winter, the effect of sitting and working on school papers.'[51]

The first five days were spent reading and discussing the play – what Stanislavski would have called 'table talk'. Salem Ludwig (Ferapont) said this gave the actors 'a mutual experience in terms of the script so that we could have something to discuss as an experience we all shared'.[52] On the sixth day, the outlines of the set were marked out on the floor of the rehearsal space. The actors were urged to use 'sense memory' to create a sense of the environment and imagine steps and walls, etc. This is a technique which asks the actor to relive sensations experienced through the five senses. A simple example: as an exercise, an actor might try to 'relive' the sensation of taking a shower. For *Three Sisters* there were a number of improvisations, at an early stage in rehearsal, which focused largely on the evocation of sense memory – 'sound, smell, and tactile sensations of the cold'.[53] In other words, Strasberg was trying to help the actors, not simply to understand the 'given circumstances' in an *intellectual* way, but to *experience* them through the senses. For Act II, for example, the actors 'had to create the sense of coming into a warm house from the frigid Russian outdoors'.[54]

Strasberg told the cast, on the very first day of rehearsals, that he would not 'block' the play, because with such an experienced cast it would not be necessary.[55] He did not want to *tell* them when and where to move; rather, he wanted them to discover their own reasons for moving. The aim was to engender a sense of spontaneity, a 'spirit of improvisation'.[56] The positions around the table for the meal at the end of Act I, for example, were never actually set. Strasberg worked for hours on this scene, and it was widely praised. 'For one thing, everyone really ate. ... While it may seem obvious, in most plays a scene like this would be faked. There's a big difference between fake eating and really eating, and I've never seen anyone fake eating convincingly.' The scene helped fuel 'the actors' sense of ensemble',[57] and to create a sense of the actors actually 'living' their roles, rather than 'acting'. 'Strasberg gave us a good thing to work on', Geraldine Page recalled. 'He said, "Go on with what you're doing when other characters are speaking; move around like normal people. Everybody go on about your business – don't stand there and be polite." That's what we all did, and the party scene had a terrific lifelike quality as a result.'[58]

Hiken recalls that Andrei's 'dance' in Act II was developed through improvisation in rehearsal. Andrei was almost teased by the others into dancing.

> All direction of that scene then became ... to maintain the feeling of Andrei being urged to get up and dance, at first rejecting it, then accepting it and then dancing spontaneously, connecting the other people in the room to that dance. ... And [Strasberg] got very angry during one performance when we had lost that quality, and it became a moment when Andrei showed off. It became something else ... [Strasberg] said, 'It's a different thing now. Now it's somebody gets up and entertains at a party. It's just the little difference of level that makes it wrong.' So understanding that, we went back to the other way ... [59]

In other words, Strasberg resisted anything that became a 'set piece'. He did not want the actors simply to repeat something that had worked before, purely for its effect. It is also clear, however, that the director visualised certain moments very strongly. Once, before rehearsals began, he showed Page (playing Olga) a Japanese print and told her, 'This is how I see the fire scene'.

> The print showed two women – one sitting on something draped and the other coming out from behind a screen with a candle, sort of listening, caught in some kind of horror. This visualization stuck like a nail in his head ... [60]

Strasberg was not, however, simply aiming for a visual effect. The screens on stage became a place for Olga to hide behind; it gave the actor 'a better opportunity to play, "I don't want to hear it" '.[61]

Similarly, Strasberg told Hiken, in his confessional speech at the end of Act III, to hold on to the back of a chair while he said certain lines. Hiken found that the action of gripping the chair created an emotional response in him. He speculated Strasberg wanted 'a courtroom feeling of confessing, standing up and confessing something, so that there was something both visual and emotional in it'.[62]

Strasberg was concerned to allow the actors the space to develop their own performances. He 'always taught directors never to demonstrate to an actor what you want them to do because they will only imitate you and not do what you really want, which is live their roles'. He did not want to inhibit the actor's 'creative and emotional force'.[63] Some actors were bemused by the degree of freedom they were given. 'Sometimes Lee would not say anything in a place where I thought I needed help', Page recalled. 'But he was right, because I figured it out for myself – and that's better than being told.'[64]

However, one result of this 'freedom' may have been some inconsistencies in the acting style. Strasberg was concerned that Kevin McCarthy was turning Vershinin into 'too charming a lady's man'; he wanted to see more of the 'lonely dreamer' in the character. After some three weeks of rehearsal, John Strasberg (who was stage-managing the production) asked his father why he did not insist more strongly on what he wanted. 'He said that it wasn't the right moment, that he was going to wait a little longer to see if Kevin would begin to do more. He would make suggestions rather than giving a definite direction.'[65] He did not *push* McCarthy or try to 'force' his performance. The actor, however, never really lost a rather 'jovial, smoking-car manner' as Vershinin[66]; and his genial style of playing did not entirely blend with the Kim Stanley's highly charged and emotional performance as Masha.

After the initial rehearsal period, Strasberg began to hold group rehearsals in the afternoons, and work with individual actors in the mornings. This included work in affective memory. Ludwig, for example, made use of an affective memory to help him sense the confusion of an old man caught up in the turmoil of the fire in Act III. Later, during run-throughs, Strasberg told him he had lost some of that feeling; and Ludwig realised he needed to go back again to that earlier affective memory work in order to recapture it.

Hiken recalled how Strasberg worked with him on the scene in Act II, when Andrei is looking through his old university lecture notes.

That was, I think, the hardest problem I had in the play. ... The thing I was furthest from, that Lee helped me the most with, was reading the Moscow lecture notes and his final suggestion of taking something strictly emotional to me, having no connection with lectures, universities or anything intellectual. Some nights it was a picture of my baby, sometimes it was a stone that had memories. Whatever I would find useful. Sometimes it was a sound. I've a memory, for example, of waves on a beach at a particular time when I was a child – a happy memory. I would remember the sound of the waves, and I would even recreate them with my mouth to make that sound that they make when they break on the shore. By coincidence, the wind in the beginning of the second Act recreated that sound. So that when Natalya's talking to me, I'm listening to that wind and trying to recapture that happy feeling of the waves on the beach, not really listening to what she's talking about, the way that you are able to listen in life when you are preoccupied with something else that is not intellectual, but emotional. ... Lee's most important work in the play was for me – I don't know about the others – in finding the human equivalent in your own experience for the scenes that you had to play.[67]

Strasberg, then, was asking the actor to draw on personal memories in order to achieve the required feeling for the scene. This feeling was not created by character's *actual situation*; rather, the primary source was 'the inner nature of the actor's self, the truth of his private emotion'. How this worked in performance can be judged by watching the film version of the production, which was made in 1965.[68] Hiken appears lost in thought, dazed, almost as if 'sleepwalking'. He sits staring ahead of him; perhaps significantly, he barely glances at the 'lecturing notes'. It could be argued that this distracted quality is appropriate for this scene. Andrei *is*, in fact, rather preoccupied, and detached from Natasha. Strasberg believed that it did not matter 'what an actor remembers, so long as it stirs the proper degree of belief and the proper stimulus to make him behave as he would under the conditions in the play'.[69] In this instance, he could, with some justification, have claimed that the internal work he did with Hiken helped the actor to do just that: it stimulated him to behave like the character. However, the fact remains that the actor was not concentrating primarily on pursuing an 'action' in the 'given circumstances'.

Asking the actor to search in their own memories for parallels or 'human equivalents' to the character's experiences might seem to be taking the role down to the actor's own level. However, Strasberg also sought to help the actor to 'ascend to the level of the character'. This emphasis was evident, for example, in the director's work with Hiken on Act IV:

> The question always was, ... given the situation of the author (and following Lee's direction), given the situation that my wife is unfaithful, I know it and everybody knows it, and I'm not talking about that – how do I do that? How do I personally behave in that kind of situation?

In other words, what would motivate the actor 'to act as the character acts'? This was Hiken's solution:

> Well, going to the kind of situation where something terrible is going on and nobody is talking about it, I don't want to talk about it, I put on the brightest face possible to discourage anybody from bringing up anything about the subject. And that led me directly to the fourth Act solution of cheeriness, of happiness, of serenity, nothing is wrong, nobody should even mention anything wrong, because I would immediately deny it. Everything is fine; ... inside I can cry about it all I want, ... but behaviour is what mattered.[70]

At one stage in rehearsal, Hiken was performing Andrei's monologue in Act IV in a depressed and melancholy tone. Strasberg felt that, from the character's point of view, this was correct; but the speech follows Tusenbach's farewell to Irina, and precedes Masha's farewell to Vershinin, and from an artistic point of view it was not advisable to have three 'downbeat' scenes in succession. Andrei's scene needed to provide a contrast; how this should be done was left up to Hiken. 'The solution he used was to have Andrei regard the situation in which he found himself to be a ludicrous one, so that he came to laugh at himself.'[71] In other words: the actor had to consider the 'aesthetic' effect. He had to find a solution that worked dramatically, but could also be justified in terms of the character's behaviour. This belies the notion that the starting point, in Strasberg's work, was whatever the actor felt was 'right', rather than the demands of the play.

Kazan argued the actors in the production 'still tended to play their scenes with themselves, not with the other actors on stage'.[72] We have to recognise, however, that Kazan was hostile to Strasberg personally. There was a strong sense, in the production, of the characters' inner lives. It was clear they were continuing to pursue their own thoughts, even while they were listening and reacting to the other characters. But this is not the same as acting in a 'miasma of self-devotion'. Geraldine Page was asked: 'In *Three Sisters*, how do you relate to the other actors, how do you get into their lives?' She replied: 'There's a conscious effort made to interrelate. I had fun seeing how Olga felt about all the different people.' She discovered, for example, 'how murderous Olga feels when Natasha starts messing around'.

> In the fire scene, the more we rehearsed it, the more I wanted to kill Natasha. I had trouble with this reaction. Olga has a line, 'Oh, it's getting all black before my eyes.' I thought I'd never be able to say a line like that without breaking up. But the more I worked, the more clearly I saw that she doesn't do anything because she's incapacitated by her titanic rage. One time, during rehearsals, when Fedor Ilich [Kulygin] said, 'Olga, if it hadn't been for Masha, I'd have married you – you have such a generous nature', I felt so guilty. I was murderous, and he thought I was generous! I'd just been thinking, 'If I could kill Natasha I would put an axe right through her; I'd slice her in half and pull the pieces apart and throw them to the dogs.'[73]

In this scene, Page poured herself a glass of water to steady herself, and then sat down – anger and tension written on her face. It was clear that, even as she was listening to Natasha, she was continuing to think her own, 'murderous' thoughts.

Frequently in the production, the characters were occupied by a task – arranging flowers, reading a newspaper, smoking a cigar, etc. – even as they continued to listen and react to what others were saying. This seemed very 'natural', and perhaps helped the actors' concentration. It was another way in which Strasberg encouraged them to 'move around like normal people'; to 'live' their roles rather than 'act'.

Kim Stanley's performance was highly acclaimed. Her Masha was like a smouldering fuse, whose feelings exploded at times with sudden and unexpected force. Take the scene in Act III, when she turned on Albert Paulsen's Kulygin, and snapped angrily: 'I can't stand it any longer... ' She pounded her forehead in her frustration; Kulygin scurried away in astonishment and fear. Some felt the performance was *too* emotional. (She 'emoted as though she were on the cross', Kevin McCarthy recalled.[74]) John Strasberg, however, has argued: 'it is not that she was overemotional but that her emotions were sometimes disturbing' – because they were so 'truthful' and 'real'. In some scenes, 'she would sometimes gasp for breath, her passion was so over-whelming'. This only seems 'excessive', he concluded, if 'someone doesn't particularly like being so immediately moved by another human being's pain and longing'.[75]

But was this the 'truth' of the character, or the truth of the actor's private emotion? Was it a revelation of character, or a revelation of self? Clurman said that Stanley turned Masha into 'a latter-day neurotic, ridden by spasms of torment caused not so much by her situation in the play as by an experience of life far more complex and sophisticated than that of Chekhov's character'.[76] Strasberg himself seemed to feel that the performance at times made the character too neurotic, and went beyond what was appropriate for the play. This was particularly true in Act IV. Stanley paced the stage restlessly, her hair down, bearing a snapped-off branch, like a riding crop, which she wielded to show her vexation. At one rehearsal, Michael Wager (Executive Administrator at the Actors Studio Theatre) turned to Strasberg and said: 'What is this? ... She looks like she's playing the mad scene from *Lucia di Lammermoor*!' Strasberg, with a touch of exasperation, said she was playing it that way because she had decided that Masha 'goes crazy' in the final Act.[77] Hiken reflected:

> I think, in some cases, there was an overevaluation of Kim's work, because she was overtly the most dramatic and, I think even she will agree, too dramatic at the opening of the run. She toned down considerably. She said her Masha *would* have gone to Moscow. I think she developed tremendously during the run a feeling of the reticence of the woman.[78]

The death of the 'Method'?

There were only some five weeks in total for rehearsal – very limited time for the kind of work Strasberg was pursuing. As Salem Ludwig saw, Strasberg could have achieved a more superficial success if he had simply told the actors what to do. But he was concerned to encourage a continual process of exploration and development, rather than settling for effective 'results'.[79]

On an *external* level, the production was rather conventional. The shadow of the Moscow Art Theatre hovered over it. (The setting was heavily realistic, and there was an extensive use of atmospheric music and sound effects.) Its strength, perhaps, was on an *internal* level: in the strong, almost palpable sense of the characters' inner lives.

When the production opened, it initially attracted enthusiastic reviews. Jerry Tallmer wrote: 'The Actors Studio talks a good deal about truth. Last night at the Morosco Theater it nailed for our lifetime the right to do so.' Later reviews, however, were more critical. Henry Hewes described it as a 'montage of acting explorations';[80] similarly, Elia Kazan wrote:

> I thought some of the actors were behaving as if they were still doing classroom exercises, competing with each other to give 'great performances' and win Lee's approval. The sorry fact is that I've come to dislike the acting of some of my Actors Studio people – even though I like them all personally. I would prefer more humour and verve and less self-indulgence, self-pity, and self-awareness. I detest emotional stripteases.[81]

The reviews for Kim Stanley's performance helped to attract audiences, and the production ran throughout the summer, closing on 3 October, after 119 performances.

Then came a fateful invitation to revive it for the second annual World Theatre Season in London in 1965. English critics and actors had long regarded the Method with suspicion; it was seen as a peculiarly American folly. This attitude is summed up by a famous anecdote. Dustin Hoffman was working on the film, *Marathon Man*. In one scene he had to appear as if he had spent three days and nights without sleep. So he decided actually to go without sleep for thirty-six hours. When his co-star, Laurence Olivier, heard about this, he said: 'You didn't sleep? Dear boy, why don't you try acting?'[82] The story is sometimes quoted as an example of the absurd lengths Method actors can go to, to achieve emotional 'truth'. But in fact it also rebounds on Olivier himself (an actor who worked largely through external technique, with very little inner 'truth').

Strasberg had in the past frequently disparaged the English stage, which he said was 'not bad, just outdated … it boasts not reality nor conviction but acting'.[83] These comments probably did not endear him to English critics, who began sharpening their collective critical knives.

There were just eleven days to revive the production. There were major cast changes. Nan Martin replaced Geraldine Page as Olga. Sandy Dennis stepped in as Irina. Meanwhile, Kim Stanley demanded that Kevin McCarthy should be replaced as Vershinin by George C. Scott, and Strasberg somewhat feebly acceded. In the event, Scott simply disappeared for three days of rehearsal; Stanley came to hate him and want McCarthy back. In London, the company were not able to rehearse on the stage at the Aldwych Theatre until the technical rehearsal, the night before the opening. They were horrified to discover that the stage was raked; all the furniture had been hired, and it was not adjusted to the rake, and so it tilted alarmingly.

The first night ran for an hour longer than usual. The audience booed; when, in Act III, Irina says, 'This has been a terrible evening', someone in the audience called out, 'It certainly has been.'[84] The next day, Herbert Kretzmer declared in the *Daily Express*: 'A cluster of celebrated Broadway names last night rendered a kind of death blow to the "Method" school of acting.' B.A. Young wrote:

> The company are prisoners of their mannerisms, and their mannerisms include all the worst features popularly attributed to Method actors. Their chief characteristic is a way of speaking as if all their lines were being extemporised, and the key words in each sentence had to be groped for, conjured out of the air.[85]

Peter Roberts parodied this style of speech in his review:

> You er must um forgive me er if this ah notice, if this notice, er reads hum, you know, reads um a bit er disjointed. Um at the end er of a whole evening with er Actors' Studio in er Chekhov's er *The Three Sisters* you ah damn–I've–lost–my–breath–fall–into– their–speech–patterns–and–hell–you–kind–of–just–can't–get–out– of–it.

The intention may have been to 'get Chekhov's lines to come out as though you just thought them up yourself. The trouble is that it leaves your audience wishing you hadn't taken the trouble.'[86]

In an interview, Strasberg conceded that 'the critics were right in some of the things they said ... We were not prepared for the travelling situation. The performance last night in no way compared with what the actors are capable of.'[87] The conditions had, in fact, badly affected the cast. Kim Stanley fell apart. For some reason she moved lethargically, 'like she was drugged', and indulged in long pauses. 'I don't know what the hell she was doing', Strasberg said. 'The movements, the speeches, the timing, everything was in halftime. It was completely thrown off.'[88] But the real problem, as Strasberg saw it, was Sandy Dennis' performance as Irina. Alan Brien wrote:

> No doubt Sandy Dennis's carefully calculated ums and ahs, repeats of phrases, pointless giggles and wriggles, stumbles and pauses, are very good exercises for her histrionic muscles. But they

reduced Irina to an inarticulate Ninny ... and must have added half an hour to the running time.[89]

It seemed almost a caricature of Method acting. Strasberg commented caustically: 'Sandy Dennis insisted on doing her junk. She's a good actress but she was just stupid.'[90]

The Actors Studio Theater closed, in many ways as a result of the London fiasco; the funding from the Ford Foundation was not renewed. Strasberg himself never directed again; he retreated to work in the classroom. Robert Brustein declared that the failure of the theatre proved the Studio itself was 'moribund, or at the least sapped of its force and vitality'.

> I did not believe I was prematurely judging a budding theatre company, since Strasberg had been working with these actors in cloistered session for more than fifteen years. No, the performance of his long-promised practical theatre cast doubt on the theory behind it ... [91]

Actually, Brustein's belief that the studio was 'moribund' was more than a little premature. His views reflected his own hostility to the Method. Seeing it as a predominantly subjective, 'psychological' and 'naturalistic' approach to acting, he campaigned to loosen its stranglehold on the American theatre, and to foster alternative traditions.

In 1965, the Moscow Art Theater returned to New York, with a new production of *The Cherry Orchard*, directed by Viktor Stanitsyn (with Alla Tarasova as Ranevskaya), and Nemirovich's production of *Three Sisters* (still in the repertoire). Audiences and critics were surprised by the energy of the acting style, and the company's 'aggressive awareness of everything physical'.[92] This seemed far from the 'internalised' acting associated with the Actors Studio. Stanitsyn told Charles Marowitz that actors at the Art Theatre were now 'encouraged to attack their roles with an uninhibited gusto, the assumption being it is better to have to tone down a performance than try to escalate it from a muttering, subjective nothingness'.[93] Brustein wrote:

> [I]t is clear enough now that, as far as results are concerned, the Stanislavski System bears about as much relation to the Strasberg Method as caviar does to hot dogs. Russian performing, as a matter of fact, forms a distinct contrast with American naturalistic acting, for it is firm, open, direct, and clearly articulated. The actors attain a high level of emotion without ever spilling over into

hysteria; they are never eccentric or neurasthenic; they change personality radically from role to role instead of repeating personal mannerisms; and although they are closely identified with their characters, they are not lost in them. While the Strasberg actor is listening most intently to himself, furthermore, the Stanislavski actor is listening most intently to others: the Moscow Art Theater obviously tolerate no star personalities, and all the actors play as if there were no such thing as minor roles.

And yet, Brustein also felt that there was now 'something old-fashioned about the Moscow Art Theatre, something a little musty and museum-like', in the predominantly realistic style of the productions. He concluded:

Perhaps it is time we stopped arguing over who is Stanislavski's legitimate heir, and founded a totally different family. It is always a difficult thing to reject a father, especially a powerful and brilliant one, but until the American theatre can break the bonds of naturalistic truth and psychological reality, there will be no real advance.[94]

Production notes

Three Sisters, directed by Lee Strasberg. The Actors Studio Theater at the Morosco Theatre, New York; first performance, 22 July 1964.

7   Andrei Serban
Upstaging the playwright?

Audiences left Andrei Serban's production of *The Cherry Orchard* (1977) in a daze, murmuring 'Is this really Chekhov?'[1] Critics were divided: was this the rediscovery of a classic – or an act of desecration that would make Chekhov turn in his Moscow grave? Walter Kerr called it 'daring, perverse and deeply original', but John Simon said it was 'consistently coarse, virtually cretinous and a total betrayal of Chekhov's basic simplicity'.[2]

Serban himself argued the production 'created an enormous controversy among the New York elite, since it was conceived upon Meyerhold's critical observations of Stanislavski's famous 1904 production. Chekhov called the play a comedy, in places almost a farce, not a drama. The whole scandal centred on the question, "Is one allowed to contradict Stanislavski?"'[3]

The set, designed by Santo Loquasto, broke with the traditional 'heavy realism' associated with Chekhov's plays. The floor of the vast stage of the Vivian Beaumont Theater was covered in white. Items of furniture were scattered over this snowscape. The characters, too, seemed adrift in a no man's land. Serban argued: 'Instead of the stage giving conventional, geographic information, ours is meant to convey sensation – even a smell. For instance, in the first Act, you feel the frost of morning and the sunlight.'[4] When Ranevskaya recalled the spring blooms of her childhood, a scrim at the back began 'to glow and to rise simultaneously, revealing row upon row of feathered May trees, not quite released from the winter's cold but iridescent with oncoming life. The vision [wrote Walter Kerr] is exquisite, and, under the formalized lighting that Jennifer Tipton has arranged, we know what we are looking at. At sunshine the colour of snow. At a mothscape. Death and life at once.'[5] Serban created a number of memorable images. When Ranevskaya recalled the death of her son, the figure of a young boy was seen wandering among the trees. At the beginning of Act II, the image of telegraph poles towering over labourers dragging an ancient plough was visible through the scrim. To reinforce Trofimov's revolutionary prophecies, 'the skyline changes once again, this time to overwhelm us with factory chimneys beneath a soot-stained red sky'.[6] Finally, the production ended with the image of a young girl, who rushed in bearing a sprig of cherry blossoms which she placed on Firs' dead body – marking the burial of the old, and the birth of the new. The image of industrialised Russia could again be seen dimly at the back. This was 'not so much a metaphor as a comment on a moment in time, a moment of change that still affects us somehow'.[7] These images were intended 'to elicit emotion rather than give information', Serban said; 'to tell you something that the mind alone cannot grasp'. He cited the sound of the snapping string in the play as an example of an effect, a 'symbolic technical device' which is similarly designed to elicit emotion rather than give information. 'It was just because this so-called realistic play contains such examples of symbolism, of elements of another nature, that I felt some freedom in approaching Chekhov and making use of images that the play suggests.'[8]

Actually, the images Serban created seemed somewhat obvious and literal-minded – the image of the factories, for example, as a portent of the future. Ironically, in some ways they recalled Stanislavski's own tendency to embellish the text with his own inventions, which were similarly designed to 'elicit emotion' rather than give information. Serban's images, moreover, were often distracting. Kerr observed: 'If scrims are rising and dazzling vistas beginning to swim in new light, while Miss Worth [Ranevskaya] is speaking', then the speech itself 'is bound to be interrupted'.[9] Throughout Act IV, articles of furniture could be seen behind the scrim as they were being carried out. Curtain rods, cases, a rocking horse, etc., seemed to be floating on air. C.K. Alexander, playing Pishchik, was upset to discover that a piano would float past during his speech. With some justification, he argued that the audience would be watching the piano, and not him.[10]

Robert Brustein sees Serban as part of the 'alternative to the tradition of Stanislavski' and 'in the non-realistic tradition of Meyerhold'; but this is a simplistic, if convenient, way of placing the director's work.[11] We will find as many echoes of Stanislavski as Meyerhold in Serban's productions. In fact, it sometimes seems as if he is deliberately 'quoting' the work of earlier directors. When Serban staged *The Cherry Orchard* again, in Romania in 1992–3, he included a group of

Plate 11 Scene from Act III of Andrei Serban's *Cherry Orchard*. Designed by Santo Loquasto (Vivian Beaumont Theatre, 1977).

peasants bearing scythes and rakes who crossed the stage in Act II – evidently a deliberate echo of Stanislavski's production plan.

The design for the New York *Cherry Orchard* actually owed more to Giorgio Strehler's production of the play, with its celebrated all-white set, than to Meyerhold.[12] The most obvious echo of Meyerhold came in the 'ball' scene in Act III. The stage was dominated by a cylindrical gazebo, which rotated like a carousel. The dancers moved at times in slow-motion, or froze completely – recalling Meyerhold's description of the scene as a puppet-show, 'a dance of death'. Harold Clurman, however, observed that the gazebo was so large that the 'main action and important dialogue are crowded onto the forestage'. As a result, the 'byplay takes precedence over the play'.[13] (We may recall that, ironically, Meyerhold criticised Stanislavski's production in similar terms – because the director's additions, such as Charlotta's magic tricks, overshadowed the play.)

A 'physical' acting style

When Serban arrived in the States from Romania in 1969, he found that, in his view, the actors were inadequately trained: they had only 'a kind of bogus Actors Studio approach, which generally is a malady, a sickness of the American stage. American actors don't have a precise Stanislavski method nor do they have a Meyerhold, body-oriented training. There is no clear, strong method of actor preparation in America, and it creates a vacuum.'[14]

Serban believes that Method acting is unsuitable for Chekhov; it is too 'internalised' and leads only to self-indulgence.[15] His own approach to directing is eclectic, and rehearsals for *The Cherry Orchard* included 'traditional' Stanislavskian work on the 'given circumstances'. (For example, he asked the actors to consider all the circumstances surrounding the characters' arrival in Act I: 'Who met them at the station? Who did they sit with in the carriage? How did it feel to see the orchard? To smell the orchard?'[16]) However, he also sought to develop a style of performance which emphasized the *physical*, rather than the psychological. The characters' 'internal states' were expressed through physical actions, which were at times quite extreme. In Act III, Lopakhin reveals that he is the new owner of the orchard. In Chekhov's text, Lopakhin at one point bangs into a table and almost knocks over a candelabra. Stanislavski wrote in his production score:

> Anton Pavlovich, fearing anything too sharp, wants to tone down this moment, and so the candelabra only *nearly* falls over. I think

this is neither one thing nor the other. The candelabra must fall over and break, but not on the stage, but there, in the room. Scarcely has it fallen to the ground, when more people (the bailiff, the telegraphist, Pishchik) rush to pick it up. But Lopakhin stops them.[17]

Thus, Stanislavski made the character's action more physical and dramatic. But Serban took the scene *even further*: Lopakhin (played by Raul Julia) exulted in violent destruction, picking up a chair and smashing it against the scenery, and throwing another across the room, while Ranevskaya lay stretched out, in a black gown on the white floor, sobbing.

The director pushed a number of performances towards a kind of grotesque and very physical farce. This was most obvious in Meryl Streep's Dunyasha. She fainted when Yasha kissed her in Act I. At the start of Act II, the two characters chased each other around the stage; Dunyasha's petticoats ended up around her ankles, and she kept tripping over and falling flat on her face. In the last Act, she even tackled Yasha to the ground. Some critics felt that the play's psychological complexities and emotional nuances were obliterated by this physical performance style. Stanley Kauffmann, for example, objected that a 'masterwork of poetic realism' was destroyed by 'a production that attacks the work with physicality, horseplay, and improvisation on the text, rather than an attempt to embody the text'.[18] The accusation of crudeness has dogged Serban's work in Chekhov; Benedict Nightingale, for example, has argued: 'His talent just doesn't seem suited to emotional variety or psychological complexity or the other qualities for which I, for one, revere Chekhov.'[19] But behind this criticism can be seen a desire for a more genteel acting style and for a more traditional Chekhov.

Serban, as he acknowledges, has gained a reputation as 'the director who destroys the classics'.[20] Partly in response to Serban's *Cherry Orchard*, Richard Gilman penned an article entitled 'How the new theatrical directors are upstaging the playwright', in which he portrayed modern directors as a kind of Mafia moving in on the theatre world.[21] Today's directors, he said, see the text as

> less in need of being faithfully served, that is to say respectfully and straightforwardly transmitted, than of being given *life*, in the problematic pursuit of which liberties are often taken of a kind that can outrage purists but also dismay the thoughtful. ... Dissimilar as their own work may be, these directors share in

regard to classics a notion of texts buried under successive layers of presentational cliché for the overthrow of which a certain degree of daring and even at times recklessness is thought to be essential.

Gilman quoted approvingly Jean Vilar, who said (regarding Shakespeare) that 'the text is there, rich in stage directions embodied in the lines themselves ... one need only have the sense to follow them. Whatever is *created*, beyond these directions, is "direction", and should be despised and rejected.' The issue, he suggested, is not 'originality vs. archaism but originality that remains in coherence with a text against that which distorts it and may even destroy its true life'. But how, exactly, can we define the 'true life' of a play?

Gilman specified Serban's *Orchard* as a

> notable instance of a directorial mind substituting itself for the playwright's, of a concept trampling over a dramatic fact. From the set design, spectacular in its own right, brilliantly calculated to draw oohs and ahs, but drastically out of keeping with Chekhov's complex, subtle realism, to the dominant farcical tone which is a perversion of Chekhov's description of the play as a 'comedy' (which he undoubtedly meant in the Dantean sense, not that of Feydeau), the intrusion of characters – the boy, the toiling peasants, the White Rock girl who kneels besides Firs at the end – unknown in the text until now, and the factory in the background to add a note of menacing industrialism where Chekhov implies no such thing, the production systematically subverts the play we have known.

Precisely – *the play we have known*. Clearly Gilman has a preconceived notion of how the play should be staged. He rejected Loquasto's set, for example, because it did not conform to his notion of Chekhovian realism. He disputed the farcical element, despite the fact that Chekhov called the play in places a farce. He objected to the image of encroaching industrialism because 'Chekhov implies no such thing'. In fact, the row of telegraph poles that stretch across the stage in Act II, and the large town which can be glimpsed in the distance, seem to signify a world in the process of change. Irene Worth, who played Ranevskaya, defended Serban's innovations: the director, she said, 'has pulled no punches; if you read the play carefully, you won't find that there is anything in this production that isn't there indigenously'.[22] But the problem, in part, might simply have been Serban's refusal to pull his punches. Rocco Landesman objected that the director 'makes dramatic points with the force of Muhammed Ali'; he 'adds so many directorial "touches" that he might as well have walked on the stage himself and with a great boxing glove punched out the audience'.[23]

Ironically, some of Serban's statements seem, in fact, to endorse Gilman's views on the need to interpret the text 'faithfully':

> when I do a play by Chekhov or Shakespeare I'm trying to understand. That's why I cannot justify any cuts, even to make the production better or more immediate, because it will always show my weakness, my incapacity to understand the fragment that I take out. So, I make it almost an obligation to myself to try and understand everything in the text and even if I don't, still to present it honestly. Because maybe somebody else will understand.[24]

Serban praised Peter Brook's production of *The Cherry Orchard* in Paris because it seemed to offer a 'straightforward' presentation of the play without any embellishments:

> ... what made it so extraordinary was the sense that at the same time the actors were on stage acting they were just being there. Somehow one really felt that the play was the experience of those actors during the time of that performance and not a metaphor, a representation or a substitute for something else. There were no theatrical effects and no aesthetic values as such. It was all done very simply, and without scenery. I don't know if you've been to the Bouffes du Nord in Paris – it's a nineteenth century theatre that's now quite deteriorated, almost a ruin. In Brook's production, the theatre itself was the old family house. So there was no need for scenery. You see, we were in the old house that had to be left, and it was much more powerful because it was the theatre itself. So what you had in that empty space was a group of actors in a direct relationship with the text and the audience and, really, the play was there. You didn't need anything more.[25]

Brook's production was actually quite conventionally 'realistic'; it was *made* extraordinary by the use of the space. Nevertheless, Serban concluded: 'I thought that my *Cherry Orchard*, in relation to his, was not all that revolutionary.'[26]

A realistic *Seagull* in Japan, and a 'Japanese' *Seagull* in New York

In 1980, Serban staged two productions of *The Seagull* – first in Japan, and then in New York. Perhaps surprisingly, in the Japanese production he moved towards a form of 'realism' in acting and design. The set (for the Shiki Theatre in Tokyo) was designed by Kaoru Kanamuri. It consisted of a vast lake of water, in which there was a platform stage in the shape of a seagull, where Treplev's play was performed. There were real rocks, real birch trees, grass and flowers. 'It was all so naturalistic', Serban later regretted. 'In the first Act, Yakov and the other workmen actually went swimming in the lake and came out dripping with water.'[27] And yet the intention was not so much to create a naturalistic set, but rather to explore the lake as a theatrical image: its magnetism, 'its power, its depth and the attraction to what we cannot see'. But as Serban saw, 'somehow water on the stage is still water on the stage. ... It's exhilarating in a certain sort of way, but the imagination is stopped from seeing further.'[28]

The production had a kind of lush romantic realism. There were beautiful and memorable images: Treplev's play took place soon after sunset, with the moon reflected in the water. In Act IV there were real waves on the surface of the lake, which became dark and dangerous. Then, when Treplev tore the pages of his manuscript into pieces, he scattered them over the lake, turning it white. Shooting himself on stage, he fell face down into the water among the torn pages.

Paradoxically, Serban felt the production he staged on his return to New York was much more 'Japanese'. The set (by Michael Yeargan) consisted of a polished wooden floor – a kind of bare, Japanese platform stage. Across the width of the stage at the back there was an elevated bridgeway which was used for entrances and exits. This was like the *hashigakari* and *hanamichi* of the Japanese theatre. It was as if Serban was incorporating, or 'quoting', elements of Japanese theatre, and using them as a point of contrast. The acting on the main stage was predominantly 'realistic'; but the action on the bridge was much more stylised. In a play which is so much about the theatre, it was as if the bridge was a 'stage' within a stage; when the actors stepped onto it, they 'presented' the drama in a much more formalised and theatrical style. Movement was slowed down, or accelerated. Thus, in Act I, Nina and Treplev met halfway across the bridge, silhouetted against the sky. (The image was repeated in Act III, with Nina and Trigorin against a setting sun.) Then, when Arkadina and the others entered, they crossed the bridge very slowly as the moon rose.

Plate 12 Scene from Act I of *The Seagull*. Directed by Andrei Serban and designed by Michael Yeargan (The Public Theater, 1980).

Serban, then, deliberately separated the main action of the drama, and the 'images' he created on the bridge – creating a kind of 'montage' effect. But again, the images could be distracting. Serban himself has said he would like to do *The Seagull* again 'because I want to understand how to do Chekhov without any beautifications, without a bridge, without a Japanese platform, without help from production elements – nothing for the eye in that sense'. The visual appeal of the production

> was unlike that of *The Cherry Orchard*, [but] it still had a shininess and beauty of its own – and none of that was Chekhov's beauty. Now, I'm very interested in beauty and it's a large part of my work even if I try to deny it, because at heart I'm a romantic. I just want to know how much the beauty of my images kills the truth and, in this respect, to what extent I'm in danger. If they support the truth, well ... then I'm alright.[29]

When, in the Japanese *Seagull*, Treplev shot himself on stage and sank into the lake, this was clearly a distortion of the play for the sake of a theatrical 'effect'. (Chekhov deliberately does not show us the death, moving the scene off-stage.) In New York, Serban originally directed Treplev, in his final scene, to tear up his manuscript, and then set it on fire and stand watching it burn. (An idea Serban actually took from Stanislavski's production plan.) Then he dropped the burning pages into a stove, and ran from the stage. 'Almost immediately', Laurence Shyer recalled, 'flames flared out the sides of the iron canister – it was a breathtaking image':

> The stage became very dark and the audience sat silently watching this fire, this mute testimony to Treplev's presence and now his absence, as it flickered to a weak flame. No sooner had the fire died out than new lights appeared from offstage – the family now entered the room carrying candelabra which wavered back and forth in the darkness. They were all laughing and chatting, like fools in the candlelight. And then came the moment of the shot, which wasn't a shot at all but an explosion. Instantly, the lights came on. The stage was suffused with harsh, white light. There was no need for Dorn to tell Trigorin his news for everyone knew immediately what had happened. You could see the realization on every face. The comedy was over. That was the only possible interpretation.

But this idea was dropped during the previews. Serban decided that 'even though it was effective', he 'didn't like what it did to the play'. The revised staging followed the text much more faithfully: Dorn took Trigorin aside and told him about Treplev's death, while the other characters continued with the card-game. This was 'much less effective but I felt it was closer to what Chekhov intended, that maybe Treplev's death doesn't mean anything ... I mean, Arkadina will have to be told at some point, but then life will go on.'[30] In this instance, then, Serban eschewed an 'effect' because he felt it did not 'support the truth'.

Some critics again objected to 'crudeness' in the performances: 'the playwright of delicate indirection is mangled once more by the master of gross misdirection', Robert Asahina wrote. The characters 'are not even permitted the dignity of pathos'.[31] John Simon complained that Dorn (F. Murray Abraham) emerged 'as a smarmy Levantine rug merchant ... whom you would not trust as far as you could throw a Bukhara the size of a mosque'. Meanwhile, 'Rosemary Harris has been directed to play Arkadina as a woman unable to utter a sincere syllable or make a natural gesture'.[32] In part these criticisms seem to arise from a desire to see a more sympathetic and endearing portrayal of Chekhov's characters – less critical and abrasive; a desire for 'delicate indirection' rather than an approach which is more direct. The actors seemed to offer less a 'realistic' performance, than a form of grotesque 'mask' of their character – a strong physical image or 'essence'. Pamela Payton-Wright, for example, as Masha, was a comic and grotesque figure, 'clumping about the stage in heavy workshoes', her shoulders stooped, 'constantly chewing a large pipe in her teeth'.[33] Ed Menta called this 'crude', but Masha *is* a rather eccentric figure (she wears black, drinks, takes snuff, etc.). The actor and director simply accentuated this eccentricity, creating a bold physical outline for the character.

Again, the characters' internal states were expressed through bold physical actions. Masha carried a long piece of white muslin – the life she trails behind her, like an endless train – which she tore into pieces as she described her hopeless love for Treplev. Similarly, Medvedenko bit savagely and angrily into an apple as he listened to Sorin and Dorn discussing Masha's drinking habits. Shamraev grabbed the hands of the ladies of the house and kissed them 'as if they were pieces of raw animal flesh'.[34] And yet, Walter Kerr felt that 'these eruptions come rarely and all too arbitrarily', and the production seemed at times 'to lapse back into the slow and moody languors of stock Chekhov'.[35] Serban himself felt that, in the last Act in particular, the acting slipped into a more internal, 'psychological' mode; as a result, the production became 'slow and heavy, and really fell apart'.[36]

Serban's *Three Sisters*: ghostly echoes of the past

Serban's production of *Three Sisters* (American Repertory Theatre, Cambridge, Mass., 1982) was played at an almost frantic pace. ('This is the most galvanic, fastest-moving *Three Sisters* you'll ever see.'[37]) The acting, then, could not slip into a more 'internal' or psychological mode. 'The director doesn't miss a moment for energizing the stage picture', Arthur Holmberg observed. Vershinin (Alvin Epstein) leapt onto a chair to philosophise, 'wigwagging his handkerchief like an SOS'. In Act IV, Irina (Cherry Jones) span round in circles, as if 'hoping to fly away like the birds overhead'.[38] Olga (Marianne Owen) frantically raked the leaves on the ground in order to avoid talking to Vershinin. Andrei (Thomas Derrah) smashed his books to the ground in rage. The actions of the characters, then, seemed driven by a kind of manic energy.

The production began in darkness. Then, 'three monolithic silhouettes take shape and, ghostlike, float across the stage bearing flowers for the dead. An eerie, disembodied voice-over fills the theatre with bits and pieces of memory skimming the surface of consciousness' – the first lines of Olga's opening speech were played on tape, while the actor (Owen) moved her lips, and then began to speak, but not quite in synch with the tape.[39] These sisters, then, were like ghosts from the past, returning to us. The voice-over perhaps recalled Krapp in Beckett's play, endlessly listening to his own voice, and fragments of his own memories, recorded on tape.

The set consisted of a series of deep red curtains, upstage, which could be rearranged in different configurations. Behind these curtains was a fake cinder-block wall, which simulated the back wall of the theatre. We were made aware throughout, then, that we were in a theatre, watching a play. (Tusenbach, Chebutykin and Soleny left for the duel by ascending the theatre's spiral staircase to the flies.) The minimal furniture and props which were used could suggest a complete room; and yet, they also seemed like chairs, props, etc., left over from a past theatre production – adrift in this empty space. The Prozorov house, then, became 'a small *theatrum mundi* onto which the familiar poor players strut and fret their hour'.[40] The designer, Beni Montresor, was actually somewhat uncomfortable with this bare look, and asked Serban: 'What country is this? This is no country in the world.' The director replied: 'Beni, it's only a play. It is a play. It doesn't have to be any country in the world.'[41] It is clear that Serban's desire to break away from realistic sets was not simply meant to allow us to concentrate on the acting. The sets for both *Three Sisters* and the New York *Seagull* emphasised that the performance was a theatrical 'event'. There was no illusion of real events unfolding.

Three Sisters again contained fragments or 'quotes' from Stanislavski's production – like ghostly echoes from the past. In Act II, Stanislavski wanted toys spread around the stage to symbolise the way Natasha and her offspring were gradually taking over the house. He suggested the characters should play with the toys at certain points; for example, as Irina talked about going to Moscow within six months, Vershinin held a Petrushka doll, and made its cymbals clash. Then, as Tusenbach philosophised about life in a thousand years, he held a toy barrel-organ, and idly turned its handle; it emitted shrill noises from time to time. Both these effects seemed to undercut the characters' hopes and dreams.

Toys also covered the floor in Act II of Serban's production; the characters played with them 'as if they were all in an oversized playpen'.[42] After Vershinin has received a note telling him his wife has tried to commit suicide, the actor turned to go – 'I'll just slip quietly away' – and immediately stumbled noisily over a pile of dominoes (a less subtle, and more farcical, way of undercutting the character).

In rehearsal, Serban and the company read Chekhov's letters and 'letters to Chekhov and snippets from the biographies and things that Stanislavski had said and things that Chekhov had said about Stanislavski'.[43] Stanislavski at one stage asked Chekhov if, at the end of the play, he could bring on a procession bearing Tusenbach's corpse; but in rehearsal, he discovered that this would be distracting. Forgetting it was his idea in the first place, he told Knipper to write to Chekhov, and ask if it was possible to dispense with it. Annoyed, Chekhov replied: 'I've already said that carrying Tusenbach's corpse across the stage during your scene would be awkward, but Alekseev [Stanislavski] insisted that nothing could be done without the body.'[44] Indeed, bringing on the corpse could only be rather melodramatic, and runs counter to Chekhov's desire to keep dramatic 'events' off-stage.

Almost certainly, Serban was aware of the exchange of letters on this issue; and yet he chose to include Tusenbach's corpse – 'quoting' Stanislavski's idea – in his production. He created a 'montage' of images for the final scene: the sisters gathered round a black baby carriage; Tusenbach's corpse was carried past; Chebutykin tore a newspaper into pieces; Olga's voice was again heard on tape: 'If only we knew, if only we knew.' These images were again intended 'to elicit emotion rather than give information'; to tell you something that 'the mind alone cannot grasp'. But Tusenbach's corpse was an extraneous addition, which clearly contradicted Chekhov's wishes. It might be argued, then, that this was another image which did not 'support the truth'.

Rats in a trap: Serban's *Uncle Vanya*

For Serban's *Uncle Vanya* (La Mama, 1983) the space was transformed into an 'environment' for the play. This recalled the way the Bouffes du Nord in Paris became the 'environment' for Brook's production of *The Cherry Orchard*. There is a line in *Vanya* which describes the rambling house where the characters live as a 'maze' ('Twenty-six huge rooms, everyone always going off in different directions. You can never find anyone.' – Serebryakov, Act III). Loquasto's set turned the theatre into a sprawling, multi-level house, a maze of corridors, rooms, stairways, covering a rectangular playing space some 50 feet by 20. In the centre there was a depressed area, like a sunken cellar, which served as Vanya's study. The set was 'something like an Escher drawing, where passageways that seem to lead somewhere lead nowhere or back onto themselves' – a *surreal* rather than real environment.[45] The characters were like rats in a trap; the maze 'overwhelms, eventually defeats the little people who scurry without purpose, without direction, through its sparsely furnished rooms, along its darkened corridors and balcony'.[46]

The space in many ways dictated the acting. Some ostensibly intimate scenes were played with huge distances between the characters – or they were separated by a stairway or a handrail (an obvious image of the distance between the characters in this Russian no man's land). The setting demanded a more physical acting style. At one moment, Sonya suddenly ran two laps around the space, before sinking abjectly to her knees. Benedict Nightingale objected to the loss of intimacy in a play which is largely about 'emotional claustrophobia – people getting on each other's nerves'.[47] And yet it is clear that this 'intimacy' is one of the Chekhovian clichés that Serban wanted to turn on its head. Jack Kroll wrote: 'By opening up the space between characters he makes us feel the electricity sputtering in that space. ... in this wooden *fin de siècle* cyclotron we feel Chekhov's houseful of failures colliding like split human atoms.'[48]

Nightingale objected to the lack of 'depth and discrimination of feeling' in the acting. One moment in particular excited the critic's wrath. In the climactic scene in Act III, when Serebryakov reveals his plans for the estate, Vanya (played by Joseph Chaikin) walked over to the professor, and perched on his knee, like a child, cuddling him and smiling, and speaking to him in a soft sing-song voice. 'Let us ask a simple question', Nightingale wrote. 'Is that the way *you* would behave at the most confused and confusing, the most gruesome and upsetting, moments of your entire existence? Or is it the way people are thought to behave by directors bent on creating original theatrical effects. The latter, I surmise.' But Richard Schechner responded that the scene represented 'hatred boiled down to its sarcastic essence'.[49]

There is, of course, no definitive way to play the scene. The obvious choice for the actor is to play sputtering anger; but clearly, Serban was deliberately rejecting the obvious choice. Perhaps he was in part simply bent on creating an original theatrical effect; but his aim was also, it seems, to make Vanya more grotesque, even absurd. The staging changed the impact of this crucial scene; it was less tragi-comic, than 'tragic–grotesque'.

A comparable moment occurred in *Three Sisters*. In Act III, a drunken Chebutykin laments his failing powers as a doctor, as he stands washing his hands in a wash-basin. In Serban's production, the actor, Jeremy Geidt, knelt on all fours, and buried his face in the wash-basin, like an animal. He drooled and rubbed his spit into the polished floor, trying to see his own reflection, as he questioned his own existence ('Maybe I'm not even human – maybe I just dream I have arms and legs and a head. Maybe I don't exist at all.'). Then, the actor stood up – and his trousers fell down. The moment was comic, even slapstick – and showed a desire to blend less the comic and the tragic, than the tragic and the grotesque, the absurd.[50]

Chekhov on speed

Serban pays particular attention to the beginning and end of the plays. On one level, perhaps, this simply reflects a desire to create memorable images; but he is also attempting to shift our relationship to Chekhov's work.

A notable ending was created for *The Cherry Orchard*. In the play, Ranevskaya surveys the nursery for one last time: 'One last look at the walls … the windows … '. But (as Kerr wrote) there were actually no walls on Loquasto's set, so Irene Worth seemed to 'inhale' the space,

> moving in a great running circle deep, deep into the unreachable horizon and then around and forward to encompass the curve of the forestage, not panting but sucking in breath as she flies,

reaching out at last to grasp the hand of the companion waiting to take her away. But she doesn't seize that hand. Instead, on impulse, she barely brushes it with her fingers and dances off again on another grand tour, eyes ablaze, lungs filled, heart broken, lips parted in what is very nearly an all-devouring smile. And then she does it one more triumphant, unbelievable time, a bareback rider on the rim of the world. When she goes, she takes it all with her.[51]

The action *externalised*, rather than internalised, the character's feelings – her desire to 'gather up' her memories. It was, as Serban observed, 'a very moving upbeat, fresh exit rather than a more traditional, melancholic end'.[52]

At the beginning of *Uncle Vanya*, Sonya entered, book in hand – reading aloud part of her closing speech ('We must rest ... '). This meant that when, at the end of the play, we returned to the speech, we viewed it somewhat ironically. Her words of comfort to Vanya had, it seemed, been memorised from a book, written presumably by Russia's answer to Patience Strong. In this scene, Vanya and Sonya sat in a well, which was like a coffin; their pens scratched across the paper like fingernails on a blackboard. Usually in the play, Telegin strums his guitar gently in the background, creating a melancholic accompaniment to Sonya's words. Here, however, the actor (Mohammad Ghaffari) played his balalaika and whirled round and round like a dervish, in ever-widening circles, apparently indifferent to Vanya's suffering. Instead of *adding* to the melancholic mood of the ending, Telegin's grotesque dance created a deliberately discordant and jarring effect.

'If you open yourself to these images', Brustein wrote, 'some of them will etch themselves indelibly on your mind, even when at first they seem gratuitous'.[53] Nightingale, however, gave his review the title: 'Would Chekhov have embraced this *Vanya*?' It is a question that is impossible to answer; but Nightingale clearly thought the answer was 'no'. The question 'suggests that the critic, not the artist, is the best reader of the playwright's intentions, the most faithful defender of his text'.[54] Richard Schechner then wrote an article defending Serban; his piece had an equally questionable heading: 'We do Chekhov right.'[55] Both critics, then, seemed to stake a proprietary claim over how Chekhov's plays should be performed – as if there could be an 'ideal' production, which could exactly realise Chekhov's intentions. They condemned, or praised Serban, according to whether they felt his work matched this 'ideal'.

When Chaikin's Vanya sat on Serebryakov's lap, was it 'wrong'? Or when Telegin danced a whirling dance at the end, was *that* wrong – simply because it contradicted our expectations of how the scene would be staged? To some extent, Serban was offending not against the text, but against traditional expectations and preconceptions. Nevertheless, at times Serban clearly strayed beyond simply 'interpreting' the text, and *re-wrote* it – becoming in some ways (to use Meyerhold's phrase) 'the author of the production'. In Serban's hands, *Vanya* became a significantly different play. Despite his declaration that he did not want to cut texts, the production was pruned to a running time of 100 minutes, without interval. This created a fast and furious pace, and again ensured the acting could not slip into a more introverted mode. By compressing the action, the production necessarily concentrated on the more 'dramatic' episodes. There was less sense of the flow of 'daily life'; instead there was a concatenation of events, progressing speedily to a climax and denouement. This significantly changed Chekhov's dramatic form. The result was Chekhov on speed.

Partly, Serban was simply employing shock tactics to make us look again at a play which had become set in a certain pattern as a rather cosy, elegiac tale of country folk. 'As usual', Jack Kroll wrote, 'his approach is brash, but loving, impudent but pertinent. And above all his Chekhov is alive.'[56] Julius Novick, however, fumed: 'Mr. Serban has freed the play from the sultry Russian gloom that so often envelops it, but he has also freed it from most of its feeling and most of its meaning.'[57]

By now, it seemed, most critics agreed with Nightingale, and thought Serban did *not* 'do Chekhov right'. Stung perhaps by the reviews, Serban retreated from directing on the New York stage. Brustein regretted that directors 'with the courage of their imaginations' were being driven from the theatre by a hostile and conservative press.

> The current passion for consensus may explain why Serban's controversial productions evoke such heated reactions: such passion presumes an authorized interpretation of the play. ...
>
> The tumult over *Vanya* reflects the traditional uneasiness between the analytical intelligence and the interpretive imagination. One does not have to believe that a play can support any harebrained or lunatic interpretation in order to recognize that theatre is not absolute, not immutable, not frozen, but rather in a

continual state of process and change, and therefore not subject to fixed concepts of authorial intention or 'definitive' production.[58]

A great play, Brustein argues, can be desecrated 'by excessive piety as much as by excessive reverence'.[59] But, in the name of protecting Chekhov's work from further 'desecration', the powerful Mafia of New York's drama critics had moved in to silence the 'impudent' experiments of Andrei Serban.

Production notes

Serban's productions in the US

The Cherry Orchard, New York Shakespeare Festival at the Vivian Beaumont Theatre, Lincoln Center, New York; first performance, 17 February 1977.

The Seagull, New York Shakespeare Festival at the Public Theatre, New York; first performance, 11 November 1980.

Three Sisters, American Repertory Theater, Cambridge, MA; first performance, 1 December 1982.

Uncle Vanya, La Mama Annex, New York; first performance, 11 September 1983.

8   The Wooster Group

Brace Up!

The Wooster Group, led by Elizabeth LeCompte, is a kind of theatrical shock-troop, mounting raids on classic texts, and reusing the material in new and unexpected ways. The company's 1984 production, *L.S.D.*, for example, incorporated extended extracts from Arthur Miller's play, *The Crucible*. LeCompte claimed that her intention was not to stage or interpret the play, but to examine it as a 'historical and theatrical document'.[1] The production questioned some of the ideas and values underpinning Miller's work. For example, the characterisation of the black servant, Tituba, now seems a dated cultural stereotype – 'more like the Aunt Jemima of fifties television commercials than a seventeenth-century slave'.[2] In *L.S.D.*, the character was played by a white actor with a painted black face, like a minstrel – instantly questioning and undermining the stereotype. The company, then, was not treating a classic text with reverence, as inviolate, and as if it contained universal 'truths', but was subjecting the work to a form of interrogation and deconstruction. It saw the text as something relative, a product of its time (the 1950s), rather than an eternal masterpiece. The company was not 'interpreting' Miller's work and trying to be 'faithful' to his intentions. Rather, the 'text' was like a site to be invaded and occupied. The company built its own performance on the ruins.[3]

LeCompte resists the notion of 'interpreting' a text: 'I think it is usually a traditional director who is trained to interpret a play, while I'm making my own play even if I'm using someone else's play.'[4] In other words, *she* is, ultimately, the 'author of the production'.

She has observed:

> When I choose texts, they're random in a way. I feel I could use any text. ... I could pick anything in this room and make a piece that's just as complete as *L.S.D.* I could take three props here: the printing on the back of that picture, this book, and whatever's in

this pile of papers, and make something that would mean as much, no more nor less, than what I've constructed in the performance space downstairs.[5]

What matters, then, is not the 'text', but the way it is used. The 'author's intention' is not even considered.

A Wooster Group production is created over many months; it evolves, almost by a process of association, an interweaving of different ideas and 'texts'. Extracts from other written sources, film clips, snippets of music, etc., are interpolated and superimposed on the play-text. ('All our pieces have been made by accumulating the texts around issues that evolve in the work.'[6]) These 'fragments' seem to be selected almost arbitrarily: 'Like a maker of collages, LeCompte takes up a found object, a fragment, that comes onto the scene without fixed meaning, and places it against other fragments.' She describes it as 'chance work, like throwing a handful of beans up in the air'.[7]

The company resists any single, fixed meaning to any of its productions. Ron Vawter, an actor with the Group until his death in 1994, argued: 'An event which can be interpreted only one way inhibits and limits the possibility. It's not that we're deliberately trying to make pieces which are mute. Just the opposite. I often see a piece as an opportunity for meaning, rather than an expression of a single meaning.'[8] Any Wooster Group production, then, contains a 'multitude' of texts, and a 'multitude' of possible meanings and interpretations. The spectator is left to construct his or her own meaning from the collage of 'fragments'.

Brace Up!

> *Three Sisters* was written in the first year of the 20th century, but passed into the canon as a great exemplar of 19th-century 'realistic' drama. The central question for us today is, what kind of existence can it have after almost a hundred years, in a theatre where realism is in retreat? *Brace Up!*, to my mind, is a stunning answer.[9]

Brace Up! (1991) was The Wooster Group's assault on Chekhov's *Three Sisters*. The play was selected, it seems, almost at random. LeCompte claims she has never actually read it. It was suggested by Vawter, and accepted simply because it 'interfaced with the company … it was easy to cast'.[10]

The set was a rectangular platform, mostly bare except for several microphones and television monitors. As the performance began, a narrator read the stage directions from the opening of the play: 'The Prozorov house. A big living room, separated by columns ... '. (Of course, the set looked nothing like this.) The narrator (played by Kate Valk) also introduced the characters, and the actors who were playing them ('Peyton Smith in the role of Olga ...', etc.); and cued the actors' opening speeches. 'Olga, how was the weather when your father died?' she inquired – as if interviewing the character for a television documentary. Olga replied: 'It was very cold, and it snowed.' Then Valk asked Irina: 'Where was it that you said you wanted to go?' 'Moscow', she replied. The audience laughed. 'Ah', Valk observed, 'that's the men laughing in the dining room.'

The actors playing the sisters were significantly older than their characters. Irina was played by a 74-year-old, Beatrice Roth. LeCompte claims the decision was arbitrary: 'In a strange way, I didn't think about age. What I was most interested in was the actress's personality and how it matched the character's. I was interested in Beatrice Roth's tone, the tone of her personality.'[11] Certain consequences followed, however. The designer Jim Clayburgh recalls: 'After Liz started to think about going against the age in the casting of the three sisters, she talked about it as almost a hospital vision. There was a sense of great aging and almost illness and how the three sisters may get dealt with almost as objects.'[12] The sisters were in fact sometimes confined to wheelchairs. The age of the actors established that there would be no 'realistic' attempt to represent the characters. Clearly, the casting also made an ironic, even comic point. These were not young people, whose youthful hopes and dreams were about to be dashed. Rather, it was as if these sisters had been stringing out their futile dreams of Moscow for years; they had grown old waiting. The basic theme of Chekhov's drama, then, was overturned, even parodied. (Similarly, when Irina talked about the need for work, the lines seemed somewhat absurd in the mouth of a 74-year-old woman in a wheelchair.)

The production was staged almost as a 'reading' or run-through of the play, rather than a full performance. The use of a narrator immediately established that the performance was anti-naturalistic – even a form of 'anti-theatre'. There was a deliberate appearance of casualness, even amateurishness. The stage-management team, sitting at the sides, casually handed the actors props as required, and grumbled that no one knew their lines. 'Mistakes' were deliberately incorporated. Valk apologised because 'the actress playing Masha isn't here yet'. She corrected actors when they went wrong. The intention behind these

Plate 13 Scene from *Brace Up!* (The Wooster Group, 1991). Kate Valk as the narrator.

Plate 14 Beatrice Roth, left, as Irina, and Kate Valk as the narrator in The Wooster Group's *Brace Up!* (1991).

strategies was to disrupt or deny theatrical illusion, and to create a sense that the performance itself was something unfinished, unstable, improvised, rather than polished and perfected.

The piece was actually flexible in structure and subject to change through the performance period. If an actor was missing, for example, due to other commitments, Valk might simply read in for them. (When Michael Stumm, who played Soleny, was missing for a period, Valk announced to the audience that he had gone on a 'little vacation' – so 'every time that he has to speak, we'll turn the TV loud'.) Ultimately, however, this was not really a 'live' event, unfolding spontaneously; even the mistakes, asides and interventions, which created the impression, the 'illusion' of spontaneity, were prepared and rehearsed. Of course, this in itself could be seen as a very 'postmodern' form of irony.

'Japan'

Before working on *Brace Up!*, LeCompte was already interested in Japanese theatre and culture. In fact, the basic idea for the production came from watching a documentary on a touring Japanese theatre company. According to Marianne Weems (the assistant director), LeCompte's original conception was that there is a Japanese troupe that performs Chekhov. There is this travelling troupe in this burned-out hotel in the middle of New York, and they are performing this Western classic that may or may not be *Three Sisters*. So we need to develop the life of the group. That's the frame for the piece.[13]

In rehearsal, the company examined a range of Japanese material including samurai films and videos of *noh* and *kyogen* theatre. There was, however, no attempt to assimilate a Japanese 'style' of performance. Rather, the production simply 'used' or 'quoted' different devices or theatrical conventions. These devices seemed incongruous when applied to a classic of Western 'realistic' drama, and again disrupted and denied any illusion of 'realism' in the performance.[14]

The stage hands, present throughout the performance, recalled the 'proscenium attendants' or *kurambo* from Japanese theatre of the sixteenth and seventeenth centuries. The set incorporated Japanese elements: there were ramps on either side (as in *noh* theatre) which created long entrances for the actors. When Chebutykin appeared in Act I with a samovar (here actually a coffee urn) he made his entrance very slowly up one of the ramps. In other words, instead of seeing an actor opening a door, and pretending to come in from outside, we saw a *stylised* or *conventionalised* stage entrance. When the actor reached a certain point, his entrance was marked 'by the chorus of men making a sound like "Uh–oh!" which is another noh element'.[15]

The costumes were an eclectic mixture – as if they had been picked at random from the theatre's costume basket: Olga wore a wide purple belt, tied at the back in a bow like an *obi*, and Masha's costume was kimono-like; but Soleny wore a 1950s-style striped shirt and black windsurfing boots. The 'world' of the play, then, was not 'Russian', it was not 'Japanese' or 'American'. It was a patchwork of different cultures, assembled it seemed almost at random. There was no attempt to represent the real historical period of the play. When Chebutykin presented Irina with a coffee-urn instead of a samovar, this seemed like a joke at the expense of productions that aspire to historical accuracy, which strive to offer a 'realistic' picture of Russian life. (The samovar, of course, has become almost a symbol of Chekhov in the theatre.)

One of the premises of The Wooster Group's work is 'to have always something that amplifies or goes against' what is happening on stage; i.e. running parallel to, and often commenting ironically on, the text.[16] In *Brace Up!*, the company incorporated extracts from popular films, played on the television monitors. These were unexpected and incongruous in a Chekhov play. The choice of clips, in fact, was often quite jokey – and one result was to undermine the seriousness of the play, and the 'reverence' it is usually given. For example, whenever Soleny appeared, the monitors showed a clip from *Godzilla*. This 'sent up' the character, by comparing him to a raging monster from a tacky horror movie. Similarly, a 'fire' scene from the film *The Harvey Girls* was used at the beginning of Act III – undermining the seriousness of the events of the play by setting them against a kitsch Hollywood melodrama. Sometimes, however, the choice of clips seemed quite arbitrary and meaningless – as if they were simply 'found objects', which had no direct relation at all to the 'context' of play, and no intentional 'meaning'. For example, at one point, a scene from a samurai film was shown without sound in slow motion, while Valk provided the soundtrack by imitating Japanese voices.

Sound effects were deliberately non-realistic. In one scene, Valk drank vodka, and after every drink, mimed smashing the glass on the floor. Each time she did this, a sound effect of smashing glass was added. Then – as if by accident – the sound was played *before* she mimed smashing the glass. Valk looked reprovingly at the sound booth, as if to say, 'That was your fault, not mine … '. Thus, the 'convention' of realistic sound in the theatre was debunked.

In a scene based on fragments from Act II, images and sounds were used to accompany and echo key words in the text: wind, snow, winter, etc. For example, a 'new-age sound-track mimicking the wind plays, while footage of a man walking in a heavy snowstorm rolls randomly on the TV monitors'.[17] At one point, Soleny (Stumm) came forward with a guitar and sang 'Blowing in the Wind'. This sequence, then, was almost a parody of 'Chekhovian' sound-effects. No 'atmosphere' was created; rather, the jokey mixture of different 'texts' (the 'new age' music, the Dylan song, etc.) again tended to deflate the air of holy reverence usually surrounding the production of a 'classic' play.

This, then, was a Chekhov of scraps and fragments, a montage of images and 'texts', thrown together, it seemed, by accident. The very title of the piece, *Brace Up!*, seemed to be arbitrary. The company 'was puzzled and intrigued by the fact that in a number of Japanese films when the hero – often a samurai warrior – is defeated by the enemy, a disciple rushes to where the hero is lying in deep sorrow and delivers a long, intense speech which is consistently translated in only two words: "*Brace Up!*" '[18] It could be said that the title ironically refers to the traditional image of Chekhov's characters as sad and defeated – as if encouraging them to cheer up a bit. But the company did not *explain* the title – leaving the audience to puzzle at the 'meaning' – or wonder, indeed, if there was any 'meaning' at all.

'Functional' acting

> *Brace Up!* is Elizabeth LeCompte's attempt to remove a hundred years of Stanislavski tradition from the text of *Three Sisters*, to find its emotional reality without recourse to Stanislavski's 'lived emotions'.[19]

At one point in *Brace Up!*, Valk asked an actor a question about her character. 'I'm not working on character', she replied.

LeCompte rejects 'acting' in the Stanislavskian sense. The actor should not attempt to 'be' the character, or 'live through' the character's experiences. The predominant style of acting in the company's work is presentational – presenting, rather than 'living' or 'becoming' the characters. Willem Dafoe played John Proctor in *L.S.D.*; he observed: 'If someone asked me about John Proctor the character, I wouldn't be able to tell him a thing.'[20] Thus, the exhaustive Stanislavskian method of acting, building up a sense of the character's whole life, was rejected. Dafoe's focus instead was on how to execute the performance on a technical level:

> I never think about John Proctor. I do think about what the effect of a certain speech should be, or a certain section should be. I do respond to 'here, you should relax a little bit more because you should have a lighter touch, he should be a nice guy here. Here, he can be pissed. Here, he's had it.' There's no real pretending, there's no transformation … [21]

LeCompte tells her actors, 'Commit yourself because there is no difference between your role and yourself.'[22] Performances are built, not around 'character', but around the personalities of the actors themselves. They present a version of their own *personae*, an 'impersonation' of themselves. In real life (Dafoe suggests) Ron Vawter was 'tense, kind of officious', and he tended to be cast in these kinds of roles. (In *L.S.D.* he played the Reverend Parris; and in *Three Sisters* he was Vershinin.) It is almost as if the Group is a stock repertory company and each actor has his or her own 'type' or theatrical *emploi*. Dafoe:

> When we make a theatre piece, we kind of accommodate what [the performers] are good at or how they read. They have functions, so it's not like we treat each other as actors and there has to be this transformation. We just put what Ron brings to a text and

formalize it: it definitely comes from Ron as we know him, as he presents himself to the world and then, of course, when you formalize it and it becomes public in a performance, that ups the stakes a little bit. That's not to say Ron is just being himself, but you're taking those qualities that he has and you're kind of pumping them up and putting them in this structure.[23]

LeCompte has stated that she is working with performers who have had different kinds of training, and have 'different ways of performing on the stage and all of them are equally wonderful to me. I don't value one over the other, I value performance, I value the stage.'[24] She draws on what each performer has to offer:

> I use so many levels of performance style. ... I'm just more inter-ested in finding the place where the performer is the most alive, where I feel the presence is real.[25]

Despite this apparent eclecticism, however, it is clear that there is a dominant tendency in LeCompte's work, which rejects the 'internal' in favour of an 'external' approach to acting. In rehearsal, she focuses on developing a series of 'tasks', which the actor then performs on a purely technical level.

> I say to the actors, 'You have information to present to the audi-ence, and you are responsible for a clear imparting of the information.' That's giving them a mental task, so they can get through the persona thing without coloring it emotionally. Often when the performer tries to decorate the text or illustrate what the text should feel like emotionally, there is a collision between what the actor is truly doing onstage and what the text is saying.[26]

LeCompte seems, in fact, to be reacting against a tendency among American Method actors to strive for emotion, and 'illustrate what the text should feel like emotionally'. In rehearsal, she uses terms like 'functional entrance' or 'utilitarian exit' in order 'to prevent the performer from pushing a heightened level of emotion (simulated or real) while executing simple tasks':

> Everybody has to be aware I don't want anyone to fill any section with emotion. I want to fill it with your presence in the space. I want you to be who you are. I want physical actions, not emotions. The emotions would be given by the overall picture. Crying is an

action not an emotion; don't manipulate your voice or feelings. If the play is boring let it be boring.[27]

LeCompte does not want the actor to experience emotion; she wants the emotion to be 'given' to the *audience* through the 'overall picture'. At one point in *L.S.D.*, Dafoe was seen to place glycerin in his eyes to simulate tears. In other words, the actor simply 'indicated' the emotion rather than actually experiencing it. The emotion was 'given' to the audience; but at the same time, our attention was drawn to the fact that the tears were not 'real' – simply a theatrical *convention*.

At one point during rehearsal for *Brace Up!*, the company looked at Stanislavski's production score for *Three Sisters*, and tried out some of his stage directions. Weems comments:

> We thought some of them absurd, some of them intriguing. ... And of course there was a lot of hilarity because Stanislavski's method was a big thing to come up against.
> However, Liz [LeCompte] and Stanislavski do have certain things in common. Liz is very obsessive about details; like Stanislavski, she creates a movement or gesture for every word in the text. He did it with a psychological slant; her slant is opposed to that. In fact, the Wooster Group is challenging the Stanislavski interpretation.[28]

In rehearsal, LeCompte focuses on tasks or physical actions in order 'to find some kind of abstract language or movement that's *not* psychological. For example, she might give the actors tasks to complete during a certain amount of time – like looking for a pillow or a flashlight. I think, basically, it was a way for Liz to explore the text while keeping people occupied.'[29] These tasks 'distract' the actors, absorb their attention and make them '*exist* in the space'. This recalls Stanislavski's own emphasis on physical tasks, especially in his Chekhov productions, which helped the actors' concentration and relaxation. However, LeCompte works through tasks which have no psychological motivation, and are often quite unrelated to the text. Thus, in *Brace Up!*, when Chebutykin entered with a coffee-urn to present to Irina, the actors played a 'game' with the narrator, Kate Valk: 'if she moves, they can move; if she stops, they have to stand still. And it's turned into this really beautiful dance.'[30] This 'dance', however, had nothing to do with the situation in the play, but was executed for its own sake. This created a strange sense of dislocation, of actions performed without meaning.

John Harrop has suggested that Stanislavski helped the actor to see a text as 'a map to action'.

> For Stanislavski, the actor's process was based upon a careful understanding and analysis of the text to gain a clear sense of the total action of the play ... The actor would gather all the information the text gave about the nature – bodily, circumstantial and emotional – of his or her character to create a physical and psychological profile of the character ... [31]

In the work of The Wooster Group, however, the 'text' is no longer the 'map'. Rather, the 'score' of choreographed movement becomes the map for performers to follow. Acting is seen as the art of 'plastic forms in space': 'the creation of solid physical scores' prevail 'over individual emotions'.[32] The performer, ultimately, is simply an 'executive artist'.

In *Brace Up!*, there was no sense of continuity or development of character. Instead, the actors simply performed a series of disconnected tasks. 'A moment of concentration and attention may build around an actor or an episode', Alfred Nordmann observed, 'but these moments are quickly dismantled and give way to other impressions.'[33] The actors were given vocal tasks to execute their speeches on a purely technical level – for example, completing a speech in a given period of time. The lines were often spoken in a flat and colourless voice – as if simply being read aloud rather than 'acted' or 'interpreted'. The 'flat' delivery of the lines, moreover, meant that there was no attempt to explore the 'subtext', the 'inner life' beneath the words. At times, indeed, it seemed as if this group of actors were simply saying their lines without any notion of their meaning. When Vershinin entered in Act I, for example, he spoke into a microphone. 'How do you do?' he said. 'I'm delighted to be here at last, delighted, believe me ... Well, well! How you've grown!' But he addressed his comments to the *audience*, not the sisters. His deadpan voice belied the emotion in his words. Then, when he announced that he is from Moscow, Irina did not look at him, but at *the narrator*, and asked: 'You're from Moscow?' This made the line seem random, arbitrary, absurd. There could be no sense that we were watching a 'real' conversation. Logic and continuity were denied.

The style of performance in *Brace Up!* was disorienting; it was 'like encountering a theatre company from outer space'.[34] It seemed to be almost a form of 'anti-acting'. The denial of *internal* action in the performances left us only with *external* action, executed it seems at random – a play of surfaces, with no inner depth.

The danger in the work of The Wooster Group is that the 'classic text' can become less a site to be occupied, than an object to be parodied. Deconstruction can easily degenerate into pastiche. (In *Brace Up!*, it was as if 'a group of smart-ass New York intellectuals were setting out to "send up" a great classic'.[35]) Paradoxically, the work of the Wooster Group does *not* really undermine the status of the 'classic text'. The text actually remains at the centre of the work. It seems, in fact, that the company feels the need to cling to the 'raft' of the conventional play-text as it floats on the sea of postmodernist confusion, collecting the flotsam and jetsam of other texts and objects which pass its way.

In *Brace Up!*, the company played on our expectations and preconceptions, and presented a series of 'ironic variations' on Chekhov's play. This could be amusing and entertaining – as Charles Marowitz saw, 'one's psyche and soma' were continually 'tantalized by novel and unexpected stimuli'.[36] Ultimately, however, this was an exercise in form without content.

* * *

As early as 1957, Robert Lewis recognised that the American Method emphasised internal work at the expense of the external means of expression. Similarly, Gordon Rogoff has argued that the cult of 'inner truth' became 'an excuse for ignoring the compelling outer realities of dramatic art'.[37] The reaction against the hegemony of the Method has led to a new emphasis on the 'physical', and a 'radical rediscovery of the body'.[38]

The Method has been associated with a predominantly naturalistic style of performance. (This is despite Strasberg's claims that it is intended as a basis for any period or style of drama.) Thus, the reaction against the Method has also led to the search for 'new forms' – to break the bonds of 'naturalistic truth and psychological reality'. Companies such as The Wooster Group have experimented with theatrical form – but have done away with the 'truth of feelings'. The result, in some ways, is a continuing split in the American theatre between art that is 'true to life but uncertain in its mastery of form, and art rich in form but poor in content'.

Production notes

Brace Up!, performed by The Wooster Group; first work-in-progress showings at the Performing Garage, New York, 10–13 May 1990. Official premiere in Seattle, 21 March 1991.

IV Chekhov in England

9 Theodore Komisarjevsky

The first production of a Chekhov play in London was a disaster comparable to the St Petersburg premiere of *The Seagull*. It was in 1911 when – as the playwright, Rodney Ackland, recalled – the directors of the London Stage Society

> decided on a production of *The Cherry Orchard* as the most auspicious way of introducing the British Public to Anton Chekhov. But when it came to it, the British Public refused to be introduced. They didn't want to know. They were quite firm about it, their reaction was unambiguous to a degree. They turned their backs and left. In ones, in twos, in threes, in parties and finally in shoals, they took off, they swep' out; until at last, by the end of the play, where poor old Firs has to totter on stage, try the door handle and groan, 'They've gone!', the unfortunate actor playing the part suddenly realised that the line had become applicable to the other side of the footlights. Gone they had. Nothing could be seen but row upon row of stalls, with nary an evening-dressed bottom to keep the seats down.[1]

It was Bernard Shaw who suggested to the Stage Society that they should attempt a Chekhov play.[2] It was presented for two performances only, after very few rehearsals. The Society's resources were limited and the production was necessarily makeshift. The set had been 'evidently raised by serf labour'[3] and the costumes were appalling. None of the actors 'seemed to know much of what it was about', Nigel Playfair (who played Simeonov-Pishchik) later recalled.[4] The audience felt that 'they were being insulted in their intelligence' by this strange play; either that, or 'their legs were being pulled'.[5]

It seemed, in fact, that Chekhov would never become popular with the great British Public. Other stage societies later tried their hands at his plays, with little more success. Then, in 1925, J.B. Fagan directed *The Cherry Orchard* at the Oxford Playhouse. John Gielgud played Trofimov. The company, as he recalled, only had a week to rehearse. 'I did not understand the play at all and there was no time for the director to explain it.'[6] The results, inevitably, were 'somewhat clumsy and tentative'.[7] Nevertheless, Nigel Playfair (by now the director of the Lyric Theatre, Hammersmith) saw the production, and determined to present it in London. The first performance was well received; indeed, there were even cries of 'Author!' in the auditorium; but the reviews were hostile. Audiences were poor, and Playfair hastily made arrangements to close the production. James Agate, however, came to the rescue. He went on the radio, to urge listeners to go to Hammersmith, and 'go now'.[8] Playfair produced a poster, quoting opposing views of the play: 'this imperishable masterpiece' (Agate); 'this fatuous drivel' (Hastings).[9] Business leaped up, and the production transferred to the Royalty Theatre, where it ran throughout the summer. Chekhov had suddenly 'arrived'.

After the success of the Hammersmith *Cherry Orchard*, 'a small-time impresario of little note and no repute (his name was Phillip Ridgeway), inaugurated an astonishing and unprecedented event: nothing more nor less than "A Season of Plays by Chekhov". Not just *one* play but one after another – a *season* of them!'[10] The first production was *The Seagull*, directed by A.E. Filmer. It was a dismal affair. ('Wave after wave of gloom rolled off the stage and swamped the audience, which soon foundered.'[11]) For the next production, Ridgeway changed directors. Theodore Komisarjevsky had directed an acclaimed *Ivanov* for the Stage Society, in December 1925. Ridgeway engaged him for the rest of his Chekhov season. (Perhaps, Gielgud suggests, he chose Komisarjevsky because he was, 'like Chekhov, supposed to be a highbrow with a Russian name'.[12]) A revival of *Ivanov* was followed by *Uncle Vanya*, *Three Sisters* and finally *The Cherry Orchard*. The productions were presented at the Barnes Theatre, a recently converted suburban cinema. Now, just fifteen years after the debacle of the Stage Society's production of *The Cherry Orchard*, people from all over London were swarming down to Barnes, and cramming themselves into the tiny theatre to see Chekhov.

Komisarjevsky (or 'Komis' as he was called) arrived in London in 1919. He was half-brother to the famous Russian actress, Vera Komissarzhevskaya (who played Nina in the original production of *The Seagull*).[13] He became a director at his sister's theatre in St Petersburg in 1906, and later worked at the Nezlobin Dramatic Theatre in Moscow, and the Bolshoi and the Mali Theatres. He also formed his own studio and school. Shaw called him 'the best theatrical director in Europe'.[14] He 'was a remarkable man', Anthony Quayle recalled; 'a draughtsman and designer as well as director'. He designed and lit his own productions: 'His was the entire and total concept.'[15] Komis himself argued, in his book *Myself and the Theatre*, for a 'Synthetic Theatre' – a form of *Gesamtkunstwerk*, in which the elements of decor, acting and *mise-en-scène* were '*synthetically* united': 'All the arts utilised on the stage of a Synthetic Theatre should convey simultaneously the same feelings and ideas to the spectator.'[16] This coherence, and synthesis, was what he aimed for in Chekhov.

> The big success of my production of *The Three Sisters* in London at the Barnes Theatre was largely due to the fact that I evolved the way to convey Chekhov's inner meaning and made the rhythm of the 'music' of the play blend with the rhythm of the movements of the actors, giving the necessary accents with the lighting and the various outer 'effects'. If this synthesis had not been completely harmonious the play might have seemed thin and even meaning-less to the audience, as indeed, it did during rehearsals to the majority of the actors until they observed the final result.[17]

Komis had not staged Chekhov in Russia. However, he had seen the Moscow Art Theatre's productions, and it is clear that he was influenced by them. 'I shall never forget', he wrote, 'the impression of the saturating atmosphere of reality and the perfect harmony of everyone and everything' in Stanislavski's production of *Uncle Vanya*.[18] Stanislavski achieved, he said, a 'symphony of feelings' – 'what is called in German "Stimmung"'.[19] As we will see, the solutions Komis found to the problems of staging Chekhov's plays, were to some extent the same as Stanislavski's solutions. (Somewhat scathingly, Rodney Ackland – who disliked Komisarjevsky personally – suggested that he simply copied the Art Theatre productions.[20])

Komisarjevsky and the Stanislavski 'system'

Komis despised the English commercial theatre. In a letter to a news-paper in Russia, he said that everything in the English theatre was blighted by 'sentimental banality' (*poshlost*): 'Theatre here now is the most detestable profiteering. ... People go to see the most stupid and banal revues and shows, musical comedies, music hall, where banality and scabrousness are camouflaged by a puritanical sentimentality.'[21]

Poshlost affected English acting too, which had degenerated into a 'stock of spiritless conventions'.[22] Commercial actors were not interested in team-work, but only in showing off and exhibiting their own personalities. At the Barnes, Komis felt he had the opportunity to present an alternative model of theatre, based around the notion of an ensemble, 'a permanent company of good, enthusiastic and vital actors', able to 'demonstrate the ideas of the producer', and trained 'into a harmonious team'.[23]

In Russia, Komis had positioned himself as an opponent of Stanislavski's theories on acting. He wrote a book about the Stanislavski 'system': *Tvorchestvo aktera i teoriya Stanislavskogo* ('The Art of the Actor and the Theory of Stanislavski', published 1917). He praised Stanislavski's work on *The Seagull*, claiming that the director discovered the methods of staging Chekhov through 'inspiration, intuitively'. However, according to Komis, when he subsequently began to develop his 'system', and attempted to analyse scientifically what he had previously created 'unthinkingly', unconsciously, he arrived at 'completely incorrect theoretical principles of acting'.[24] Komis accused Stanislavski of advocating a form of 'psychological naturalism'. The 'system', he said, was based on a fallacy: it assumed that the actor could only play himself on stage, and only portray feelings which he or she had experienced in life. This, Komis concluded, ignored the most important quality in acting: the power of the *imagination*.

But Komis had never actually worked with Stanislavski, and his book was based purely on hearsay and conjecture. Stanislavski filled the margins of his own copy with angry comments: 'Lies!', 'How vile!', 'I say exactly the opposite!' He was particularly incensed by the suggestion he downgraded the importance of imagination – when this was the *centre* of his work as an actor and director: 'What a scandalous slander and lack of understanding.' Komis also attacked 'affective memory'. But according to Stanislavski, he had misunderstood the whole concept. The starting point, the very basis of the argument, was wrong – and so the rest was just superfluous: 'I could cross out everything written in the book.'[25]

Paradoxically, Komis' approach to acting was in fact based, to some extent, on Stanislavskian principles. Like Stanislavski, he was strongly opposed to the 'conventionalities of the stage and all the stereotyped forms, habits and mannerisms connected with it'.[26] He believed it was wrong to try to impose external forms of expression on the actor, because this could only lead to empty clichés:

> the 'inside' of an actor, call it 'soul' or 'consciousness,' or whatever you like, is a very complicated and delicate instrument. That

instrument is what matters most on stage, and only an extremely sensitive and careful producer can play on it without hurting the freshness of the actor's conception of the part and his own creation of it.[27]

First and foremost, he said, the director must be able to reveal the inner life of a play to the actors, and the inner feelings, the 'inner life' of the characters; and then, help them to find the external means to express these feelings: 'For me, the most important thing … is the correct experience of the role. When the soul of the actor is transformed through the work, then his ability to master clearly and accurately the form of expression is also transformed.'[28]

Komis stressed to actors the need to know the 'whole background' of the characters, 'besides the moments we actually see them'.[29] The 'life of a human being', he wrote, 'is continuous, without intervening gaps', and so 'the acting of an actor on the stage must be continuous'.[30] In other words, there must be a 'through-line.'

Komis also emphasised the importance of concentration and relaxation, and sought to develop communion between the actors on stage (although he did not actually use that term). An actor, he said, must 'listen to his partner, when he is supposed to hear him, look at him, and actually see him'.[31]

When Komis came to work in England, he became the means whereby elements of the Stanislavski 'system' were transmitted to English actors. Warren Jenkins, who received acting lessons from Komis, observed that the director 'brought with him something of the Stanislavskian approach to acting. He encouraged you to probe much deeper into the character's emotions and inner life than English actors were used to.'[32] Quayle argued: 'Everything was to do with reality and the truth of human relationships. This is what he was endlessly on about.'[33]

'Until I worked with Komisarjevsky', Gielgud recalled, 'I was always showing off, either in a romantic or hysterical vein.'[34] But now, he 'began to realise how a part should be lived from within'. Komis

> was an enormous influence in teaching me not to act from outside, not to seize on obvious, showy effects and histrionics, not so much to exhibit myself as to be within myself trying to impersonate a character who is not aware of the audience, to try to absorb the atmosphere of the play and the background of the character, to build it outward so that it came to life naturally. This was something I had never thought of and it seemed to me a great relaxing exercise. … This relaxation is the secret of good acting.[35]

He learnt to act, in other words, as if behind a 'fourth wall'.

Charles Morgan wrote that Komis, in his Chekhov productions, was able to achieve 'a kind of natural simplicity of treatment. He permits no actor to indulge in heroics; he sets his face against any kind of theatricality; everyone has an air of strolling about the stage at his ease.'[36] Gielgud joined the Barnes company to play Tusenbach in *Three Sisters*.

> I remember our first rehearsals in someone's Bloomsbury flat, with the floor marked out in bewildering lines of coloured chalk – the groupings, entrances and exits all most accurately planned – though at first we could none of us imagine why we were being shuffled about in such intricate patterns of movement.[37]

Komis' production plan is preserved in his prompt-book. We can witness the 'intricate patterns of movement' he created in, for example, the opening of Act II. Natasha entered from downstage right; she moved upstage right, then downstage left, sat at the table in the centre, then rose, and exited downstage right. In the same scene, Andrei entered upstage left, crossed the stage and sat downstage right; then crossed to another chair, downstage left.[38] Reading Komis' production plan today, it might seem as if he included too much movement and activity. Clearly, at first, the cast could not understand the moves they had been given. However, the 'score' helped to create a sense of continuous life on stage. Through his blocking, Komis carefully captured the 'minutiae of comings and goings, of groupings and dispersions' so that 'the illusion of the social scene may be complete'.[39] In Act I of *Three Sisters*, the stage was set with the dining room visible through trellis-work of a verandah. In the very first scene, during Olga's monologue, Irina was occupied in the dining room, helping the maid to set the table. There was, then, a use of simultaneous action, to create a sense of the everyday life of the household. This also helped to create a sense that the actors were continually 'living' their roles. (Desmond MacCarthy, who insisted that the 'underlying unity' of a Chekhov play could only be achieved 'by keeping every actor and actress on the scene continuously alive and simultaneously acting', said that 'Mr Komisarjevsky's productions of Chekhov are beyond comparison successful because he insists upon this simultaneity'.[40])

The staging, however, was never 'casual' or 'haphazard': at any moment, the grouping was 'perfect' and 'deliberately formal'.[41] *The Times* wrote that 'the great beauty, even if it appeared a trifle mannered, of the groupings in *The Three Sisters* was clearly the result of a deep sensibility to the atmosphere of Chekhov's most poetic play'.[42] Agate recalled Irina in Act III, with her arms entwined about her sisters, as she bursts into a storm of weeping: 'The grouping here is pyramidal, and it is as … much the visual effect as the skill of the words which gives an effect of dolour such as may not be compassed by the precis-writer'.[43] Norman Marshall concluded: 'I have seen nothing more lovely in the theatre than the stage pictures Komisarjevsky created on that cramped little stage at Barnes.'[44]

Komis wanted a 'musical ensemble of the actors' who could find the rhythm to express the play's 'emotional content'.[45] He argued that 'every play, even the most naturalistic one, has music concealed in it'.[46] The 'rhythm' of the play is the 'expression of the "inner life"', now quick, now slow, now soft, now loud'. Finding the rhythm was a way of 'reaching the emotion' of a scene or role.[47] (Warren Jenkins recalls that in rehearsal, the director would sometimes stop to play the piano, and say to the actors: 'This is the mood.')

Komis 'knew exactly what he wanted a production to be: he knew the tempo, the interpretation, the precise musical rhythm of a play'. Like Stanislavski, he made extensive uses of pauses, 'the timing of which he rehearsed minutely'. His favourite word, indeed, was 'pawse'; he was determined to orchestrate his productions 'as significantly in the silences as in the dialogue'.[48] (There was a famous 'pawse' in Act 1 of *The Seagull*, which according to Alec Guinness lasted four minutes.[49])

Reviewing *Three Sisters*, John Shand said the production 'has been tuned to a pitch that allows every modulation of tone, every nuance of emotion, its proper value. Each change of rhythm has been so perfectly timed that the throb of one's heart acknowledges the truth of the altered beat. Each new scene is a new movement which is valid in its own right, and yet is given an additional worth and beauty by its difference from and in relation to the scenes which precede and follow it.' Agate admired the way Komis created a 'whole web of sight and sound' in his productions, 'so that the play becomes an orchestrated score. This is beauty in which dramatist and producer have an equal hand.'[50] Again like Stanislavski, Komis filled pauses with atmospheric sound-effects.[51] Take, for example, the opening of *The Cherry Orchard*: atmospheric lighting, the 'mingled lamplights and moonlight on white walls, already flushed with the roseate hues of dawn', was combined with sound, 'the distant tinkle of sleighbells warning the sleepy watchers of the emigres' return'.[52]

In his stage settings, Komis was much more concerned with 'mood' than with realism: 'his lighting, soft, rich and mellow, was romantic

Plate 15 Scene from Act I of Komisarjevsky's production of *The Seagull* (1936). 'Mr Komisarjevsky's direction has been brilliant and his scenery fascinates ... he restates the case for the old decorative style: there is soft music in his branches and his willows truly weep.' (Ivor Brown)

rather than realistic, and with the skill of a painter he made dramatic use of highlights, shadows and half-tones to give emphasis to his beautifully composed groupings and ensembles'.[53]

Komis liked to use light which appeared to emanate from natural sources – from candles and lamps on-stage; through windows, or open doorways. ('M. Komisarjevsky can throw a light through a window that will tell you the season of the year and the time of day.'[54]) But this was less for the purposes of 'naturalism' than to create a 'mood'. (One critic even complained about his 'obsession of strange lighting for the sake of pictorial effect'.[55]) Thus in *Uncle Vanya* (1921), light shone through stained glass windows onto a darkened stage. The result was that 'the twilight melancholy in which the play is bathed was made almost visible'.[56]

In Act II of *Three Sisters*, the wintry mood was evoked by the lighting. A shaft of light fell across the stage through the doorway at the rear. 'See how beautifully the pictures fulfil the action', wrote

'H.H.'; 'how the light from the kitchen (where life has entrenched its forces) glows into the room where Masha and her lover lay bare their hearts in the twilight'.[57] At the end of Act III, Olga and Irina retire to bed, behind the screens at the rear of the stage. At this point in Komis' production, the lighting was almost expressionistic: 'The younger sister's flood of passion is not yet stilled, and as you listen to the last of its ebb you see the giant shadows of these two figures of grief thrown by the candle upon the upper wall and ceiling.'[58] Effects such as this were novel enough to attract comment from critics: 'Who but a genius would have ventured to have had one of the most pathetic scenes played so that only the distorted leaping shadows of the speakers were seen by the audience?'[59]

Komis, then, orchestrated or 'synthesised' the elements of the production, in order to 'convey simultaneously the same feelings and ideas to the spectator'. It is clear that he achieved miracles with minimal resources at his disposal. Later productions of Chekhov were criticised for lacking some of his effects. When the Group de Prague performed *Uncle Vanya* in 1928, 'H.H.' complained that the 'externals of the production were less charming': 'Here was none of Komisarjevsky's visual poetry'.[60] On the other hand, reviewing the Group de Prague in *The Cherry Orchard*, Agate wrote:

> The play was acted before some miserable scenery, the miserableness of which did not even begin to matter. The lighting was not particularly good, and this matters more. Or am I sentimentalising? M. Komisarjevsky certainly sentimentalised when he bathed that last scene in a glow of afternoon sunshine filtering through the shutters.[61]

It seems that critics and audiences were seduced, to a certain extent, by the 'externals' of Komis' productions.

Chekhov through a 'mist of loveliness'

The most successful production at the Barnes was *Three Sisters*. The *Evening Standard* said it was one of 'the deepest and loveliest things that modern drama has done'. C. Nabokoff had seen the play at the Moscow Art Theatre, but he had 'no hesitation' in saying that Komis' production 'was likewise an unforgettable one'.[62]

The production evoked a melancholic mood 'as sadly beautiful as autumn itself yet graced with spring-time flash of merriment'.[63] Peggy Ashcroft said: 'one knew that one was seeing something the like of which had not been seen on the English stage before: everyday life recreated with total fidelity'. For Rodney Ackland, the experience was overwhelming: 'I saw, as if for the first time, the beauty and wonder of ordinary life.'[64]

And yet, it was 'ordinary life' seen through a romantic haze. Komis, we can now see, distorted Chekhov's play, in order to make it more appealing to English audiences. 'To suit the public's taste', he argued, 'life on the English stage had to be shown through a mist of loveliness.'[65] He said this disparagingly; but he himself presented Chekhov through a 'mist of loveliness'. The women in *Three Sisters* were dressed in 'bustles and chignons', which 'looked very attractive and certainly heightened their picturesque appearance'.[66] Komis changed the period of the play to the 1870s, creating a certain nostalgic charm, rather like a BBC classic serial: 'the dressing sets the emotions back in time and indicates a world which is no more'.[67]

Irina, played by Beatrix Thomson, was 'an exquisite creature, like one of Christina Rossetti's maidens, in a drawing by Arthur Hughes'. She had a 'delicate, flower-like beauty'.[68] Ivor Brown wrote that when she submits to her 'loveless, ill-fated match' with Tusenbach, 'it is like the withering of some perfect flower'.[69] Komis, meanwhile, cut all references to the Baron being an ugly man. He told Gielgud to play him as a 'romantic juvenile',

> with a smart uniform and side-whiskers, looking as handsome as possible. I have never been able to discover why he did this – but I have a suspicion that he felt that a juvenile love-interest was essential in any play that was to appeal to an English audience.[70]

Margaret Swallow as Masha 'represented the pathos of romance *manque* in the unhappily married woman. A faded air of Gounod made her live for one moment passionately, and then the spirit seemed to die again.'[71] Ivor Brown urged his readers: 'Go then to see the love of Masha and Vershinin glowing at the heart of the play, for Mr. Ion Swinley and Miss Margaret Swallow are nobly kindled by the flame.'[72]

Komis, then, romanticised the characters, turning the sisters into tragic heroines, and the play into the bitter-sweet story of two doomed love-affairs. He distorted Chekhov – but critics, by and large, were still not very familiar with the plays, and did not notice the changes he made. In any case, as Michael Redgrave observed, everyone assumed that he knew what he was doing and they 'took his word as gospel'.[73]

Komis returned to Chekhov in 1936 with his production of *The Seagull*. It was, in many ways, the apotheosis of his approach to the plays. 'This, in fact, is the first time *The Seagull* has been produced on the grand scale', the *Daily Mirror* announced.[74] At the Barnes, Komis had minimal resources to work with; but now, he was working in the West End, and he spent extravagantly (insisting, for example, on silk leaves on the trees for Act I). The result was a *'de luxe* production'.[75] The cast included John Gielgud, Edith Evans, Peggy Ashcroft, Leon Quartermaine and George Devine. The critic from the *Daily Sketch*, in a piece called 'It's the Star Cast That Matters', wrote: 'People won't go to see this play, but they *will* go to see the star cast – probably for ever and ever.'[76]

The production combined an 'atmosphere of brooding melancholy, alleviated by gleams of humour'. The settings, especially for Act I, were 'enchanting'.[77] Ivor Brown said that Komis 'restates the case for the old decorative style' of staging: 'there is soft music in his branches and his willows truly weep'.[78] The costumes were also charming. In one journal, a spread of photographs from the production was accompanied by the caption: 'Not a fashion page of 1894, but Edith Evans in *The Seagull*'.[79]

Again, the characters were simplified and romanticised. Komis insisted that Gielgud should play Trigorin as an elegant figure in evening-wear. (He told Gielgud that 'each of the three fine Russian actors he had seen as Trigorin had been dressed elegantly – Dalmatov at the Imperial Stage, Stanislavski at the Moscow Arts and Bravich at his sister's theatre'. Stanislavski, it is true, first played the role 'in the most elegant of costumes' and could not understand it when Chekhov told him that Trigorin should wear torn shoes and checked trousers.[80]) The performance was 'an exquisite exhibition of sensitive Gielgudry', the character pining after Nina 'as Dante did after Beatrice'.[81]

Agate called the production 'endlessly beautiful'. 'J.G.B.' in *The Evening News*, however, wrote: 'somehow, it is all a little too carefully, too elaborately done, beautifully, but too beautifully. There is no waywardness, no rawness, nothing that is not competent and controlled.'[82] Bernard Shaw hated it. In seems that Komis, like Stanislavski, reduced the last Act to a crawl:

> I went to *The Seagull* and disliked it extremely. ... Komisar has lost his old Russian touch: he filled the last Act with pauses of the sort that are bearable only in a first Act when there is no hurry and the audience is willing to speculate a little on dumb shows. And anyhow the dumbshows were unintelligible and uninteresting.[83]

Komis argued that the English theatre offered 'a kind of stagey pretty chocolate box reproduction of life – and false romanticism'.[84] It is paradoxical that, while despising the commercial English theatre, and the way it pandered to its audiences, he made his own compromises with English tastes, and distorted Chekhov's plays, to offer us something closer to a 'chocolate box reproduction of life'.

'I think Komisarjevsky is very much responsible for the love that English people have for Chekhov', Peggy Ashcroft claimed.[85] In some ways he had set the tone for Chekhov on the British stage; it would be hard, in the future, to shed that 'mist of loveliness' in which he submerged the plays. As Ivor Brown wrote, reviewing *The Seagull*, critics and audiences had come to love 'the exquisite rhythm of Chekhov's laments for an old way of living, the pattern of the figures in their period clothes, the tingling sense of a civilization in its autumn mood with the winds of winter at the door'.[86]

Production notes

Komisarjevsky's productions

Uncle Vanya, Incorporated Stage Society at the Royal Court Theatre, London; first performance, 27 November 1921.

Ivanov, Incorporated Stage Society at the Duke of York's Theatre, London; first performance, 6 December 1925.

Uncle Vanya, Barnes Theatre, London; first performance, 16 January 1926.

Three Sisters, Barnes Theatre; first performance, 16 February 1926.

The Cherry Orchard, Barnes Theatre; first performance, 28 September 1926.

The Seagull, New Theatre, London; first performance, 20 May 1936.

10 Jonathan Miller

In 1976, fifty years after Komisarjevsky's *Three Sisters*, Rodney Ackland went to see Jonathan Miller's production of the play, during its run at the Cambridge Theatre in London. He recalled: 'as soon as I entered the auditorium my heart sank'. There was a platform stage, a plain grey backcloth, and 'naked, unconcealed spotlights hanging from the fly'. Such drabness, he reflected, may be a modern trend in stage design, 'but that Chekhov, of all dramatists, should be subjected to it!' This was only the first shock he experienced: no sooner had the lights gone up on *Three Sisters*, 'than I realized it was not going to be a question merely of accepting a mode of presentation I was allergic to, but of jettisoning a whole lot of Komisarjevsky – derived ideas about the play itself'. Hilary Spurling agreed: 'it is hard to imagine anything more different from the tradition handed down via Stanislavski and Komisarjevsky ... than the uncompromisingly anti-romantic bias of this production'.[1]

Miller's approach to Chekhov can be seen, in part, as an attempt to strip away, once and for all, the 'mist of loveliness' surrounding the plays. In England, he suggests, Chekhov can 'all too easily become embalmed in a monumental melancholy'.[2] When another style is introduced, and his work 'is played much more rapidly, casually, even shabbily', people think 'that a beautiful work has been violated. This seems to me to misunderstand what is remarkable about Chekhov – that his work takes such pleasure in what is unbeautiful and mundane about life.'[3]

Chekhov, we will recall, declared: 'On stage everything should be just as complicated and just as simple as in life. People eat, just eat, and at the same time their happiness is being decided or their lives ruined.'[4] Taking his cue from this, Miller suggests that Chekhov's plays should, on the surface, appear quite 'ordinary, casual, even slipshod – like real life': 'The plays float on a rather indolent tide of undirected chit-chat.' This element, 'together with the comedy, needs to be brought out'.[5]

Miller describes his productions as 'stabs at a form of naturalism': 'Chekhov is quite clearly more realistic than Shakespeare. The characters speak lines that are very like those that ordinary people speak when conversing with one another. There are ways of enhancing that sense of being in the presence of reality, and it is most important to attend to what are called "the rules of conversation".' There are rules 'of listening, of not speaking until the other person has finished, learning how to take your turn', and so on.[6] Conversations 'are in fact complicated competitions to speak next, in which, during the time when someone is speaking, you are waiting to get in'. In any conversation, 'there is – to use a musical term – a 'stave' of non-verbal sounds and noises, and that is part of the *design* of conversation'. However, speeches on the page of a playscript lack the 'hesitations, the incompletenesses and overlaps you might find on a tape-recording of the conversation'. In order to achieve a 'natural' quality to the performance, these details 'must be consciously restored'. 'All these little characteristics of speech take a long time to recreate on stage, but when the actors manage it the audience feels as if it is in the presence of a real conversation.'[7]

In Millers' productions, characters sometimes interrupt each other; they interject with agreements, or mumble some comment which isn't heard. Speeches may overlap; at times, characters all speak at once. The aim, then, is to create a sense of idly trickling colloquy, 'the chronic coming and going of fairly undirected discourse'[8] – emphasizing the *ordinariness* of the drama. 'It was all incredibly normal', Miller suggests. 'I took twenty minutes off the running time of *Three Sisters* simply by having people talk as if they were really *talking* to each other.'

Redesigning the characters

When Miller directed *Three Sisters*, 'he discovered that the three girls pining for Moscow are very far from being stylish, glamorous, sensitive heroines'.[9] Irving Wardle wrote:

> To varying degrees, every other performance I have seen falls into the trap of presenting the action from the sisters' own viewpoint: three Grade-A girls, well-equipped for life in Moscow, but pathetically defeated by the mediocrity of provincial life, and too high-minded to protect themselves against a wastrel brother and his ruthlessly acquisitive wife.[10]

Miller comments:

> The fact that the play is called *Three Sisters* might incline you to
> see events from their viewpoint. But there are no minor characters
> in Chekhov. It is often thought, for example, that Masha is the
> central character in the play – but she is no more interesting to me
> than Olga, Irina, or the old nanny, filled with panic at the thought
> of losing her job. I think Chekhov was actually interested in three
> quite ordinary young women, who had views of themselves as
> rather better than the society in which they lived.

Miller, then, emphasises the *ordinariness* of the characters' situation.
The sisters' failure to get to Moscow 'is *not* tragic; they simply have to
continue having a dull suburban life – with an affair now and again –
as time passes by'.[11] John Shrapnel, who played Andrei, concluded:
'Chekhov was portraying the boredom of everyday lives, not three
tragic heroines demonstrating some Universal Truth to the rest of the
world through their own suffering.'[12]

Masha has often been seen as the play's romantic heroine. David
Magarshack, for example, called her 'the most poetic and sensitive of
the three sisters'; in the unfolding of her love for Vershinin, he wrote,
'Chekhov reveals her truly poetic nature'.[13] Miller, however, argues:

> I think this is probably the opposite of what Chekhov intended.
> What began to emerge in rehearsal was the affectation, the preten-
> tiousness of Masha – her contempt for people she thinks are
> beneath her, for her poor commonplace husband. She thinks she is
> much more sensitive and intelligent than she really is. She is
> leading a boring life in a boring garrison town. Quite suddenly an
> officer arrives. Vershinin is usually played as a silver-haired,
> romantic figure. He is not romantic. He isn't even particularly
> handsome. He is always worrying about his wife, his two little girls.
> His philosophical speculations are dull and repetitive. He's a bore.

The director, Miller contends, 'has to be careful not to follow or fall
into stereotypes. There are no "romantic leads" in Chekhov. There is
no-one particularly commendable or villainous. They are just foolish,
at times ridiculous, and lovable, as most people are.' Subsequently, 'the
characters need to be fairly radically redesigned so that they are
neither too romantic, nor too attractive, nor too melodramatic. The
ordinariness must be emphasised with the humour'.[14]

It has been suggested that Miller retains a critical distance from the characters in the plays. (They are presented 'objectively and with a comic edge' – Wardle.[15]) 'I am a doctor, like Chekhov', he comments, 'and I *look* at people. It is sometimes assumed that when you look at people, you are detaching yourself from them. In fact, it is the way you *attach* yourself to them: you see them for what they are.' Discussing Miller's work, Robert Cushman has concluded: 'We look at Chekhov's characters now, not patronisingly, which with Chekhov would be the unforgivable sin, but harshly. Because their weaknesses are our own, we have to; and because they are so fully drawn, they can stand it.'[16]

The most startling performance in Miller's production – 'the real eye-opener'[17] – was the portrayal of Irina, played by Angela Down. In Komisarjevsky's production, as Ackland recalled,

> and, in my mind, unquestioned since the day I saw it, Beatrix Thomson as the youngest of the sisters, tender, sensitive and vulnerable, infinitely feminine and infinitely appealing, was, in terms of tragedy and emotion, the centre of the play's design. Even now, sitting in front at the Cambridge, all these unimaginable years later, I could perceive, quite clearly in my mind's eye, an image of Trixie Thomson as she was in the first Act with her delicate, flower-like beauty and her tremulous hopes of happiness, a perfect paradigm of all of Chekhov's pure young girls, the 'little victims' who, all unconscious of their Fourth Act doom, do, in the First Act, play. This, surely, was the only possible Irina, the True Irina of Chekhovian intent. But here, before my present eyes, was a determined young person in a stiff and starchy high-necked dress, abrasive and unyielding in manner as the material the dress was made of. And she, too, according to Dr. Miller and Miss Angela Down, was supposed to be Irina. I found this difficult to accept. I resisted it. I hated it. But gradually, reluctantly and fighting every inch of the way, I was won over.[18]

Miller comments:

> I know that Irina is often played as this sweet innocent child, this delicate flower. I had to consider: is this necessarily the case? Olga tells her how attractive and radiant she looks – but this may tell us more about Olga than about Irina. Older sisters often cosset and praise a younger sister in this way. Chebutykin calls Irina 'my child,' 'my sweet girl' – but he is a sentimental old fool, who happens to dote on Irina. I have always imagined her as very hard, worn-down and impatient.

Miller 'discovered this interpretation was realisable on stage by redesigning the delivery of one short line at the end of the play': 'Usually when the Doctor enters with the news that Tusenbach has been shot, there is a melancholy and sad surrendering "*I* knew *it, I knew it* ... ". Instead I had her suddenly bite and slam her fist on the ground, spitting out the words as though shouting an expletive' – as if she is furious at Tusenbach for having been such a fool, and for blighting her chances of escape. 'This totally transformed the character and retrospectively we had to reconstruct her.'[19]

Ackland saw that by the end of Miller's production, 'a different pattern' had emerged 'behind the one we have been conditioned to see'.[20] The 'tragic stature' of the sisters was diminished. If the 'sympathetic' characters were viewed more dryly, then the 'unsympathetic' were treated with greater warmth and lenity. Natasha has been seen as the embodiment of vulgarity, intent on destroying the sisters and their world. David Magarshack spoke of her 'devilish nature' and of the 'stark horror' she must evoke.[21] In June Ritchie's performance, however, the character emerged as comic rather than villainous. (As Janet Suzman commented, Natasha 'is always going to be a total pain in the ass, but here she also became very funny indeed – her vulgarity was stunningly comic'.[22]) She had an 'officious clockwork strut'[23] and breezed through the house on whirlwind tours of inspection, carrying a candle before her like a miniature Olympic torch, and checking every corner to make sure nothing was out of place, with rapid nods of her head in all directions.

Similarly, Soleny (played by Peter Bayliss) was no 'wonderful, sinister duelling villain' but a slightly absurd, 'drunken, resentful, solitary and harassed figure'[24] who stood lurking in corners, inhaling deeply on fat cigars and surrounded by a halo of smoke. Bayliss exposed the character's social incompetence. When he proposed to Irina, he stood some distance from her. It was as if this was something he had steeled himself to do, probably with drink: he was stiff with fear and unable even to look at her. 'I love you', he said. 'I can't live without you.' His words were full of passion but there was no emotion in his voice; it was as if he was reciting lines he had learned beforehand. 'Oh, it's such a delight just to look at you', he declared – still with his eyes resolutely averted. The scene was comic, painful, and absurd.

Reinstating the comedy

In *My Life in Art*, Stanislavski recalled Chekhov's anger at the description of *Three Sisters* as a 'tragedy'; he insisted it was a comedy. This has puzzled many critics, however, who have continued to see the play as a tragedy. In Miller's production, a strong vein of irony and humour, and a 'lightness of touch', counteracted this reading. What Miller has done, Sheridan Morley concluded, 'is simply and boldly to reinstate *Three Sisters* as a comedy first and last'.[25]

Miller observes that, in Chekhov's work, one mood is continually undercut by another: 'one moment the characters are crying, and the next they are hysterical with laughter'. These unexpected changes and ironic reversals were a major source of the comedy in the production. In Act II, for example, Masha and Vershinin were seated together at a table. 'Let's do a bit of philosophising', Vershinin suggested; and the two of them leaned closer together, anticipating an intimate *tête-à-tête*. They were disappointed, however. 'Yes, let's!' said Tusenbach enthusiastically – and settled himself down between the two of them. Simultaneously, Masha and Vershinin both turned away, a look of dismay on their faces.

On the night of the fire, Tusenbach fell asleep, with his head slumped on a pile of clothes which had been left on the table. Irina woke him, he stirred, and immediately launched into a fresh declaration of his love for her: 'You're so pale, so beautiful, so fascinating … Your pallor seems to light up the darkness around you …'. When she heard this, Masha let out a groan – 'Oh, *God!*' – and buried her head under a pillow. The emotion in Tusenbach's line, then, was immediately undercut by Masha's reaction.

Irina's breakdown in Act III had a 'savage force'.[26] Then Natasha entered on one of her tours of inspection. She walked briskly through the room, without even looking at the sisters, and left without saying a word. In Miller's production, Irina then stood, and imitated her sister-in-law: waddling along, nose in the air, nodding her head in all directions. The sisters laughed helplessly together. It was as if Irina, having recovered a little, wished to reassure both herself and her sisters. In an instant, the mood of the scene had been reversed. And then, Masha (Janet Suzman) confessed her love for Vershinin. As she began the speech, she unexpectedly started to giggle – nervously at first, but then almost uncontrollably. 'I love everything about him', she declared, flinging her arms out wide; 'his voice, his misfortunes, even' – and she burst into laughter again – 'even his two little girls'. Suzman observed: 'Masha's confession can be a very grand piece of theatre if you don't watch it. I seem to recall we all arrived one day at the very true perception that often you get the giggles when you're saying the most important thing in your life.'[27] At the end of the scene, the giggling fit subsided. She sat back on the sofa, looking thoughtful, even a little puzzled – as if the wave of nervous emotion that welled up within her had just as suddenly passed away.

These variations in mood, Miller suggests, create an 'opalescent surface' to the work, and 'audiences are vastly entertained, even though they are seeing people in distress'.

Subliminal details

In *Subsequent Performances*, Miller writes that Chekhov's stories are 'probably the best prefaces to the plays'; they

> are full of accounts of gesture, and tiny physical detail. It is as if, confronted by a play script by Dickens, you found inspiration for details in its performance by looking at the novels, which are full of wonderful vignettes, like the one of Mr. Pocket, Herbert Pocket's father, who is seen picking himself up by the hair.[28]

Dickens and Chekhov, Miller argues, 'both excel in providing unexpected oddnesses of behaviour, which, incorporated into a play, can be quite breathtaking'. He cites the example in *Three Sisters* of Soleny dabbing his hands with cologne – 'rather a Dickensian oddity'.[29] It is a surprising detail – intriguing, and faintly ludicrous. It is only in the fourth Act that we learn the reason for his behaviour. Soleny is about to face Tusenbach in a duel. He stands dabbing his hands with scent. 'I've used up a whole bottle today', he says, 'and they still smell. They smell like a corpse.' Suddenly, we are given a glimpse into the macabre workings of Soleny's mind. The detail functions at once as a curious and even comic objectification of character, and an 'ephemeral' insight into character psychology. 'What makes any Chekhov production lift off', Miller contends, 'is this morbid sparkle of tiny subliminal details, idiosyncrasies that are curious but never extraordinary.'[30]

These 'subliminal details' can be both illuminating, and comic; they can expose the contradictions in a character's behaviour. In 1973–4, Miller staged *The Seagull*; Robert Stephens played Trigorin. Here was no 'suave literary gent' but an 'embarrassed, shambling figure – rather dazed in the unfamiliar countryside and out of depth with its inhabitants'.[31] Stephens 'sets the tone of his performance exactly when, just after his first entrance, he gives a little discreet cough of boredom as he crosses to seat himself by Arkadina'.[32] When it came to arranging Nina's seduction, he scribbled his address for her 'in a hand shaking as much with guilt as desire'[33]; and then he kissed her – but with one eye nervously open, in case Arkadina should suddenly come in and catch them.

Reviewing *Three Sisters*, Michael Billington argued that Miller 'has the first-rate Chekhovian director's ability to illuminate character through tiny behaviourist detail'. Suzman's Masha, for example, 'positively luxuriates in Vershinin's cigarette smoke while a moment later testily scything her way through Soleny's unbearable cigar fumes'.[34] 'It is details of this kind, pervading the show, that compel one's assent', Wardle suggested.

> Sebastian Shaw, as the drunken doctor, making his desperate confession while vainly looking for somewhere to pour away the water in which he has just tried to drown himself; Peter Bayliss' Soleny saying yes to another brandy and secretly adding it to the one he has got already; Peter Eyre delivering the Baron's final request for coffee as a firm order to keep Irina away from the duel.[35]

The actors, John Elsom concluded, 'are good enough to make the various points directly, efficiently and with throwaway rapidity. Miller seems to have caught that element in Chekhov's art which Stanislavski missed, the love of economy and precision, of the quick detail instead of the slow portrait.'[36]

'I approach Chekhov on the stage with a certain amount of clinical detail', Miller suggests. 'By clinical I do not mean pathological. I am interested in the nuances of physical behaviour.' In *The Seagull*, Treplev was played by Peter Eyre. Rather than the usual 'moody Hamlet substitute',[37] here was a natural pedant: gloomy, dreadfully earnest, prematurely aging; a sickly figure, perhaps, with his gaunt, haunted face. In the final Act, he wore a black suit to match the blackness of his mood. Treplev's final act before committing suicide was 'to rearrange his desk with obsessive Freudian tidiness'.[38] Miller observes:

> I had to consider how Treplev should behave in this scene. People who are preparing for suicide often leave traces, in order to let others know how injured they have been. Most suicides are pedantic about the actual act. Chekhov has an interesting note

about the scene: he wants it to take about two minutes for Treplev to tear up his papers. If you take that literally, it is a very long time on stage. In my production, Treplev begins by tearing up the papers and putting some in the wastepaper basket; then he stuffs some in his pocket, so that when the body is found, traces of his own romantic failure as a writer will be found on him. Then, he looks around the room, to see that everything is set as he wants it. He suddenly remembers he had given some water to Nina; the glass is still half-full. He drinks down the rest, shakes out the drops and places the glass on top of the carafe, so that no trace of her presence will be left. Then, he checks the room once more. When he is ready, he goes out to shoot himself.

When the sound of the explosion is heard, there should be a terrible noise. Everyone on stage freezes; the time the doctor is out of the room should seem interminable. Then he returns – and clearly, he has had to recompose himself, and consider what he will say. He decides to make a joke. 'Oh, that's right', he tells them, 'one of my ether bottles has exploded.' And then, he actually makes the sound: 'Pop!' And again, to reassure them: 'Poff!'

Then the doctor walks around the room. He has to consider how he is going to get Arkadina away, and he also has to look around the room to see if there is any evidence which would lead them to guess what has happened. Casually, he pulls the drawer out of the desk, and sees that there are torn papers there. 'Ah,' he thinks, 'that makes sense. It was inevitable. Why didn't we notice it before?' That has given the time he needs.

The whole scene takes some seven minutes. Sometimes it is necessary to draw out time on the stage, and recognise how long it can take people to do things. The action can be compressed elsewhere, and can even be taken at quite a headlong pace.

The staging of the scene, then, was based on a precise sequence (or 'score') of physical actions. The steps leading to Treplev's suicide attempt were built logically, through an attention to realistic detail, to the nuances or 'small truths' of behaviour. Each detail, such as tearing the paper, or drinking the glass of water, was both an 'ordinary, small, natural action', and a subliminal sign, offering us an insight into the workings of the character's mind.[39]

The metaphor of photography

The settings designed by Patrick Robertson for both *Three Sisters* (1976) and *The Seagull* (1973–4) were simple, not to say austere. There was no attempt to evoke a 'mood.' Miller observes:

> Chekhov himself had become exasperated by the quantity of visually and acoustically realistic detail which Stanislavski had introduced. They were extraneous and only served to clutter the productions. What is important in Chekhov is the encounter between characters and the web of relationships that develops. To make it easier to concentrate on that, I opted for a simple setting. There was very little in the way of accessory realistic detail.

In the absence of a decorative set, Elsom saw, the main element in Miller's visual composition 'is provided by the actors themselves'. The design for *Three Sisters*

> splits up the stage into unusual acting spaces and, above all, depths. Miller brings out the lights and shadows of the play often by the simple device of placing his actors on a distinctive part of the stage; but to do so, he had to delineate carefully the background, foreground, and the various grades between.[40]

At the beginning of the play, for example, Olga stood centre-stage. She was the centre of the action and the focal point of the stage-picture. Irina and Masha sat motionless in the foreground, and the group of men stood by the table in the background.

Stanislavski's production used a wide stage, and a 'wide-angle lens', to capture the comings-and-goings in the house. With Simov, the director divided the stage into distinct areas, including the dining room, through an archway at the back, and a small bay or verandah, forestage-right. At the opening of Act I, Masha was seated on the divan, on the extreme left; Olga and Irina occupied the bay on the opposite extreme. The men entered and stood by the dining table. Chekhov cuts from Olga's speech to snippets of conversation between Chebutykin, Tusenbach and Soleny.

OLGA: When I woke up this morning and saw this flood of sunshine, all this spring sunshine – I felt so moved and so happy! I felt such a longing to go back to Moscow!

CHEBUTYKIN: (*to Soleny and Tusenbach*) Not a chance in hell.

TUSENBACH: It's nonsense, I agree.

It is clear that the men's lines are a deliberate device, which comment ironically on Olga's dreams of Moscow. In Stanislavski's staging, however, their words became part of a naturalistic 'background' hum of conversation – mingling with the sounds of Anfisa laying the table in the dining-room, and Andrei playing the violin off-stage.

Miller's staging was slightly more formal and non-naturalistic. Different elements in the stage-picture were held 'in-shot', and juxtaposed, at the same time. Olga's speech is full of warmth and sentiment – but we only had to glance at Irina and Masha, in the 'foreground', to see that they were only half-listening, if at all. Their indifference offset her enthusiasm. When the men spoke, it was as if the background of the picture suddenly came into focus for a time, and then receded. The staging emphasised the fact that Chekhov's juxtaposition of the officers and the sisters is a deliberate formal device, which makes an ironic point.

The slight element of formality in the staging counteracted, to a certain extent, the production's 'naturalistic' surface. Certain moments were 'frozen' in order to isolate them from the surrounding 'flow' of 'fairly undirected discourse'.[41] In *Subsequent Performances* Miller recalls:

> In the process of rehearsing *Three Sisters*, we discovered the recurrent themes of memory. There are references to the passage of time and the impermanence of strong feelings on almost every page. ...

> As in Proust, the metaphor of photography is used to emphasize the experience of time. A group photograph is taken at the end of the first act and at the beginning of the last – two moments enjoyed and perhaps remembered by the participants but whose visual record will be impenetrable and enigmatic to anyone looking at it hereafter.[42]

At the end of Act I, the company, gathered for Irina's name-day, pose for the camera. As Miller observes: 'In those days, it could take some thirty seconds to expose a photograph.' The prolonged pause in Miller's production allowed the audience time to scan the faces of the characters. They all seemed a little wary of the camera, a little self-conscious – except Masha, who stared back without flinching. Natasha, on the other hand, seemed to be on the verge of tears. Once the picture was taken, the group broke into applause – as if they had just 'performed' for the camera, and were looking forward to seeing themselves in the finished print.

Another metaphor of time in the play is provided by the spinning top, which Fedotik presents to Irina. In Miller's production, as the guests at the table turned to watch the top, they again froze. The only sound was the toy's prolonged hum. It was 'as though time had dropped a stitch'.[43]

> They all turn – as, in photographs, you can see people turning to look over their shoulders. As they watch the top spinning away, each person confronts it with their own thoughts – some with no thoughts at all.
>
> The top is an epitome of human life: it represents an organism, set going by a form of energy supplied to it, and active as long as the energy lasts. It falls silent and finally slows to a standstill.

Plate 16 The opening scene from Jonathan Miller's *Three Sisters* (1976).

Plate 17 The guests, gathered to celebrate Irina's name-day, pose for the camera, in Act I of *Three Sisters* (Jonathan Miller, 1976).

Suddenly the company – gathered to celebrate someone's name-day – see their own lives winding down in miniature.

The play begins, Miller notes, with the recollection of a 'moment in time', an image from the past. Olga recalls the death of their father a year before: 'I felt then as if I should never survive his death', she tells Irina, 'and you had fainted and were lying quite still, as if you were dead'; and yet,

> a year later, they can talk about it so easily, and Irina is 'radiant' with happiness. Even grief, it seems, passes with time. At the end of the play, we reach another moment of grief, when it seems the sisters are inconsolable, that they will never recover. And yet, we know that they *will* recover, and that, a year later, one of them will look back on that day and say, 'Do you remember how we all were when Tusenbach died?'

In Miller's production, the action was frozen briefly at the beginning and end of each Act. This established a certain sense of 'distance' – it was as if we were looking at an old photograph, at something distanced from us in time. At the start of the play, the sisters were arranged in a 'triangular' shape. Throughout, Miller created a number of variations on this familial 'triangle,' culminating in a final 'tableau' at the end of Act IV. As the news of the Baron's death sinks in, Irina sat staring ahead of her – frozen into immobility; Masha sat, slumped forward, shoulders hunched, her head on her knees, lifeless; and Olga stood over them both. It was as if this was another moment to be recorded forever in a photograph.

'Things are soon forgotten', Miller suggests, 'our lives pass with someone growing ill, having a stroke or dying.'

> One of Trigorin's lines in *The Seagull* captures Chekhov's preoccupation with time: 'So we are going? More railway carriages, stations, refreshment bars, veal cutlets, conversations.' ...

... Conversations and veal cutlets – that's all there is to life.[44]

Production notes

Miller's productions

The Seagull, Chichester Festival Theatre; first performance, 22 May 1973. Revived: Greenwich Theatre, London, 30 January 1974.

Three Sisters, Triumph Theatre Productions; first performance, Yvonne Arnaud Theatre, Guildford, 20 April 1976.

Miller also directed *The Seagull* at the Nottingham Playhouse in 1969.

11 Mike Alfreds

I first talked to Mike Alfreds about his work on Chekhov in the after-math of his 1982 production of *The Cherry Orchard* with the Oxford Playhouse Company. It was a production that had received some scathing reviews, and yet, as Robert Cushman saw, a 'new idea of the play was plainly *there*'.[1] I next tracked him down when he was directing the play again for the National Theatre in 1985. I later sat in on rehearsals for *Three Sisters* (Shared Experience, 1986); and followed the tour of his latest production, *Cherry Orchard* (Method & Madness, 1998).

Alfreds rejects the notion that Chekhov's work is 'naturalistic'. In contrast to Jonathan Miller, he argues that there is 'nothing *casual* in the plays'. The characters never 'just sit around making chat. Everything Chekhov writes is highly selective and has many reso-nances and implications. Almost every line of text serves more than one purpose.' Take, for example, the moment in Act IV of *The Seagull*, when Arkadina says to her brother, Sorin: 'Petrusha, are you bored? [*Pause*] He's asleep.' This might appear to be (and is often played) as a simple piece of conversational chit-chat, 'to pass the time'. But Alfreds points out that Arkadina has returned home, knowing that her brother is seriously ill – so she is, in fact, checking to make sure he *is* only asleep, and has not died. The line cannot, therefore, simply be treated as a conversational *non-sequitur*. In a 'naturalistic' production, however, 'lines are often thrown away, and moments are simply not examined'.[2]

Alfreds' aim is to create a 'heightened' performance style, which is both physically bold, and psychologically complex; full of energy and emotion – and at the same time full of subtlety and detail. Work with actors in rehearsal has a Stanislavskian basis. 'We plan an inner life for our characters, starting with actions and objectives.' The acting, then, is based on an inner, 'psychological' realism; but it is also *heightened*, highly kinaesthetic and 'physically expressive'. The actors are encouraged to 'produce a vivid and bold *externalisation*' of the character's inner life.

Efros, we will recall, believed that whatever is going on inside a character 'must come out in the flesh'.[3] Alfreds observes:

> My emphasis in rehearsals used to be on the *internal*. I believed that if the actor played the character's objectives strongly, then the body would be transformed by the inner drive. But I now realise that the actor might be thinking and feeling quite deeply, but the audience sees nothing, because the body is not programmed to release the emotion. I might say to an actor, 'You are not reacting. Someone is giving you the most extraordinary piece of news, and you are simply standing there.' And they will say: 'Oh, but I was listening.' And I say: 'Yes, but in some way, your body has to take on your reaction and express it.'

In a 'naturalistic' production, Alfreds argues, the performances are 'turned *in* and *away*' from the audience. In contrast, he is looking for ways in which the emotional undercurrents in the play can be brought to the surface and 'shared' with the audience.

> I am aiming for a form of "super-realism". What I have in mind can be seen in the films of Ingmar Bergman, where the inner lives of the characters are vividly revealed. I hope that a very strong, open, emotional level of playing will have the same effect as a cinematic close-up.[4]

Observing the work of the actors, in Alfreds' productions, one is aware of how they are striving to reach a 'heightened' level of playing. 'It takes a great act of courage', he suggests, 'to break out of what is usually demanded: effective sub-realism.'

The Shared Experience *Seagull*

Alfreds staged *The Seagull* in 1981, with Shared Experience. Anne McFerran called it by far 'the most heightened evening in London Theatre'. The characters seemed to be driven by urgent, even frantic passions. This was expressed through a bold, and comic, physicality. Sandra Voe's Polina, for example, 'manically attacks her lover the Doctor'; and Jonathan Hackett's Trigorin 'pounces on Nina as if to devour her innocence as fodder for his art'.[5]

In physicalising the performances, the actors accentuated the idiosyncratic in each character's behaviour. Details such as Masha's snuff-taking, which in other productions might be thrown away, were enlarged upon. For example, Chekhov indicates that Trigorin always carries a notebook – a sign of his obsession with writing. In Alfreds' production, this obsession was 'heightened': the character became a walking filing-cabinet, his pockets overflowing with papers and manuscripts.

At first the tone of the performances struck Cushman as 'over-emphatic'; but, he concluded, the production finally 'delivers the truth. We are beginning to learn that Chekhov can take tough handling'.[6]

The balance between farce and feeling: *The Cherry Orchard* at the Oxford Playhouse

The Oxford *Cherry Orchard* began with Dunyasha and Lopakhin running on to the stage, giggling like a pair of excited children. This was an unusually energised opening to the play. (The first scene is ordinarily quite subdued and downbeat.) The characters' inner excitement and nervousness were expressed physically: Dunyasha stood nodding her head eagerly, and tugging at her dress like a child.

On the entrance of Ranevskaya, the whole household seemed swept up in a mood of child-like delight. Everyone gathered in a huddle around Pishchik when he threatened to swallow Ranevskaya's pills – and yelped with delight when he did. The degree of physical contact in the company was unusual, including one delightful moment when Ranevskaya led the whole company off-stage in one long, snaking line, hand-in-hand.

The actors had developed a strong physical life for their characters, again selecting and heightening certain characteristics. Trofimov, for example, was a gangling figure in ill-fitting trousers, continually wringing his hands. Michael Billington, however, objected that 'almost every character is played on the same note of hectic frenzy. Thus, Varya ("a serious and religious girl" according to Chekhov) here becomes an eye-popping, hand-clasping, knee-bending hysteric.' Similarly, Ned Chaillet wrote: 'Each performance strains to paint each character in primary colours, accentuating whatever characteristic is most dominant.' The characters, Michael Coveney complained, were turned into a 'bunch of neurasthenics'.[7] Alfreds responds:

> I'd be the first to agree that the actual performance did not fully realize the conception. Quite a few of the company had great diffi-

culty (not unwillingness) in reaching a 'heightened' level of playing. There was less rehearsal time than I felt was necessary. It was never the intention to present one-dimensional caricatures or cartoon characters. But in the process of 'heightening' the performances to take them out of naturalism, there is a stage when it might appear that the work is slightly crude.

In developing a physical life for the character, the actor will probably focus on one aspect: a particular walk or gesture, which will be repeated. Usually, the actor will emerge from the rehearsal period with this work absorbed. The performances grow and become subtle and multi-layered. Perhaps this was a stage we did not reach.

Alfreds wanted to stress the play's farcical qualities; but in performance, he felt the balance was lost 'between farce and feeling, and the result was somewhat frenetic'.

He directed the play again in 1985, at the National Theatre, working with a group of actors led by Ian McKellen and Edward Petherbridge, and including Sheila Hancock and Roy Kinnear. He observed at the time:

One of the reasons I felt the play would be very good with the company is that they are strong, comic and individualistic actors capable of very bold performances. I felt that they would bring these qualities to bear on the work. I would not *need* to stress the farcical element too much.

Russian volatility

Alfreds argues that in performing Chekhov, it is important to try to replace

our Anglo-Saxon mode of emotional expression by a more extrovert, Slavic one. For English people, the main way of handling emotion is to underplay, to understate – to withhold and repress. With Russians emotional release is more available. It is not a matter of one nationality being capable of more or less feeling, but of how an emotion is expressed.

When David Jones was directing productions of Gorky and Chekhov for the Royal Shakespeare Company in the 1970s, he was influenced by watching Mark Donskoi's film versions of Gorky's autobiographical trilogy (*My Childhood*, *My Apprenticeship* and *My Universities*) where he saw

> an ability to move quickly and in extremes from a tragic mood into a comic mood, or to be absolutely vicious to somebody one moment and terribly sweet the next. It's a sort of volatility of temperament which is not English – English actors as a rule want to smooth out their emotional shape. I tried to encourage them to have the nerve to be extreme, exploring emotional limits to the characters.[8]

Alfreds comments:

> We know in our heads that Russians are more emotionally volatile, and go from tears to laughter to anger in a split second. That's not difficult to understand intellectually. It *is* difficult for actors to achieve. Discovering that volatility in performance, however, makes *sense* of certain moments in the text which would otherwise remain obscure. The gear shifts are extraordinary. For instance, when Ranevskaya comes home and sees the nursery, she cries and she laughs and she cries again. Every other line is a huge jump – what *we* would think of as a huge jump – in emotion.

You cannot 'bring English attitudes to these plays', Alfreds insists. He is looking for ways to help actors to inhabit a different psychology – a different way of thinking and feeling. 'You are trying to get inside the psychology of a virtually alien society, with different attitudes and values, and to *change yourself.*'

In his production notes for *The Cherry Orchard* at the National, Alfreds defined Russians as 'volatile, prone to emotional display and physically expressive'.[9] How volatile *are* Russians, exactly? This is a moot point. They *are* more volatile than the English, but then most races are.[10] Indeed, it might be argued that Alfreds is not so much aiming for a physical and emotional mode of expression that is specifically 'Russian', than seeking to break conventional Anglo-Saxon reticence and reserve. 'We English don't use our bodies', he argues, 'we don't gesticulate, we don't touch each other very much, and it affects our whole way of playing. We deal in irony and understatement.'[11]

The notion of 'Russianness' is, in fact, one of the ways in which Alfreds encourages the actors to be 'physically expressive' – so that whatever is going on inside a character will 'come out in the flesh'. The focus in rehearsal is in part on physical work which will begin to shift the actors – to change their patterns of movement, and ways of expressing themselves physically. Sheila Hancock recalls that, rehearsing *The Cherry Orchard* at the National, 'we did many things to try to shed our nationality, including starting each day with vigorous Russian dances'.[12] These dances were seen by Alfreds as a form of 'physical research' which would give the actors a sense of the 'physical temperament', and a shared 'physical language', which would then be carried over into performance.

Alfreds resists the word 'style', because 'it implies an imposition from the outside'. He prefers to speak of the 'world' of the play.

> I want to see a consistent 'world' on the stage. In too many productions, there is very little unity: every actor seems to move, speak, handle the text in a different way. Instead of working with individual actors on separate scenes, I always keep the company together throughout the rehearsal process. This helps to create a sense of an 'ensemble' – a sense of actors living together in the same 'world'.

In Alfreds' Chekhov productions, it is partly the notion of 'Russianness' which creates this sense of actors living together in the same 'world'.

> What I'm trying to do, in fact, is to create a world which actually does not exist. English actors cannot be Russian. On the other hand, they should not remain English. What I hope we achieve is a created 'world' which captures a different way of moving and relating, a different psychology and temperament.

When Alfreds staged *Cherry Orchard* again, with Method & Madness in 1998, the actors performed in Russian accents. As Alfreds observes: 'The way we speak is so organic to the way we move and express ourselves.' It was another way of encouraging the actors to 'change' themselves.

'A light, elegant "clown show"'

Rehearsing at the National, Alfreds wanted the cast to 'heighten' their acting 'so that it became almost surreal. The play is like a kaleidoscope and the colours need to be flashing and bright.'[13]

I visualise *The Cherry Orchard* as a light, elegant 'clown show.' I am using 'clown' in the broadest sense of the word, as someone whose unhappiness pushes him or her into ludicrous behaviour. The cue for this comes from Charlotta's character. She is a 'clown' who dresses up in funny clothes, and performs to make people laugh – and she is desperately unhappy. Epikhodov is a 'clown': he is permanently accident-prone, but he also takes himself very seriously.

There is a freshness, a colourful quality to *The Cherry Orchard*. Although the inner life of the play is intense, the surface is light. It is much more elusive, elliptical than other Chekhov plays. There are more things said apparently out of the blue, and there are very few scenes which the actors can seize and play through in a conventional manner. The play's surface almost 'bubbles' or 'flickers'.

Alfreds wanted this 'freshness' to be reflected in the set. Paul Dart's design was influenced by the paintings of Boris Kustodiev. Alfreds notes: 'Kustodiev's work is intensely colourful and full of light. His skyscapes are extraordinary. We used a similar form of background – a bright blue sky with clouds. It is very fresh and lyrical.' Within the surrounding skyscape, white curtains were used around and above the acting space, to create a 'box' effect – 'to suggest the fragile world in which the characters live. The curtains expand to different shapes for each Act, like an exploding box.'

At the end of the play, the final sound of a breaking string was sharp and metallic, rather than distant and sad. The curtains fell from their hangings and floated like blossom to the ground, covering Firs like a shroud. All of the brilliant colour of the Kustodiev – style skyscape was revealed for the first time. This, then, was not the usual, melancholic ending; rather, there was a 'metaphorical explosion of sunshine and hope'.[14]

The design, then, was 'non-realistic'. Within this, however, the actors were encouraged to use the space, and relate to the furniture, 'realistically'. They created a 'realistic' environment in their imaginations. When the actors first came to work on the set, however, they were taken back. Hancock recalls:

> During the previous seven weeks in the anonymous surroundings of the rehearsal rooms, I had created in my imagination such a vivid idea of my Russian estate and home that a few floating curtains and blue back cloth with sugar-pink clouds were a rude shock. … The whole thing just did not feel right.

It was difficult, then, for the actors to move from internal work, visualising the environment in their imaginations, to acting on this non-realistic or 'conceptual' set. Hancock, however, suggests another reason for the company's initial resistance.

> Despite all our work on lightness not to mention seeing the model of the set at the start of rehearsal and approving it, we were still not genuinely prepared for the revolution away from our English perception of subtle colours and heavy furniture in Russian plays.

The 'pink ice-cream cone clouds' were slightly toned down, but the rest stayed. And, Hancock concluded, Alfreds 'was right to keep it'.[15]

'Chekhov with the gloves off'

Reviewing the production, Michael Billington wrote:

> I have seen *The Cherry Orchard* in Paris, Moscow, Chicago and at least nine times in Britain over the last two decades; but I have never seen such an emotionally full-blooded or deeply affecting version as Mike Alfreds' new production at the Cottesloe. This is Chekhov with the gloves off.[16]

There was, again, an unusual degree of sensuousness and physical contact among the company – hugging, kissing, touching, etc. There was also a sense that all the actors were continually swept up in the action. For instance, in Act I, Sheila Hancock's Ranevskaya showed her excitement at her homecoming by waving her hands in the air; all the other characters on stage, caught up in the moment, copied her and half-waved too.

Each character was 'vividly realised' and given a strong, distinctive physical life. These were slightly larger-than-life, almost clown-like performances. Take, for example, Dunyasha (Selina Cadell), 'with her dry, squeaky laughter and sliding eyes, repairing herself with panic dabs of powder at every excessive excitement and social reverse'[17]; or Epikhodov, whose 'description of himself as "some sort of insect" proved uncannily apposite in the performance of Greg Hicks, who contorted his fingers with insectile angularity to suggest the pain in the character's struggle to express himself'.[18]

Alfreds felt the production had come close to realising his conception of the play as a light, elegant 'clown show'. 'I don't think you could go further', he concluded, 'unless, perhaps, you were working for six months with a group of trained clowns.'

The rehearsal process

Underlying Alfreds' approach to the theatre 'is a fascination with the *process* of acting'.[19] In rehearsal, he makes fewer interventions than most directors. He does not 'direct', in the conventional sense of working for results. Initially, he approaches each play through steps in a process which is aimed at developing a thorough grasp and shared understanding of the text: 'Our rehearsals are concerned with "input", filling ourselves up with the material, which is then released as honestly as possible in performance. We analyse the play in a very active and emotional way; it is not a dry intellectual process.'

The text is used, then, as a 'map to action'. Alfreds begins by breaking the play down into Stanislavskian 'units' – each unit marking a single event. (For example, the first unit in *The Cherry Orchard* might be, 'Lopakhin and Dunyasha confirm the train's arrival'; the second, 'Lopakhin recalls his past relationship with Madame Ranevskaya.') This sets out a detailed 'plot' of the play in clear, simple terms. He then asks the actors simply to define the *actions* (not the 'objectives' at this stage) which the characters perform. At the beginning of *The Cherry Orchard*, for example, these actions might be 'I enter with a candle', 'I enter with a book', 'I express relief that the train has arrived.'

In a radio programme, *Actors' Workshop*, Alfreds explained this method to the student actor, Peter Wingfield. They defined Treplev's actions, in the scene with his mother from Act III of *The Seagull*:

ALFREDS: What are you doing ... ?
WINGFIELD: I'm trying to –
ALFREDS: No, what are you *doing*. Not your objective, what are you doing. Try to find the simplest, least interpretive word you can find.

Alfreds offered several examples: 'I explain to you ... ', 'I point out to you ... ', 'I remind you ... ', etc.[20] The focus, then, at this stage, is on *action*, rather than motivation, or feelings. The approach recalls Stanislavski's 'Method of Physical Actions'. In the first days of rehearsal, Alfreds and the company break down the text in this way, and then attempt to run each Act – using *only* the 'actions,' not the lines of the play. The actors both state the actions, and perform them physically (e.g. 'I enter with a candle'). 'At this point, you have to assume you know nothing about your character or the play. All you know is what the characters *do*. You do not know *why* they do these things, or how you will do them.'

The actors, then, are beginning to physicalise their roles – 'they are virtually acting on Day One'. Finally, the company is ready to run the whole play, using only the 'actions,' and without reference to their scripts. 'We are establishing the spine on which we will build the flesh and muscles and blood of the play. This work gives us a rough, full view of the whole of the play, very early on.'

Alfreds also asks the actors to prepare a 'character study'. They each produce four 'lists' based on a close reading of the text:

i.   concrete facts about the character
ii. what the character says about himself
iii. what other people say about the character
iv. what the character says about other people.

Again, then, this exercise simply asks the actors to analyse, rather than 'interpret', the factual information in the text.

> Approaching the play in this way avoids the double danger of a director imposing an interpretation which ignores the facts and the evidence in the play, or an actor imposing a woolly vision of the character, which has less to do with what the playwright has provided and more to do with what the actor would like to play.

The actors then read the lists before the whole company. ('The lists disclose patterns which may otherwise be hidden', Alfreds suggests. 'For example, in *Three Sisters* it becomes clear how often Olga says, "I'm tired", or "I have a headache".') Only then do they begin to speculate on what the information implies about a character's motivation. Alfreds emphasises that this is a shared process, with each actor free to contribute to the discussion. 'Everyone is exposed to the problems of the play as a whole, and not just that of their own character. I have found this a very quick way of getting accurately to the content of the play, and also ensuring that the whole company is going through the same process.'

I watched rehearsals for the Shared Experience production of *Three Sisters* (1986). In an early session, Philip Voss read out the 'lists' he had prepared for the character of Chebutykin. 'Facts' included:

He is billeted on the family.

He goes to a club and gambles.
He has a drink problem (though he hasn't drunk for two years).

After studying the lists, the company began to speculate about the character's motivation. Again Alfreds urged them to base their observations on what the character actually *does*. Voss saw that Chebutykin 'mocks people's philosophical ideas. To justify his own failure, he has to prove other people's aspirations are ridiculous. He encourages Andrei to gamble. He kills a woman. He smashes the clock. He goes to a duel without caring. He wants to destroy everything.'

'Is there anything positive?' Alfreds asked.

'His relationship with Irina.'

Voss and Alfreds then discussed the character's 'main lines of action' through the play – again, looking at what the character actually *does*. They outlined three points:

to minimise others, to belittle them.
to cling to his relationship with Irina.
to convince himself that his existence is a mirage.

Alfreds next discussed the role of Irina with Chloe Salaman. They examined the character's 'given circumstances'; for example:

> Irina is 20. She was nine when she left Moscow. The death of her father, a year ago, was a significant turning point. The sisters had to reconstruct their lives. She has not worn white for a year (during mourning); now she is in white. (etc.)

The company also discussed how they saw the character, in physical terms, and tried to define this, using Rudolf Laban's 'efforts'.[21] Irina, it was suggested, tends to 'float; her movements are light, and indirect'. 'The character changes during the play', Alfreds suggested. 'At the beginning, she's excited, radiant, optimistic. As the play goes on, she becomes disillusioned, tired, fretful, dried-up. So there is a wide emotional and physical range.'

After each character has been discussed, Alfreds encourages the entire company to begin to explore the character's physical life. Here, for example, he suggested they should choose a particular aspect of Irina to focus on: when she is elated, or when she is depressed; at the beginning of the play, or the end.

The actors separated again to different parts of the room, and began to experiment, trying to find physical expression for the character's feeling states. One of them sat gazing through a window, running her fingers around the edges of the frame. Some tried a light, 'floating' movement; others sank into tiredness. This encouraged the actors to reflect on the emotional range in the role. It also ensured that the 'character analysis' did not remain abstract or intellectual, but was translated into physical form. After about fifteen minutes, the company came together again, to discuss what discoveries they had made.

'She's very intense. Life has got to be exciting all the time.'

'I have a sense of a scream inside.'

'The pull between the child and the woman is very strong, I think.'

'I have an image of her waiting at a train station. She looks at her watch a lot, and then thinks, "Oh, that train's not coming – I might as well marry the Baron and catch the next one".'

'Chloe Salaman may use or discard these suggestions as she sees fit', Alfreds told me later. She did in fact assimilate much of this work in performance – in the contrast, for example, between the character's exuberance, her lightness of movement, in Act I, and her lassitude in Act II. There was a moment in Act I when Irina, telling Chebutykin of her happiness, spread her arms out wide and swirled round. The boldness of the gesture seemed to emerge from the work the company had undertaken on physicalising the character's 'intense inner states'.[22]

To Alfreds, the key to the actor's performance lies in understanding the character's 'superobjective':

> As an actor, you can never really be at a loss on the stage if you knows what your *intention* is. For example, Ranevskaya's motivation in life, her superobjective, is to be loved, to be adored, to go where she will get the most love. So the actor has to relate to people in such a way – intellectually and emotionally – that she will achieve the response she needs.

The 'superobjective' is usually very broad – 'to be loved', 'to succeed in life', etc. As Alfreds observes, 'this is not actable, because it is too generalised. Only smaller, specific scene objectives can be acted'. But the superobjective 'gives the actor something to hold on to, or a track to travel down' – a 'through line'. Ranevskaya's desire 'to be loved, to be adored' represents a continuing need in her, which is then worked out, concretely, in particular situations (for example, in Act III, when she tries to elicit sympathy from Trofimov: 'You're a good man, kind man. Have pity on me … ').

Playing the moment

No two performances, Alfreds believes, should ever be quite the same. The actors should continue to explore the text in performance.

> You must give the actors room to breathe. You cannot say of a great play, by which I mean something complex, multi-layered and ambiguous, 'I want you to do the line this way' or 'This is what this scene is about'. Every night should be freshly created and the actors should be free to go wherever they want, physically and emotionally. It means they have to be tremendously open to each other.

This has its base in Stanislavski: the need for truthful 'adaptation' (although it does not seem likely that Stanislavski ever allowed his actors the freedom to change moves). 'Acting is, in essence, very simple,' Alfreds suggests. 'You go on stage with an objective. You *want* something. You have different tactics or strategies to pursue, to try to get what you want. And you see what happens.' The actors must know the characters' *objectives* in a scene – but this does not tell them *how* to play it; 'it gives them a guide-line as to what to pursue during it'.[23] 'How' can vary, to a greater or lesser degree, from performance to performance: 'you know what you want, but how you try to get it is really an improvisation'. In other words, the actor plays the *inner score* of the role, rather than a fixed 'external' score. Take, for example, the scene between Treplev and Arkadina in Act III of *The Seagull*. At one performance, the actor playing Treplev might be more 'babyish' and 'clinging'. If the actor playing Arkadina responds briskly, Treplev must adapt, and find ways to win her round.

The method makes great demands on the actors, both technically, and emotionally.

> What I am asking is that the actors should play truthfully the moment as it occurs. If you are exploring a new aspect of your character, then your performance will be subtly altered. If you receive a certain impulse, a certain energy from your partner in a scene, you must respond to that, at that moment.

> Instead of being able to rely on a previously structured vocal and physical pattern, they are asked to play the moment as truthfully as they can. They should not strain for something that is artificial, or falsely effective. Unfortunately we have become accustomed to

seeing cleverly simulated emotion on the stage. Rarely is there any sense of risks being taken, of emotional danger to the performances. Emotional truth is very rare, and it is difficult to achieve. If there are half a dozen truthful emotional moments in a performance, then that is extraordinary. However, we need to distinguish between honest intentions in performance and effective results. If we accept a theatre which thrives upon simulated emotion, then we are compounding a dishonest theatre.

In rehearsal, the aim is to 'create an inner structure and discipline' to the work, so that performance can become a kind of 'controlled improvisation'. Hancock recalls the intensive preparation needed for *The Cherry Orchard*:

> We had to know everything possible about the person we were playing as well as the others in the piece, allowing at the same time for the unpredictability of human nature, to be so inside our characters that if someone else on stage did something different we would respond on the spur of the moment exactly as our character would. We had, in short, to *be* the person.[24]

Half of your task as an actor, Alfreds believes, is building your own character; the other half is supporting the performances of those around you. In order to strengthen and clarify the relationships between the characters, he undertakes a series of run-throughs of the entire play, in which all the actors focus upon one particular character each time – 'relating to them directly, and/or always thinking intensely about them'. Often the text does not provide much dialogue between some of the characters in a scene, 'but since they appear on the stage together, the actors must explore their attitudes to one another. This particular exercise gives the actor the opportunity to do so.'

Alfreds also runs each Act over and over again, giving the actors each time a different 'point of concentration'. For Act I of *The Cherry Orchard*, for example, these included: 'the time, 2 am'; 'it is five years since Ranevskaya went away'; 'Grisha's death'; 'the cherry orchard'; 'the nursery', etc.[25] This exercise ensures a collective awareness of the 'given circumstances' of the play. (It is not enough, Alfreds realises, simply to *list* the 'given circumstances', as a series of indigestible facts; they have to be absorbed into an actor's experience.)

Hopefully, through this intensive rehearsal process, the actors will have absorbed the material until it becomes subconscious knowledge for them: a body of thoughts, images and feelings that will underpin the performances. It is a method of working that demands great trust between the actors and the director. The actors may not always feel confident that they can bring it off: it does place a great responsibility on them, for the play and the performances.

While he was working with the National company, Alfreds was at times concerned that the actors might not really be taking in what he was asking them to do – not really believing that he ultimately wanted such 'freedom' in performance.

Probably the greatest problem is that most actors are used to being told by directors what to do, especially in external terms. They are not used to allowing themselves the right – they think it is a privilege if it is offered to them, but it is their right – to try things, to explore, to take risks.

Michael Ratcliffe saw that Alfreds' method creates 'an electrifying keenness and sensitivity' between the actors. Here is his description of McKellen's performance as Lopakhin on two consecutive nights:

The grieving triumph of the peasant Lopakhin at the purchase of Ranevskaya's estate was the more moving when ... the victorious and the defeated fell weeping into one anothers' arms, but it made equal theatrical sense within Chekhov's character and McKellen's characterization for the boorish Lopakhin to whirl the keys to the house around his head like a cowboy, kick over the daybed, and scatter the vase of scarlet flowers, together with Ranevskaya ... to the very edge of the white room.[26]

Hancock recalls that playing scenes with McKellen

was like a marvellous duel. In the scene where he announces that he has bought the cherry orchard I never knew what he would do and every night it was a fresh earthquake. Sometimes he would crush me into a bear-hug and kiss away my tears, sometimes he would hurl hatred at me. Underlying all our actions were gauntlets thrown down to see if the other could pick them up.[27]

Plate 18 Ian McKellen as Lopakhin in *The Cherry Orchard* (National Theatre, 1985).

During the course of the play's run, however, some of the moves tended to become 'fixed,' as they would be in a conventional production. Actors were also sometimes guilty of taking moments which had 'worked' with audiences on previous occasions, and repeating them. It was the opposite of Alfreds' intentions – it was playing for 'results', rather than 'playing the moment':

> Actions and gestures can become automatic very quickly on the stage. There is nothing wrong with an actor making the same choice, as long as it has a real impulse behind it. However, if there is no inner justification, only the repetition of an effect, then I have to intervene to break those patterns.

After one performance, Alfreds wrote an angry note to the cast: 'You have made your contributions to Deadly Theatre. Would you please return to Lively Theatre. Please all think and prepare before all performances. You can't just go on … '[28]

Three Sisters: a sense of emotional danger

Alfreds adapts his working methods, and introduces new exercises, according to the demands of a particular play, or the needs of the company. For example, his approach to *Three Sisters* for Shared Experience in 1986 was quite different from his interpretation of *The Cherry Orchard*.

'Chekhov's plays tend to be discussed as if they were all written in a similar style,' he argues. 'In fact, each play is quite different, and demands a careful appraisal and an individual approach. Chekhov calls *Three Sisters* a drama. It has many comic moments and it is full of bitter ironies – but it is much darker, bleaker and more painful than *The Cherry Orchard*.'

Paul Dart's set was dark and brooding and created a sense of 'doomed predestination'.[29] Four columns, off-white and stained with a black grain, suggested both the colonnade in Act I, and the birch trees outside in Act IV. The backcloth was scored with broad black brush stokes; it was 'darkly violent', [30] even expressionistic.

Jonathan Miller, as we have seen, stressed the *ordinariness* of the sisters' situation. In contrast, Alfreds argues:

> Although the action of the play covers three and a half years, the characters are almost always in crisis. Today, if you had to deal with that degree of pain, you would be rushed off to an analyst. One of the problems of staging *Three Sisters* is that it is very demanding emotionally. What I tried to do in rehearsal was to exercise the actors so that they could sustain that degree of intensity through the length of the performance.
>
> The play was at times disturbing to work on. The actors took great risks in rehearsal in coming to terms with the painfulness of the characters' experiences. There needs to be, in performance too, an emotional danger, and a sense of a desolate emotional landscape.

In the National *Cherry Orchard*, Alfreds encouraged a 'lightness and delicacy' in the playing. Here, however, he was aiming for a different physical quality:

> As the play moves deeper into crisis, it takes on a tragic dimension. The performances need to be concentrated and intense. Some of the long speeches are almost like Shakespearian monologues: they are not realistic at all. In rehearsal, I asked the actors to

choose a speech and try to heighten it – to attain a classic, almost 'heroic' level. Some of this work has been absorbed into the performances. I felt the actors needed to find a stillness at these moments. The casual movement that goes with a realistic performance had to be selected and distilled.

We can see an example of this, in the performance of Jonathan Hackett as Andrei. Flustered and fidgety in company, the character became thoughtful and still in his Act IV monologue, as he sat, his eyes fixed on the child in the pram he pushes. As a fleeting image of a more hopeful future gripped him, he looked up, a bright, almost imbecilic smile on his face. 'My sisters!' he cried, and threw his arms out wide as if to embrace them. But then, Natasha interrupted: 'Who's that talking so loudly out here?' The vision faded, and he sank back into silence.

Alfreds' production avoided the 'gentility' of most English productions. Billington praised the emotional danger in some of the performances. Philip Voss, for example, played Chebutykin not as some 'mellow old party stroking his beard', but as a 'man of incredible manic anger who looks as if he might break the bowl in which he is washing his face at one point'.[31]

Nevertheless, *Three Sisters* received mixed reviews. Alfreds felt that, on the first night, the actors' nervousness slightly affected the performance. It meant they could not be quite so responsive and 'open' to each other. (Significantly, perhaps, critics who saw later performances were generally more enthusiastic.) But there was also some resistance to the 'line' Alfreds had taken on the play. Thus, Billington complained that the production 'loses some of Chekhov's spontaneous humour. Clearly this is the result of a deliberate decision since this is the most unrelievedly tragic *Three Sisters* I have seen for some time.'[32] Alfreds responds: 'People seem very proprietary in their view of how Chekhov should be staged. Critics speak about a "Chekhovian balance". I fear that what they mean is that a performance of Chekhov should be moving, but not too emotional; funny, but not too comic; sad, but not too tragic.'

Chekhov, of course, insisted to Stanislavski that the play was a comedy – but he also told Vera Komissarzhevskaya that 'its mood is darker than dark'.[33] There were numerous touches of humour and irony in Alfreds' production (Nigel Andrews, for example, noted the way that, during Vershinin's philosophical speeches, 'everyone starts metaphorically looking at their watches'[34]); but it was also, as Helen

Plate 19 Philip Voss as Chebutykin in *Three Sisters* (Shared Experience, 1986).

Rose saw, 'suffused with doom from the outset'[35] – its mood, indeed, 'darker than dark'.

The Seagull and the metaphor of 'theatre'

In 1991, Alfreds returned to *The Seagull*, this time with the Oxford Stage Company. All of the characters in the play, Alfreds argues, 'are in some ways playing roles, "performing" their lives'. It is as if they see themselves as characters in a play or novel. Masha, for example, '*is* unhappy, but she also "performs" her unhappiness. The feelings are real, but the way she deals with them is ludicrous and comic. She indulges them, and makes a drama out of them. And a number of the characters do this: they "perform" the pain of their lives, in a way that makes it bearable and manageable.'

Paul Dart's set included a false 'proscenium arch' at the front. The classical white pillars suggested an elegant nineteenth-century theatre. A rich red half-curtain descended at the end of each Act, again echoing the theatres of an age when *grande dames* like Arkadina trod the boards. But this was only a façade: on one side of the stage, the façade was stripped away, to reveal the wooden frame beneath the classical pillars. There were no 'walls' to the set: actors were visible in the wings before they entered. The set, then, was intended to underscore the play's central metaphor of the 'theatre'. It ensured that the audience was always aware that the characters were 'performing'.

The production highlighted moments when the characters are self-dramatising. When Masha told Trigorin (in Act III) what he should write as a dedication in the books he sends her, for example, she pressed her hand dramatically to her breast. It was a kind of grand, self-dramatising statement by Masha on her life – inspired, perhaps, by a little too much vodka.

There is a moment in Act II, when Polina grabs a bunch of flowers which Nina has given to Dorn, and jealously tears them up. In the Oxford production, Polina flew into a rage, and the characters continued to wrestle maniacally over possession of the flowers, as they exited. Polina was 'theatricalising', '*performing*' her feelings, for Dorn's benefit. Thus, the action was *internally motivated*. And yet, we could also see how ludicrous and self-dramatising she was being. We were given a certain ironic perspective from which to view the character's behaviour.

'The psychological and the physical'

Again, some critics felt the acting was at times over-emphatic. Benedict Nightingale complained that the actors 'bring out emotions like semaphore flags and flourish them'. Little, if anything, he said, 'is happening in places that matter a great deal to Chekhov: that is, beneath the words and behind the eyes'.[36] Clearly, however, he was looking for a quite different, and more 'naturalistic' style of performance – 'turned *in* and *away* from the audience'; where the feelings of the characters are delicately hinted at, rather than 'brought out in the flesh'.

'Truth and realism still seem to be confusedly thought of as synonymous', Alfreds comments. 'The fact that the acting style is "bold" does not mean that there is nothing happening beneath the surface, and no inner "truth".'

Alfreds' most recent Chekhov is *Cherry Orchard* for Method & Madness, which opened at the Northcott Theatre, Exeter, in January 1998.[37]

The set, designed by Peter McKintosh, seemed to contain echoes of Meyerhold. There was a circular playing area, like a circus-ring, surrounded by a number of ladders at the back, rising out of sight into the flies. The ladders suggested the circus, as well as an orchard of trees, telegraph poles, railways lines and so on. At the beginning of the performance, all members of the company entered quickly, and arranged the set for Act I. The music was bright, even circus-like. The actors acknowledged the audience with a smile. Immediately, then, it was established that these are 'performers' – almost like circus artistes – who were going to 'perform' for us.

Rehearsals had included some clown work; and when the production first opened, the performance style was highly physical. The actors did cartwheels and pratfalls. Epikhodov performed a circus roll, as he stumbled when he entered. When Trofimov saw Anya at the end of Act I, he did a cartwheel to express his joy. At the end of Act II, when Trofimov is alone with Anya, they climbed the ladders together – the energy of the action expressing a heightened state of excitement. Similarly, when Varya tried to chase Epikhodov from the ball in Act III, he climbed one of the ladders, and she followed him. He moved across to another ladder, and then descended by sliding (clown-like) down the sides. The actors, then, had been encouraged to use the set, almost like a Meyerholdian 'machine for acting'. They were finding ways of expressing the characters' 'inner states' through bold, physical actions.

At this stage, however, Alfreds felt that the performances needed to become more emotional. A break in the tour allowed the company time to work again on actions, objectives and points of concentration. When I saw the production again, some six months after the opening, the *physical* dimension was far less apparent. There were no cartwheels or pratfalls. The acting was more internalised. Alfreds commented:

> The change is a step in the show's development. I have no intention of giving up on the physical work – far from it. But that is the stage we have reached at the moment. What happens is that if the performance becomes athletic and playful, it loses its inner life; if it is fuller internally, it loses its physical vitality.

After a year on tour, some of the 'physical vitality' had returned. The excitement of the homecoming in Act I, for example, was expressed in sudden and unexpected ways – such as the moment when Ranevskaya, seeing Dunyasha again for the first time, lifted her off the ground and spun her round (much to Dunyasha's evident surprise and satisfaction). Alfreds felt that the performances had become 'more organic': 'The journey in all acting is to unite the internal and external,

Plate 20 Scene from Act II of *Cherry Orchard* (Method & Madness, 1998).

the psychological and the physical. Gradually, the actors are bringing the two sides together.'

'I am sure I will continue to return to Chekhov', Alfreds concludes. 'The plays are rich in insight, complex in form, and make great demands on performers and audiences alike. I am always making new discoveries. As you uncover one layer to the text, you find another layer beneath.

'There are limitless depths to be explored.'

Production notes

Alfreds' productions in the UK

The Seagull, Shared Experience; first performance, Crucible Theatre, Sheffield, 12 September 1981.
The Cherry Orchard, Oxford Playhouse Company; first performance, Roundhouse Theatre, London, 9 August 1982.

The Cherry Orchard, National Theatre, London; first performance, Cottesloe Theatre, 10 December 1985.

Three Sisters, Shared Experience; first performance, Theatre Royal, Winchester, 20 February 1986.

The Seagull, Oxford Stage Company; first performance, Warwick Arts Centre, 23 January 1991.

Cherry Orchard, Method and Madness; first performance, Northcott Theatre, Exeter, 22 January 1998.

Conclusion

Running through this book, like a 'red thread', has been the question of the 'internal' and 'external' in acting.

Chekhov in the West has become associated with a certain style of performance: a gentle form of 'naturalism,' where the subtext, the inner thoughts and feelings of the characters, are intimated through tiny, glancing details of behaviour, 'by oeillades and tentative gestures'.[1] This style of performance has even been dubbed 'Chekhovian'.

As we have seen, there have been a number of attempts, in recent years, to break the grip of 'naturalism', and develop a more 'expressive' performance style in Chekhov. These attempts tend, however, to be resisted by critics, who argue that a more 'physical' or expressive' style can seem crude and lack Chekhov's 'subtlety'. But behind these comments lies a belief that 'subtle' must necessarily mean 'small' and 'naturalistic'.

Mike Alfreds recognises the danger that acting which is very *external* risks having no 'inner life'; but on the other hand, work which emphasises the *internal* risks being weak in terms of physical expressiveness. The question remains: how should the 'inner life' of Chekhov's characters be expressed in external form? Should the 'inner drama' remain buried, and suggested obliquely, through tiny, 'naturalistic' details? Or should it be brought out 'in the flesh'?

Chekhov was opposed to purely 'external' forms of acting. When he saw Sarah Bernhardt perform in Moscow, he attacked her acting as a series of 'tricks': 'every sigh, her tears, her death throes, all of her acting – is nothing other than an impeccably and cleverly prepared lesson. A lesson, reader, and nothing more!' There was 'no spark in her, which alone can move us to passionate tears and make us swoon'. In other words, there was no 'inner life'. Moreover, in her acting, 'she seeks, not the natural, but the unusual. Her goal is to startle and surprise and dazzle you.'[2]

When Chekhov saw rehearsals of *The Seagull* at the Aleksandrinski Theatre, he objected that the actors 'act a lot, there should be less acting'. He urged them: 'the main thing ... is not to be theatrical. Everything should be simple, quite simple. They are all simple, ordinary people.'[3] He was concerned to counter the actors' tendency to work through purely 'external' means, with no inner life. Stage tradition encouraged them to be 'theatrical', to seek the unusual, to startle and dazzle the audience.

Chekhov insisted that subtle feelings 'must be subtly expressed in an external form'. But did this mean he advocated a form of 'naturalism' in performance? Certainly, he directed actors to observe the way people actually behave (witness, for example, the advice he offered to Kachalov on playing Trigorin). It seems that he wanted characters to be created, in part, through precise attention to the details of physical behaviour. The actions of Chekhov's characters, however, are never simply 'naturalistic'. An apparently simple action can express a deep inner psychological significance. When Treplev tears up his manuscripts in *The Seagull*, for example, this is a 'psychophysical' action, which expresses the inner feelings of the character in a subtle external form. In fact, every detail in Chekhov is at once as 'simple and as complex as in life'. The challenge for actors is to work through these ostensibly 'simple' actions, and communicate the inner complexity and depth.

Maurice Baring reported that the actors in an early London production of *The Seagull* could not execute the actions of their characters with any sense of the inner meaning. He cited the moment in Act III, when Treplev tears a bandage off his head, in the course of an argument with his mother.

> The company had, I suppose, read the stage direction, which says: 'Man removes bandage', but the words of the scene were spoken without any emotion or emphasis. At one moment, the man quietly removed his bandage and dropped it on the floor, as though it were in the way, or as if he were throwing down a cigarette which he had done with.

The act of discarding the bandage was performed, in other words, as if it was simply a 'naturalistic' detail, without any sense of its 'inner' significance. The 'external' physical action did not express the inner psychological action.

Baring, however, had seen the Moscow Art Theatre, where 'every effect was made to tell'.[4]

Stanislavski has been castigated for embalming Chekhov's plays in a heavy form of naturalism; but as we have seen, he saw his productions, not as exercises in realism or naturalism, but as attempts to reveal the 'inner life' of Chekhov's characters. The devices he developed, such as sound effects, were intended, not to create an external naturalism, but to reveal 'the human soul'.[5]

Chekhov's characters, Stanislavski observed, 'often feel and think things which they do not express in words'.[6] In his work with actors, he was concerned to find ways that the 'inner action', the 'subtext' could be revealed and expressed. He was attempting to move away from conventional forms of 'visualised' or external acting, which *demonstrated* the characters' feelings – and looking for more subtle ways of *expressing* inner feelings in external form. In *The Seagull* production plan, he created a 'score' of physical actions. In the scene when Treplev burns his manuscripts, for example, a series of simple actions was used to express the complex inner psychology of the character, as he prepares for suicide.

At times, as we have seen, Stanislavski's methods in *The Seagull* could seem a little crude, when he reverted to 'demonstrating' the characters' feelings externally or 'visually'. Moreover, there was a certain lack of selectivity in details – at times, it seemed that Stanislavski was simply filling the stage with 'naturalistic' business. Nevertheless, it is clear that the focus on physical actions helped the actors to achieve an unusual depth of involvement in their roles, helping them to 'live' on stage.

In later years, Stanislavski developed the 'Method of Physical Actions'. He realised that working through a logical 'score' of concrete physical actions would help to guide the actor's performance. The aim was never, however, to create the naturalistic surface of behaviour. Stanislavski insisted: 'we need the truth of physical actions and our belief in them not for the sake of realism or naturalism, but in order to stimulate in us the inner experience of the role' and 'to convey on the stage the living, human, spiritual essence of the characters'.[7]

Stanislavski recognised that complex feelings could be expressed in simple actions. When Lady Macbeth tries to wash the blood from her hands, the action is both simple, and complex. Working through the Method of Physical Actions was a way of helping actor to go 'from the simple to the complicated, from simple physical actions to complex psychological experiences'.[8] Stanislavski made this 'Method' the centre of his 'system' in the 1930s; but it is clear he was working through physical actions from a much earlier date. In 1916, he called for acting to be based on a 'score of vital, dynamic physical and psychological tasks'.[9] We have seen how, in rehearsing *The Seagull* in 1917, with Tarasova and Mikhail Chekhov, he tried to create this 'score' for each scene. Every action, such as the moment when Treplev kisses his mother, was both *psychological* and *physical*. It was not an 'incidental' detail; it was explored for its inner significance. It was both a simple action, and yet complex. The aim was to create a unity of the 'internal' and 'external', the psychological and the physical – which Stanislavski termed 'organic action' on the stage.[10]

'Let everything on stage be just as complicated and just as simple as in life', Chekhov declared. It is necessary, he argued, 'that life should be shown exactly as it is, and people exactly as they are'. He added, however, that it 'is not a question of naturalism or realism. It is not necessary to keep within such limits'.[11] Showing life 'as it is', then, and people 'as they are', does not necessarily mean working in a naturalistic form.

One of the keys to performing Chekhov lies in the 'physical actions' of the characters. The danger in any naturalistic production is, as Alfreds has argued, that moments 'are simply not examined'; the significance is missed. We are left, then, only with the surface 'simplicity' of life, without the complexity within.

There are, ultimately, no final answers to the way Chekhov should be performed. But we cannot accept any narrow and restricting definitions of what *is* 'Chekhovian' and what *isn't*. Throughout his life, Stanislavski continued to explore the demands of performing Chekhov. He was irritated and perplexed when people seemed to dismiss the writer's work – as if it was already thoroughly understood, and there was nothing new to discover. Theatre practitioners, he insisted, must continue to study and learn from the techniques of Chekhov's drama; it demands new means of expression, and 'a new psychology of acting':

> That is why the chapter about Chekhov is still not finished. It has not been read as it should, its essence has not been grasped. The book has been closed too soon.
>
> It should be opened again, studied and read through to the end.[12]

Notes

Abbreviations used

Chekhov, *PSS*: A.P. Chekhov, *Polnoe sobranie sochineni i pisem v tridtsati tomakh* (complete works in thirty volumes), Moscow, Nauka, 1974–84.
Stanislavski, *SS*: K.S. Stanislavski, *Sobranie sochineni v devyati tomakh* (collected works in nine volumes), vols 1–7, Moscow, Iskusstvo, 1988–95.

Introduction

1 Reported by I.L. Leont'ev (Shcheglov), 'Iz vospominani ob Antone Chekhove' in E.D. Surkov (ed.), *Chekhov i teatr*, Moscow, Iskusstvo, 1961, pp. 219–20.
2 *Peterburgski listok*, 18 October 1896, no. 288; quoted in Chekhov, *PSS*, vol. 13, p. 372.
3 A. Suvorin, *Dnevnik A.S. Suvorina*, Mikh. Krichevski (ed.), Moscow and Petrograd, L.D. Frenkel', 1923, p. 125.
4 *Peterburgski listok*, 18 October 1896, no. 288; quoted by A. Anikst in *Teoriya dramy v Rossii ot Pushkina do Chekhova*, Moscow, Nauka, 1972, p. 571.
5 Suvorin, *Dnevnik*, p. 125.
6 Quoted by A. Skaftymov, 'Principles of Structure in Chekhov's plays' in Robert Louis Jackson (ed.), *Chekhov: A Collection of Critical Essays*, Englewood Cliffs, NJ, Prentice-Hall, 1967, p. 69.
7 A. Smirnov, 'Teatr dush' in *Samarskaya gazeta*, 9 December 1897, no. 263; in Chekhov, *PSS*, vol. 13, p. 378.
8 S. Vasil'ev, 'Teatral'naya khronika' in *Moskovskie vedemosti*, 1 January 1890, no. 1; in Chekhov, *PSS*, vol. 12, p. 391. I.I. Ivanov, *Artist*, February 1890, part 6, pp. 124–5; in *PSS*, vol. 12, p. 392.
9 Maurice Maeterlinck, 'The modern drama' in Bernard F. Dukore (ed.), *Dramatic Theory and Criticism*, New York, Holt, Rinehart & Winston, 1974, p. 734.
10 N.V. Gogol', 'Peterburgskie zapiski 1836 goda' in *Sobranie sochineni*, S.I. Mashinski and M.B. Khrapchenko (eds), vol. 6, Moscow, Khudozhestvennaya literatura, 1978, p. 176.
11 Chekhov, 'Modny effekt' in *Chekhov i teatr*, p. 192.

12   D. Gorodetski, 'Iz vospominani ob A.P. Chekhove' in *Chekhov i teatr*, pp. 208–9.
13   A. Gurlyand, 'Iz vospominani ob A.P. Chekhove' in *Chekhov i teatr*, p. 206.
14   T.L. Shchepkina-Kupernik, 'O Chekhove' in *Chekhov i teatr*, p. 243.
15   A. Smirnov, 'Teatr dush' in *Samaskaya gazeta*, 9 December 1897, no. 263; in Chekhov, *PSS*, vol. 13, p. 378.
16   N. Efros, '*Chaika*' in *Novosti Dnya*, 31 December 1898.
17   Smirnov, 'Teatr dush' in Chekhov, *PSS*, vol. 13, p. 378.
18   N.S. Butova, 'Iz vospominani' in *Chekhov i teatr*, p. 346. It appears Butova's memory is slightly at fault here. Sonya actually says 'Papa, you must be merciful' *before* a single pistol shot is fired. It is not, then, a 'continuation' of the shooting.
19   Leonid Andreev, 'Second letter on the theater' in Laurence Senelick (ed.), *Russian Dramatic Theory from Pushkin to the Symbolists*, Austin, University of Texas Press, 1981, pp. 258–9.
20   Chekhov, letter to Ol'ga Knipper, 2 January 1900; in *Chekhov i teatr*, p. 110.
21   Chekhov, letter to Ol'ga Knipper, 2 January 1901; in *Chekhov i teatr*, p. 118.
22   P.P. Gnedich, quoted by Laurence Senelick in *The Chekhov Theatre*, Cambridge, CUP, 1997, p. 31.
23   Chekhov, reported by Evtikhi Karpov, 'Istoriya pervogo predstavleniya *Chaiki*' in *Chekhov i teatr*, p. 238.
24   V.I. Nemirovich-Danchenko, *Rozhdenie teatra*, Moscow, Pravda, 1989, p. 79.
25   M.M. Chitau, 'Prem'era *Chaiki*' in N.I. Gitovich (ed.), *A.P. Chekhov v vospominaniyakh sovremenikov*, Moscow, Khudozhestvennaya literatura, 1986, p. 354.
26   Chekhov, letter to Suvorin, 22 October 1896; in *Chekhov i teatr*, p. 88.
27   Nemirovich-Danchenko, *Rozhdenie*, p. 52.

Part I: Chekhov and Stanislavski

1 'The theatre of mood': the Moscow Art Theatre

1   Stanislavski, *SS*, vol. 1, p. 254.
2   Stanislavski, *SS*, vol. 1, p. 193.
3   Stanislavski, *SS*, vol. 5, book 1, p. 141.
4   Ol'ga Knipper, 'O A.P. Chekhove', in N.I. Gitovich (ed.), *A.P. Chekhov v vospominaniyakh sovremennikov*, Moscow, Khudozhestvennaya literatura, 1986, p. 615.
5   See Chekhov, letter to Suvorin, 18 October 1896; in I. Vinogradskaya (ed.), *Zhizn' i tvorchestvo K.S. Stanislavskogo*, vol. 1, Moscow, VTO, 1971, p. 195.
6   V.I. Nemirovich-Danchenko, letter to Chekhov, quoted in *Rozhdenie teatra*, Moscow, Pravda, 1989, p. 130.
7   Nemirovich-Danchenko, *Rozhdenie*, p. 136.
8   Nemirovich-Danchenko, *Rozhdenie*, p. 131.

9 Stanislavski, letter to Nemirovich, 10 September 1898; in Stanislavski, *SS*, vol. 7, pp. 275–6.
10 Nemirovich-Danchenko, *Rozhdenie*, p. 145.
11 Nemirovich-Danchenko, *Rozhdenie*, p. 162.
12 Ol'ga Knipper, 'O A.P. Chekhove', p. 619. Knipper said that this occurred after the first two acts, but other memoirs suggest it occurred after Act I.
13 Meyerhold, 'Naturalisticheski teatr i teatr nastroeniya' in *V.E. Meierkhol'd: stat'i, pis'ma, rechi, besedy*, Moscow, Iskusstvo, 1968, vol. 1 (1891–1917), p. 122.
14 *Russkaya Mysl'*, quoted by S.D. Balukhaty in *'Chaika' v postanovke Moskovskogo khudozhestvennogo teatra*, Leningrad and Moscow, Iskusstvo, 1938, p. 66.
15 Balukhaty, *'Chaika'*, p. 121.
16 David Magarshack, *Stanislavsky: A Life*, London, MacGibbon & Kee, 1950, pp. 172–3.
17 Stanislavski, *SS*, vol. 1, p. 291.
18 Balukhaty, *'Chaika'*, p. 167.
19 Nemirovich-Danchenko, *Rozhdenie*, p. 162.
20 Stanislavski, *My Life in Art*, translated by J.J. Robbins, Harmondsworth, Penguin Books, 1967, p. 331. This passage, which appeared in the first American edition of *My Life in Art*, was cut by Stanislavski for the Russian edition.
21 Stanislavski, *SS*, vol. 1, p. 292.
22 Stanislavski, *SS*, vol. 1, p. 345.
23 Meyerhold, 'Naturalisticheski', p. 120.
24 Stanislavski, *Rezhisserskie ekzemplyary K.S. Stanislavskogo*, vol. 3, Moscow, Iskusstvo, 1983, p. 195.
25 Stanislavski, *Rezhisserskie*, vol. 3, p. 203.
26 Chekhov, letters to Ol'ga Knipper dated 20 and 17 January 1901; in E.D. Surkov (ed.), *Chekhov i teatr*, Moscow, Iskusstvo, 1961, p. 120.
27 Nemirovich-Danchenko, *Rozhdenie*, p. 146.
28 Balukhaty, *'Chaika'*, p. 253.
29 Balukhaty, *'Chaika'*, p. 97.
30 Balukhaty, *'Chaika'*, p. 259.
31 Balukhaty, *'Chaika'*, p. 261.
32 Nemirovich-Danchenko, *Rozhdenie*, p. 146.
33 Balukhaty, *'Chaika'*, p. 56.
34 Balukhaty, *'Chaika'*, p. 273.
35 A.R. Kugel', *Peterburgskaya gazeta*, 19 October 1896, no. 289; in Chekhov, *PSS*, vol. 13, p. 376.
36 Sergei Glagol' (pseudonym of S. Sergeev), quoted by Laurence Senelick in *The Chekhov Theatre*, Cambridge, CUP, 1997, p. 47.
37 David Richard Jones, *Great Directors at Work*, Berkeley, University of California Press, 1986, pp. 66–7.
38 Ol'ga Knipper, 'Iz moikh vospominani o Khudozhestvennom teatre i ob A.P. Chekhove' in *Chekhov i teatr*, p. 334.
39 Laurence Senelick, *Anton Chekhov*, London, Macmillan, 1985, pp. 73–4.
40 *Novosti Dnya* and *Teatr i uskusstvo*, quoted Balukhaty, *'Chaika'*, pp. 64–5 and p. 67.

2 'Stanislavski has ruined my play … '

1 Stanislavski, *SS*, vol. 1, p. 305.
2 Jean Benedetti, *Stanislavski: A Biography*, London, Methuen, 1988, p. 86.
3 N.K. Mikhailovski, quoted by Robert Louis Jackson in his introduction to *Chekhov: A Collection of Critical Essays*, Englewood Cliffs, NJ, Prentice–Hall Inc., 1967, p. 8.
4 Evtikhi Karpov, 'Dve poslednie vstrechi s A.P. Chekhovym' in E.D. Surkov (ed.), *Chekhov i teatr*, Moscow, Iskusstvo, 1961, p. 373.
5 Aleksandr Serebrov [A.N. Tikhonov], 'Vremya i lyudi: O Chekhove' in *Chekhov i teatr*, pp. 370–1.
6 Aleksandr Kugel', quoted by Nick Worrall in *The Moscow Art Theatre*, London, Methuen, 1996, p. 162.
7 Kugel', quoted by A. Anikst in *Teoriya dramy v Rossii ot Pushkina do Chekhova*, Moscow, Nauka, 1972, p. 615.
8 Stanislavski, *Rezhisserskie ekzemplyary K.S. Stanislavskogo 1890–1930: 'Dyadya Vanya' A.P. Chekhova, 1899*, ed. I.N. Solov'eva, Moscow, Phoenix, 1994, p. 133.
9 In Worrall, *Moscow*, p. 117.
10 In Worrall, *Moscow*, p. 117.
11 Desmond MacCarthy, *New Statesman and Nation*, 13 February 1937; in Victor Emeljanow (ed.), *Chekhov: The Critical Heritage*, London, Routledge & Kegan Paul, 1981, p. 399.
12 Stanislavski, *Rezhisserskie (Dyadya Vanya)*, pp. 101–3.
13 Stanislavski, quoted by Nikolai Efros in *Moskovski khudozhestvenny teatr: 1898–1923*, Moscow, Gosudarstvennoe izdatel'stvo, 1924, p. 232.
14 Stanislavski, *Rezhisserskie (Dyadya Vanya)*, p. 133.
15 In Efros, *Moskovski*, p. 232.
16 Stanislavski, *SS*, vol. 4, p. 134.
17 Meyerhold, quoted by Laurence Senelick in *The Chekhov Theatre*, Cambridge, CUP, 1997, p. 59.
18 Simov, quoted by Edward Braun in *The Director and the Stage*, London, Methuen, 1982, p. 70.
19 Simov, quoted by M. Stroeva in *Chekhov i khudozhestvenni teatr*, Moscow, Iskusstvo, 1955, p. 130.
20 Stroeva, *Chekhov*, p. 114.
21 Stanislavski, *SS*, vol. 1, p. 306.
22 Stanislavski, *SS*, vol. 1, pp. 306–7.
23 Stanislavski in I.N. Vinogradskaya (ed.), *Stanislavski repetiruet*, Moscow, STD RSFSR, 1987, p. 200.
24 Stanislavski, letter to N.V. Drizen; in I.N. Vinogradskaya (ed.), *Zhizn' i tvorchestvo Stanislavskogo*, vol. 2, Moscow, VTO, 1971, p. 209.
25 Blok, quoted by Viktor Borovsky in 'Discord in *The Cherry Orchard*: Chekhov and Stanislavsky' in *Encounter*, January/February 1990, p. 67.
26 S.D. Balukhaty, *Problemy dramaturgicheskogo analiza Chekhova*, Leningrad and Moscow, Academia, 1927; reprinted Munich, Wilhelm Fink, 1969, p. 146.
27 Andreev, quoted by Worrall, *Moscow*, p. 127.
28 Borovsky, 'Discord', p. 70.

29 Rolf-Dieter Kluge, *Anton P. Čechov*, Darmstadt, Wissenschaftliche Buchgesellschaft, 1995, p. 120.
30 Chekhov, letter to M.N. Alekseeva [Lilina], 15 September 1903; in *Chekhov i teatr*, p. 149.
31 Stanislavski, letter to Chekhov, 22 October 1903; *SS*, vol. 7, p. 505.
32 Stanislavski, letter to Chekhov, 23 November 1903; *SS*, vol. 7, p. 519.
33 Senelick, *Chekhov Theatre*, p. 71.
34 Stanislavski, *Rezhisserskie ekzemplyary K.S. Stanislavskogo*, vol. 3, Moscow, Iskusstvo, 1983, p. 317.
35 Stanislavski, *Rezhisserskie*, vol. 3, p. 315.
36 Stroeva, *Chekhov*, p. 187.
37 Stanislavski, *Rezhisserskie*, vol. 3, p. 315.
38 Nemirovich-Danchenko, letter to Ol'ga Knipper, before 17 January 1904; in V.I. Nemirovich-Danchenko, *Izbrannye pis'ma*, vol. 1 (1879–1909), Moscow, Iskusstvo, 1979, p. 354.
39 Stanislavski, *Rezhisserskie*, vol. 3, p. 413.
40 Stanislavski, *Rezhisserskie*, vol. 3, p. 297.
41 Aleksandr Amfiteatrov, quoted by Worrall, *Moscow*, p. 161.
42 Stanislavski, letter to Chekhov, 31 October 1903; *SS*, vol. 7, p. 510.
43 Stanislavski, *Rezhisserskie*, vol. 3, p. 319.
44 Stanislavski, *Rezhisserskie*, vol. 3, p. 331.
45 Stanislavski, *Rezhisserskie*, vol. 3, p. 333.
46 Heywood Braun, 'The new plays' in *New York World*, 23 January 1923; quoted by Sharon Carnicke in 'Stanislavsky's production of *The Cherry Orchard* in the US' in J. Douglas Clayton (ed.), *Chekhov Then and Now*, New York, Peter Lang, 1997, p. 24.
47 Carnicke, 'Stanislavsky's production', p. 25.
48 See O.A. Radishcheva, *Stanislavski i Nemirovich-Danchenko*, Moscow, ART, 1997, p. 226.
49 Stanislavski, *Rezhisserskie*, vol. 3, pp. 423–5.
50 Senelick, *Chekhov Theatre*, p. 71.
51 L.M. Leonidov, 'Proshloe i nastoyashchee' in *Chekhov i teatr*, pp. 351–2.
52 Kugel' in Anikst, *Teoriya*, p. 613.
53 Kugel' in Stroeva, *Chekhov*, p. 199.
54 Stroeva, *Chekhov*, p. 199.
55 Stanislavski, *SS*, vol. 1, p. 347; Nemirovich, letter to Efros, after 21 December 1908, quoted by M.N. Stroeva in *Rezhisserskie iskaniya Stanislavskogo 1898–1917*, Moscow, Nauka, 1973, p. 121.
56 See *Teatr i iskusstvo*, no. 12, pp. 246–7 and no. 13, pp. 262–5, 1904.
57 In Anikst, *Teoriya*, pp. 612–4.
58 Kugel', 'Zametki o Moskovskom khudozhestvennom teatre' in *Teatr i isskustvo*, no. 15, 11 April 1904, p. 304.
59 Kugel' quoted by Borovsky, 'Discord', p. 71.
60 Ol'ga Knipper, letter to Chekhov, 5 April 1904; in V.Ya. Vilenkin (ed.), *Ol'ga Leonardovna Knipper-Chekhova*, Moscow, Iskusstvo, 1972, vol. 1, p. 365.
61 Valeri Bryusov, 'Nenuzhnaya pravda' in *Sobranie sochineni*, vol. 6, Moscow, Khudozhestvennaya literatura, 1975, p. 68.
62 Bryusov, *Sobranie*, vol. 6, p. 71.

63 See Stanislavski, *SS*, vol. 1, p. 398. Stanislavski's productions of symbolist dramas caused a sensation, and Leonid Andreev considered his staging of *The Life of Man* (1907) was superior to Meyerhold's. (See Jean Benedetti, *Stanislavski: A Biography*, London, Methuen, 1988, p. 167.)
64 Vl. I. Nemirovich-Danchenko, *Rozhdenie teatra*, Moscow, Pravda, 1989, pp. 368–9.
65 Meyerhold, 'Naturalisticheski teatr i teatr nastroeniya' in *V.E. Meierkhol'd: stat'i, pis'ma, rechi, besedy*, Moscow, Iskusstvo, 1968, vol. 1 (1891–1917), p. 113.
66 Stanislavski, letter to Chekhov, 19 November 1903; *SS*, vol. 7, p. 518.
67 Stanislavski, *Rezhisserskie*, vol. 3, p. 337.
68 Stanislavski, *Rezhisserskie*, vol. 3, p. 339.
69 Stanislavski, *Rezhisserskie*, vol. 3, p. 357.
70 Stanislavski, *Rezhisserskie*, vol. 3, p. 361. According to Vakhtangov, Chekhov protested vehemently against the mosquitoes in *The Cherry Orchard*. See Nikolai Gorchakov, *Rezhisserskie uroki Vakhtangova*, Moscow, Iskusstvo, 1957, p. 49.
71 Stanislavski, *Rezhisserskie*, vol. 3, p. 369.
72 Meyerhold, 'Naturalisticheski', p. 118.
73 Meyerhold, letter to Chekhov, 8 May 1904; in *V.E. Meierkhol'd*, vol. 1, p. 85.
74 Stanislavski, *Rezhisserskie*, vol. 3, p. 374.
75 Stanislavski, *Rezhisserskie*, vol. 3, p. 375. Meyerhold argued that the characters in Act III are careless and indifferent, and do not sense the impending disaster. But the Art Theatre 'wanted to portray boredom. That's a mistake. One must show indifference. That is not the same. Indifference is more active. Then the tragedy of the act will emerge in a concentrated form.' (Letter to Chekhov, 8 May 1904; in *V.E. Meierkhol'd*, vol. 1, p. 86)
76 Stanislavski, *Rezhisserskie*, vol. 3, p. 391.
77 Stanislavski, *Rezhisserskie*, vol. 3, p. 411.
78 Vera Gottlieb, *Chekhov in Performance in Russia and Soviet Russia*, Cambridge, Chadwyck–Healey, 1984, p. 30.
79 Gottlieb, *Chekhov*, p. 30.
80 Worrall, *Moscow*, p. 156.
81 Chekhov, letter to N. Leikin, 15 November 1887; in *Chekhov i teatr*, p. 26.
82 Chekhov, letter to Ol'ga Knipper, 15 October 1900; see Jean Benedetti, *The Moscow Art Theatre Letters*, London, Methuen, 1991, pp. 84–5.
83 Chekhov, quoted by Radishcheva, *Stanislavski*, p. 230.
84 Simov, quoted by Radishcheva, *Stanislavski*, pp. 227–8.
85 Stanislavski, letter to V.V. Kotlyarevskaya, 26 December 1903; *SS*, vol. 7, p. 521.
86 Nemirovich-Danchenko, quoted by Radishcheva in *Stanislavski*, p. 229.
87 Radishcheva, *Stanislavski*, p. 236.
88 Nemirovich-Danchenko, letter to Stanislavski, before 26 October 1899 in *Izbrannye pis'ma*, vol. 1, p. 198. (And yet, photographs of the production suggest that Stanislavski kept his handkerchief.)
89 Nemirovich-Danchenko, letter to Chekhov, 22 January 1901; in *Izbrannye pis'ma*, vol. 1, p. 230.

90 Chekhov, letter to Stanislavski, 23 November 1903; in *Chekhov i teatr*, p. 160.
91 Stanislavski, letter to Chekhov, 19 November 1903; in *SS*, vol. 7, p. 518.
92 Chekhov, letter to Knipper, 23 November 1903; in *Chekhov i teatr*, p. 160.
93 Chekhov, letter to Stanislavski, 23 November 1903; in *Chekhov i teatr*, p. 160.
94 Chekhov, letter to Knipper, 29 March 1904; see *Chekhov i teatr*, p. 164.
95 Reported by A.S. Yakovlev in *Chekhov i teatr*, p. 465.
96 S.G. Skitalets, quoted Radishcheva, *Stanislavski*, pp. 235–6.
97 Chekhov, letter to Knipper, 18 March 1904; in *Chekhov i teatr*, p. 163.
98 Jean Benedetti, *The Moscow Art Theatre Letters*, London, Methuen, 1991, p. 170.
99 Evtikhi Karpov, 'Dve poslednie vstrechi s A.P. Chekhovym' in *Chekhov i teatr*, pp. 372–3.

3 'The line of intuition and feeling': Chekhov and the Stanislavski 'system'

1 Stanislavski, *My Life in Art*, translated by J.J. Robbins, Harmondsworth, Penguin Books, 1967, p. 329. This passage was cut from the Russian edition.
2 Stanislavski, *SS*, vol. 1, pp. 290–1, 295.
3 Stanislavski, *SS*, vol. 2, p. 297.
4 Stanislavski, *SS*, vol. 1, pp. 292, 294–5.
5 Stanislavski, *My Life*, p. 331. This sentence was cut from the Russian edition.
6 Nemirovich-Danchenko, *Rozhdenie teatra*, Moscow, Iskusstvo, 1989, p. 147. Photographs of the production do not really convey this sense of gloom; the lighting was probably altered for the photographer.
7 Stanislavski, *SS*, vol. 2, p. 299.
8 Stanislavski, *My Life*, p. 331. This sentence was cut from the Russian edition.
9 Nemirovich-Danchenko, *Rozhdenie*, p. 147.
10 Laurence Senelick, *The Chekhov Theatre*, Cambridge, CUP, 1997, p. 43; Ol'ga Knipper, quoted by E. Polyakova in *Stanislavski*, Moscow, Iskusstvo, 1977, p. 152.
11 Stanislavski, *SS*, vol. 1, p. 267.
12 Stanislavski, quoted in *Rezhisserskie ekzemplyary K.S. Stanislavskogo*, vol. 2, (1898–1901), Moscow, Iskusstvo, 1981, p. 6.
13 S.D. Balukhaty, *'Chaika' v postanovke Moskovskogo Khudozhestvennogo teatra*, Leningrad and Moscow, Iskusstvo, 1938, p. 129.
14 Raymond Williams, *Drama in Performance*, Harmondsworth, Pelican Books, 1972, p. 119.
15 Nemirovich-Danchenko, *Rozhdenie*, pp. 145–6.
16 Meyerhold in *Meierkhol'd repetiruet*, M.M. Sitkovetskaya (ed.), vol. 2, Moscow, ART, 1993, p. 274.
17 Miroslav Krleza, quoted by Jovan Hristic in '"Thinking with Chekhov": The evidence of the notebooks' in *New Theatre Quarterly*, no. 42, p. 179.
18 Michel Saint-Denis, *Theatre: The Rediscovery of Style*, London, Heinemann, 1960, pp. 41–3.

19 *Meierkhol'd repetiruet*, vol. 2, p. 274.
20 Dieter Hoffmeier, 'Die Regiebücher Stanislavskijs' in *Konstantin Stanislawski: Neue Aspekte und Perspektiven*, Günter Ahrends (ed.), Tübingen, Gunter Narr Verlag, 1992, p. 16.
21 V.I. Kachalov, 'Iz vospominani' in *Chekhov i teatr*, E.D. Surkov (ed.), Moscow, Iskusstvo, 1961, pp. 349–50.
22 O.A. Radishcheva, *Stanislavski i Nemirovich-Danchenko*, Moscow, APT, 1997, p. 229.
23 Stanislavski, reported by V. Toporkov in *Stanislavski na repetitsii*, Moscow, Iskusstvo, 1950, p. 145.
24 In Toporkov, *Stanislavski*, p. 136.
25 Stanislavski, *SS*, vol. 2, p. 235.
26 Stanislavski, reported by Nikolai Gorchakov in *Rezhisserskie uroki K.S. Stanislavskogo*, Moscow, Iskusstvo, 1951, p. 151.
27 In Toporkov, *Stanislavski*, p. 71.
28 Stanislavski, *SS*, vol. 1, pp. 288–9.
29 A.R. Kugel', *Peterburgskaya gazeta*, 19 October 1896, no. 289; in Chekhov, *PSS*, vol. 13, p. 376.
30 In Balukhaty, '*Chaika*', p. 159. Something similar can be seen in the production plan for *The Cherry Orchard*: in Act II, for example, Stanislavski notes: 'Whenever it is possible, Trofimov feasts his eyes on Anya.' (*Rezhisserskie ekzemplyary K.S. Stanislavskogo*, vol. 3, Moscow, Iskusstvo, 1983, p. 361.)
31 N. Efros, '*Chaika*' in *Novosti Dnya*, 31 December 1898.
32 Balukhaty, '*Chaika*', p. 291.
33 Balukhaty, '*Chaika*', p. 165.
34 Balukhaty, '*Chaika*', p. 253.
35 *Ezhegodnik Moskovskogo Khudozhestvennogo teatra 1944*, p. 290; quoted by Senelick in *Chekhov Theatre*, p. 47.
36 Balukhaty, '*Chaika*', p. 227.
37 Chekhov, letter to Ol'ga Knipper, 30 September 1899; in *Chekhov i teatr*, p. 105.
38 Stanislavski, *Rezisserskie ekzemplyary Stanislavskogo 1898–1930: 'Dyadya Vanya' A.P. Chekhova, 1899*, ed. N. Solov'eva, Moscow, Phoenix, 1994, p. 99.
39 Chekhov, reported by N.S. Butova in 'Iz vospominani' in *Chekhov i teatr*, p. 346.
40 Jean Benedetti, *Stanislavski: A Biography*, London, Methuen, 1988, p. 131.
41 Stanislavski, *Rezhisserskie*, vol. 3, pp. 325–7.
42 Stanislavski, letter to Chekhov, 31 October 1903; *SS*, vol. 7, p. 510.
43 Stanislavski, *Rezhisserskie*, vol. 3, pp. 421–5.
44 Nemirovich, letter to Stanislavski, 14 January 1904. See Radishcheva, *Stanislavski*, p. 233.
45 Stanislavski worked on *The Seagull* over a period of, altogether, some five months, between September 1917 and June 1918. However, the only notes available cover just four of the rehearsals. Vinogradskaya suggests that the main interest in the production for Stanislavski was the casting of Alla Tarasova and Mikhail Chekhov as Nina and Trepler. See I.N. Vinogradskaya, *Stanislavski repetiruet*, Moscow, STD RSFSR, 1987, p. 190.

46 In Vinogradskaya, *Stanislavski*, p. 197.
47 In Vinogradskaya, *Stanislavski*, p. 202.
48 In Vinogradskaya, *Stanislavski*, p. 202–3.
49 In Vinogradskaya, *Stanislavski*, p. 197.
50 In Vinogradskaya, *Stanislavski*, p. 205.
51 Stanislavski, *SS*, vol. 2, p. 239.
52 In Vinogradskaya, *Stanislavski*, p. 206.
53 N. Gorchakov, *Rezhisserskie uroki K.S. Stanislavskogo*, p. 52.
54 Tarasova returned to Chekhov and *The Seagull* – but not until 1960, when she took on the role of Arkadina at the Art Theatre. She was also Masha in Nemirovich's 1940 production of *Three Sisters*.
55 Stanislavski, *SS*, vol. 1, p. 459.
56 Evgeni Vakhtangov, 'S khudozhnika sprositsya' in *Evg. Vakhtangov: Materialy i stat'i*, eds L.D. Vendrovskaya and G.P. Kaptereva, Moscow, VTO, 1959, pp. 166–7.

Part II: Chekhov in Russia: after Stanislavski

4 Vakhtangov and Meyerhold

1 N. Gorchakov, *Rezhisserskie uroki Vakhtangova*, Moscow, Iskusstvo, 1957, p. 30.
2 Gorchakov, *Rezisserskie uroki Vakhtangova*, p. 11.
3 Konstantin Rudnitsky, *Russian and Soviet Theatre*, London, Thames & Hudson, 1988, p. 21.
4 Stanislavski, *SS*, vol. 1, p. 436.
5 Quoted by Meyerhold in 'Sverchok na pechi, ili U zamochnoi skvazhiny' in *V.E. Meierkhol'd: stat'i, pis'ma, rechi, besedy*, vol. 1, Moscow, Iskusstvo, 1968, p. 263.
6 Meyerhold, 'Sverchok', pp. 263–4.
7 See 'K istorii i tekhnike teatra' in *V.E. Meierkhol'd*, vol. 1, pp. 105–42.
8 Ruben Simonov, *S Vakhtangovym*, Moscow, Iskusstvo, 1959, p. 95 and p. 162.
9 Meyerhold, quoted by Aleksandr Gladkov in *Meierkhol'd*, vol. 2, Moscow, STD RSFSR, 1990, p. 236.
10 Stanislavski, *SS*, vol. 2, p. 62.
11 Vakhtangov noted that, during improvisations with his students, held in December 1914, the question arose 'as to whether or not a production should be stylised. At this stage, the decision had been to reject the idea in the interests of a felt need to concentrate on the demands of an "intimate–psychological" and "subjective–naturalist" theatre.' (Quoted by Nick Worrall in *Modernism to Realism on the Soviet Stage*, Cambridge, CUP, 1989, p. 90.)
12 S.V. Giatsintova, quoted by I. Vinogradskaya in *Zhizn' i tvorchestvo K.S. Stanislavskogo*, vol. 3 (1916–26), Moscow, VTO, 1973, p. 61.
13 A. Diki, quoted by M.N. Stroeva in *Rezhisserskie iskaniya Stanislavskogo, 1917–1938*, Moscow, Nauka, 1977, p. 15.
14 Giatsintova, quoted by Vinogradskaya, *Zhizn'*, vol. 3, p. 88.

15 Vakhtangov, letter to A.I. Cheban, 3 August 1917; in *Evg. Vakhtangov: Materialy i stat'i*, L.D. Vendrovskaya and G.P. Kaptereva (eds), Moscow, VTO, 1959, p. 79.
16 See Stroeva, *Rezhisserskie iskaniya, 1917–1938*, p. 16.
17 See Jean Benedetti, *Stanislavski: A Biography*, London, Methuen, 1988, p. 229.
18 Vakhtangov, 'S khudozhnika sprositsya' in *Evg. Vakhtangov*, pp. 166–7.
19 Vakhtangov, in *Evg. Vakhtangov*, Lyubov Vendrovskaya and Galina Kaptereva (eds), translated by Doris Bradbury, Moscow, Progress, 1982, p. 141. (This passage was omitted from the Russian edition of the book.)
20 Vakhtangov, 'Dve besedy s uchenikami' in *Evg. Vakhtangov*, pp. 207–8.
21 Worrall, *Modernism*, p. 77.
22 Vakhtangov, 'Dve besedy', p. 208.
23 Boris Zakhava, *Vakhtangov i ego studiya*, in *Jewgeni B. Wachtangow: Schriften*, Dieter Wardetzky (ed.), Berlin, Henschelverlag, 1982, p. 294.
24 Zakhava, *Vakhtangov*, p. 300. Similarly, Brecht saw Vakhtangov as the 'meeting point' between Stanislavski and Meyerhold. (See *Brecht on Theatre*, John Willett (ed.), London, Methuen, 1978, p. 238.)
25 Vakhtangov, 'Dve besedy', p. 214.
26 Vakhtangov, *Kul'tura teatra*, no. 4, 5 April 1921; in *Evg. Vakhtangov*, p. 185.
27 Gorchakov, *Rezhisserskie uroki Vakhtangova*, p. 187 and p. 177.
28 Stanislavski, 'Iz poslednego razgovora s E.B. Vakhtangovym' in *Moe grazhdanskoe slyzhenie Rossii*, M.N. Lyubomudrova (ed.), Moscow, Pravda, 1990, pp. 486–7.
29 Vakhtangov, notebook entry for 26 March 1921; in *Evg. Vakhtangov*, p. 188.
30 Zakhava, *Vakhtangov*, pp. 292–3.
31 There were two versions of the production. It was first staged in 1920, and then revised in 1921.
32 Gorchakov, *Rezhisserskie uroki Vakhtangova*, p. 43.
33 Simonov, *S Vakhtangovym*, p. 21.
34 Simonov, *S Vakhtangovym*, p. 25.
35 Gorchakov, *Rezhisserskie uroki Vakhtangova*, p. 30.
36 Zakhava, *Vakhtangov*, p. 296.
37 Simonov, *S Vakhtangovym*, p. 46.
38 Gorchakov, *Rezhisserskie uroki Vakhtangova*, p. 40.
39 Gorchakov, *Rezhisserskie uroki Vakhtangova*, p. 41.
40 Simonov, *S Vakhtangovym*, p. 62.
41 Simonov, *S Vakhtangovym*, p. 28.
42 Vakhtangov, *Evg. Vakhtangov*, p. 187.
43 Simonov, *S Vakhtangovym*, p. 29.
44 Simonov, *S Vakhtangovym*, p. 53.
45 Zakhava, *Vakhtangov*, p. 296.
46 Simonov, *S Vakhtangovym*, p. 56.
47 Simonov, *S Vakhtangovym*, p. 127.
48 Mikhail Chekhov, quoted by Laurence Senelick in *The Chekhov Theatre*, Cambridge, CUP, 1997, p. 120.
49 Meyerhold, quoted by Norris Houghton in *Moscow Rehearsals*, London, George Allen & Unwin, 1938, p. 117.

50 Meyerhold, quoted by K. Rudnitski in *Rezhisser Meierkhol'd*, Moscow, Nauka, 1969, p. 475.
51 Meyerhold, '33 obmoroka. Beseda s narodnym artistom respubliki Vs. Meierkhol'dom' in *Pravda*, 25 March 1935.
52 Meyerhold in *Meierkhol'd repetiruet*, Moscow, ART, 1993, vol. 2, p. 151.
53 Meyerhold, *Meierkhol'd repetiruet*, vol. 2, p. 152.
54 Igor Il'inski, *Sam o sebe*, Moscow, Iskusstvo, 1984, p. 248.
55 Houghton, *Moscow*, p. 123.
56 Aleksandr Fevral'ski, quoted by Konstantin Rudnitsky in *Meyerhold the Director*, Ann Arbor, MI, Ardis, 1981, p. 526.
57 Meyerhold, 'Moya rabota nad Chekhovym' in *V.E. Meierkhol'd: stat'i, pis'ma, rechi, besedy*, Moscow, Iskusstvo, 1968, vol. 2 (1917–39), p. 316.
58 Meyerhold, 'Akter budushchego i biomekhanika' in *V.E. Meierkhol'd*, vol. 2, p. 488–9.
59 Aleksandr Gladkov, *Meierkhol'd*, Moscow, STD RSFSR, 1990, vol. 2, p. 239.
60 Houghton, *Moscow*, p. 127.
61 Gladkov, *Meierkhol'd*, vol. 2, p. 296.
62 Lunacharski, quoted by Nikolai A. Gorchakov in *The Theater in Soviet Russia*, New York, Columbia University Press, 1957, p. 287.
63 From an editorial, 'Znamenatelnoe piatiletie' in *Teatr*, no. 1, 1937, p. 7; quoted by Gorchakov, *Theater*, p. 356.
64 Yuri Lyubimov, *Le Feu Sacré*, Paris, Fayard, 1985, p. 31.
65 Sharon Marie Carnicke, 'Stanislavsky Uncensored and Unabridged' in *The Drama Review*, vol. 37, no. 1 (T137), Spring 1993, p. 22.
66 Lyubimov, *Le Feu*, p. 32.
67 Stanislavski, 'S narodnoi tribuny' in *Pravda*, 7 November 1937.
68 Stanislavski, *SS*, vol. 1, p. 487.
69 Reported by Aleksandr Gladkov in *Meierkhol'd*, vol. 2, p. 237.
70 Anatoli Efros, *Prodolzhenie teatral'nogo romana*, Moscow, Panas, 1993, p. 52.
71 In Rudnitsky, *Meyerhold*, p. 540.
72 In Rudnitsky, *Meyerhold*, pp. 539–40.
73 Meyerhold in Gladkov, *Meierkhol'd*, vol. 2, p. 233.
74 Yu. Bakhrushin, 'Stanislavski i Meierkhol'd' in *Vstrechi s Meierkhol'dom* L.D. Vendrovskaya (ed.), Moscow, VTO, 1967, p. 589.

5 Efros and Lyubimov

1 V.I. Nemirovich-Danchenko, *Rozhdenie teatra*, Moscow, Pravda, 1989, p. 424.
2 G. Tovstonogov, 'Chekhov's *Three Sisters* at the Gorky Theatre' in Eugene K. Bristow (ed.), *Anton Chekhov's Plays*, New York, W.W. Norton, 1977, p. 328.
3 Anatoly Smeliansky, *Is Comrade Bulgakov Dead?*, London, Methuen, 1993, p. 293.
4 T. Knyazavskaya, 'Providcheskoe u Chekhova' in *Teatral'naya zhizn'*, 1994, part 4, p. 11.
5 V. Komissarjevsky, *Inside Moscow Theatres*, Moscow, 1959, p. 124. (Publisher unknown.)

6 Quoted by Michael Walton in 'If only we knew' in *New Theatre Magazine*, Autumn 1968, vol. 8, no. 1, p. 34. Significantly, Nemirovich cut Chebutykin from the play's final scene, so his negative, nihilistic refrain, 'Nothing matters ... ', did not disturb the note of triumphant hope.

7 Tovstonogov, 'Chekhov's *Three Sisters*', p. 328.

8 Nikolai A. Gorchakov, *The Theater in Soviet Russia*, New York, Columbia University Press, 1957, p. 394.

9 Stanislavski himself was partly responsible for this development. He had been saddened and puzzled by the way Chekhov's work, in the years following the Revolution, was dismissed as part of the 'old' world; he could not understand 'why people say he would not have understood the revolution and the new life it has created'. He was reacting, in part, against the opinion, still prevalent, 'that Chekhov was a poet of everyday life and grey people; that his plays reflected a drab side of Russian life, and were evidence of the country's spiritual decay. Dissatisfaction, paralysing all endeavour; hopelessness, killing energy. ... These were seen as the motifs of his dramatic works.' Instead, Stanislavski stressed Chekhov's optimism, and portrayed him almost as a 'fellow-traveller' in the cause of the Revolution. He claimed Chekhov sided with progressive people who 'were preparing public opinion, spreading new ideas, explaining the rottenness of the old life'.

> Time was passing. Chekhov, who was always striving for progress, could not mark time. On the contrary, he marched along with life and the age. ...
>
> ... He was one of the first writers at the turn of the century to sense the inevitability of the revolution, at a time when it was only at an embryonic stage, and society continued to bathe in luxury. He was one of the first to sound the alarm. Wasn't it he who began to cut down the beautiful, blooming cherry orchard, recognising that its time had passed, that the old life was doomed?
>
> (Stanislavski, *SS*, vol. 1, pp. 350–1)

10 N.K. Mikhailovski, quoted by Robert L. Jackson, introduction to *Chekhov: A Collection of Critical Essays*, Englewood Cliffs, NJ, Prentice-Hall, 1967, p. 8.

11 Alexander Solodovnikov, 'The Moscow Art Theatre Today' in: *Moscow Art Theatre: A Symposium* by A. Solodovnikov, N. Volkov, V. Vilenkin and G. Zayavlin. London, Soviet News Booklet no. 27, 1958, p. 11.

12 B.I. Aleksandov, quoted by Jackson, *Chekhov*, pp. 14–15.

13 Anatoli Efros, *Repetitsiya – lyubov' moya*, Moscow, Panas, 1993, p. 266.

14 T. Knyazevskaya, 'Providcheskoe', p. 11.

15 M. Stroeva, 'Voennaya musyka' in *Teatr*, 1982, part 10, p. 119.

16 Knyazevskaya, 'Providcheskoe', p. 11.

17 Knyazevskaya, 'Providcheskoe', p. 11.

18 Efros, *Repetitsiya*, p. 33.

19 Efros, quoted by Henry Popkin, *The Times*, 17 July 1968.

20 Efros, *Professiya: rezhisser*, Moscow, Panas, 1993, pp. 93–4.

21 Efros, 'O Chekhove i o nashei professii' in *Moskovski nablyudatel'*, 1993, part 11–12, p. 8.
22 Efros, 'O Chekhove', p. 7.
23 Efros, quoted by Spencer Golub in 'The theatre of Anatolij Efros' in *Theatre Quarterly*, 1977, vol. VII, no. 26, p. 33.
24 Efros, 'O Chekhove', p. 7.
25 In Golub, 'Theatre', p. 22 and p. 31.
26 Alla Demidova, *Teni zazerkal'ya*, Moscow, Prosveshchenie, 1993, p. 73.
27 Efros, quoted by Aleksandr Gershkovich in *Izbrannoe*, Moscow, ULISS/Teatral'naya zhizn', 1994, p. 36.
28 Reported by Golub, 'Theatre', p. 24.
29 Golub, 'Theatre', p. 25.
30 Efros, quoted by Anatoli Smelyanski in *Nashi sobesedniki*, Moscow, Iskusstvo, 1981, p. 293.
31 Smelyanski, *Nashi*, p. 296. Interestingly, Smelyanski found this 'unChekhovian'.
32 Smelyanski, *Nashi*, p. 296.
33 Smelyanski, *Nashi*, p. 297.
34 Golub, 'Theatre', p. 25.
35 Demidova, *Teni*, p. 132.
36 Gershkovich, *Izbrannoe*, p. 27.
37 Efros, 'O Chekhove', p. 4.
38 Gershkovich, *Izbrannoe*, p. 26.
39 *Moskovskie novosti*, 25 February 1990; in Gershkovich, *Izbrannoe*, p. 30.
40 Gershkovich, *Izbrannoe*, p. 38.
41 Yuri Lyubimov, 'Portrety na stenakh i zhivye traditsii' in *Stanislavski v menyayushchemsya mire*, Moscow, Blagotvoritel'ni Fond Stanislavskogo, 1994, p. 160.
42 Lyubimov, quoted by Marina Dmitrevskaya in 'Yuri Lyubimov: "Ya ne proryvami zanumalsya … "' in *Peterburgski teatral'ny zhurnal*, 1995, no. 8, p. 102.
43 Lyubimov, *Le Feu Sacré*, Paris, Fayard, 1985, p. 36.
44 Lyubimov, *Le Feu*, p. 34.
45 Lyubimov, 'The Algebra of Harmony: A Meditation on Theatre Aesthetics' in *The Theater of Yuri Lyubimov* by Alexander Gershkovich, New York, Paragon House, 1989, p. 203.
46 Lyubimov, 'Algebra', p. 202.
47 Lyubimov, quoted by Aleksandr Gershkovich in *Teatr na Taganke*, Moscow, Solyaris, 1993, p. 7.
48 Paola Dionisotti, who acted in Lyubimov's London production of *Crime and Punishment*, has observed that the director sees himself very much 'as a choreographer, and us as dancers, his job to teach us the steps, ours to memorize them'. (Paola Dionisotti, quoted by Birgit Beumers in *Yuri Lyubimov at the Taganka Theatre 1964–1994*, Amsterdam, Harwood Academic Publishers, 1997, p. 223.)
49 Lyubimov, 'A note on actors and the acting profession' in Gershkovich, *The Theater of Yuri Lyubimov*, p. 214.
50 Lyubimov, quoted by O. Mal'tseva in *Akter teatra Lyubimova*, St Petersburg, LenNar, 1994, p. 55.
51 In Mal'tseva, *Akter*, p. 47.

52 Mal'tseva, *Akter*, pp. 47–8.
53 In Mal'tseva, *Akter*, p. 54.
54 Smelyanski, *Nashi*, p. 293.
55 Yuri Pogrebnichko rehearsed the production for about a year. Then Lyubimov stepped in, and made significant changes. It seems he completed the production in just twelve days. See Beumers, *Lyubimov*, p. 302.
56 Stroeva, 'Voennaya', p. 121.
57 Stroeva, 'Voennaya', p. 125.
58 Gershkovich, *Teatr na Taganke*, p. 99.
59 Knyazevskaya, 'Providcheskoe', p. 11.
60 Knyazevskaya, 'Providcheskoe', p. 11.
61 A 'speed-run' is a rehearsal technique, in which the actors are asked to run swiftly through the whole play, 'indicating' all the actions, without any emotion.
62 A. Karaulov, 'Rekviem' in *Teatr*, 1982, part 10, p. 117.
63 Marie-Luise Bott, 'Die *Drei Schwestern* in Moskau – Eine Groteske: Zur bisher letzten zugelassen Inszenierung Jurij Ljubimows am Taganka-Theater' in *Theater Heute*, March 1984, p. 20.
64 Marina Litavrina, 'Klyuch ot royalya' in *Moskva*, 1983, part 7, p. 178.
65 Karaulov, 'Rekviem', p. 117.
66 See Beumers, *Lyubimov*, p. 183.
67 G. Zamkovets, 'Variatsii pod orkestr' in *Tealtral'naya zhizn'*, 1981, part 23, p. 29.
68 Pessimistically, Smelyanski has concluded that the two trends 'cannot merge into one'. (Smelyanski, *Nashi*, p. 299.)
69 Stanislavski, *SS*, vol. 1, p. 489.

Part III: Chekhov in America

6 Lee Strasberg: truth in acting

1 *New York American*; quoted by Foster Hirsch in *A Method to their Madness*, New York, Da Capo Press, 1984, p. 54.
2 Oliver M. Sayler, *The Russian Theatre*, London, Bretano's, 1923, pp. 46–7.
3 Kenneth MacGowan, 'And again repertory: the Moscow Art Theatre and Shakespeare divide New York honors' in *Theatre Arts Magazine*, April 1923, vol. VII, part 2, p. 90.
4 Alan Dale, *New York Journal*; quoted Hirsch, *A Method*, p. 56.
5 Percy Hammond, *New York Tribune*, 30 January 1923.
6 Maida Castellun, *New York Call*; quoted by Christine Edwards in *The Stanislavsky Heritage*, London, Owen, 1966, p. 231.
7 Hammond, *New York Tribune*, 30 January 1923.
8 Sayler, *Russian*, p. 52.
9 Strasberg in Robert H. Hethmon (ed.), *Strasberg at the Actors Studio*, New York, Theatre Communications Group, 1991, p. 74.
10 Miriam Kimball Stockton, quoted by J.W. Roberts in *Richard Boleslavsky: His Life and Work in the Theatre*, Ann Arbor, UMI Research Press, 1981, p. 108.

11 Richard Boleslavsky, 'Living the part' in *Actors on Acting*, Toby Cole and Helen Krich Chinoy (eds), New York, Three Rivers Press, 1970, p. 511.

12 Statement by the trustees of the American Laboratory Theatre; quoted by Sharon M. Carnicke in 'Boleslavsky in America' in Laurence Senelick (ed.), *Wandering Stars*, Iowa City, University of Iowa Press, 1992, p. 120.

13 Stella Adler, quoted by Hirsch in *A Method*, p. 62.

14 Harold Clurman, quoted by Roberts in *Boleslavsky*, p. 165.

15 See Mel Gordon, *The Stanislavsky Technique: Russia*, New York, Applause, 1987, pp. 45–6 and pp. 120–1.

16 See Roberts, *Boleslavsky*, pp. 165–6.

17 Letter to Stanislavski, 5 January 1933. See *Ezhegodnik Moskovskogo Khudozhestvennogo teatra 1943*, Moscow, Iskusstvo, 1945, p. 610.

18 Harold Clurman, *The Fervent Years*, New York, Da Capo Press, 1983, p. 44.

19 Lee Strasberg, 'Acting and the training of actors' in John Gassner (ed.), *Producing the Play*, New York, Holt, Rinehart & Winston, 1941, p. 144.

20 Strasberg, quoted by Lorrie Hull in *Strasberg's Method as Taught by Lorrie Hull*, Woodbridge, Connecticut, Ox Bow Publishing, 1985, p. 84.

21 Strasberg, interview with Richard Schechner, 'Working with live material' in *Tulane Drama Review*, vol. 9, no. 1, Fall 1964, p. 134.

22 Phoebe Brand and Margaret Barker, quoted by Hirsch in *A Method*, p. 77.

23 Elia Kazan, *Elia Kazan: A Life*, London, Andre Deutsch, 1988, pp. 706–7.

24 Stanislavski, quoted by Hirsch in *A Method*, p. 78.

25 See *A Player's Place* by David Garfield, New York, Macmillan, 1980, p. 33.

26 I. Rapoport, 'The work of the actor', in *Acting: A Handbook of the Stanislavski Method*, Toby Cole (ed.), New York, Three Rivers Press, 1995, p. 67.

27 In Hirsch, *A Method*, p. 79.

28 Strasberg, quoted by Cindy Adams in *Lee Strasberg*, New York, Doubleday, 1980, p. 179.

29 Strasberg, 'Working', p. 133.

30 Adler, quoted in Hirsch *A Method*, p. 79.

31 Strasberg, 'View from the studio' in *New York Times*, 2 September 1956.

32 Strasberg, 'View' in *New York Times*, 2 September 1956.

33 Strasberg, in *Strasberg at the Actors Studio*, p. 368.

34 Robert Brustein, quoted Garfield, *A Player's Place*, p. x.

35 Robert Lewis, 'Method – or madness?', *New York Times*, 23 June 1957.

36 Harold Clurman, 'There's a method in British acting', *New York Times Magazine*, 12 Jan 1964, sec.6, p. 62.

37 Charles Marowitz, letter to the author, 6 August 1986.

38 Strasberg, on *Reputations: Lee Strasberg*, BBC Television documentary, broadcast BBC2, 23 July 1997.

39 Strasberg, 'Working', p. 129.

40 Strasberg, in *Strasberg at the Actors Studio*, p. 309.

41 Strasberg, 'Working', p. 129.

42 Strasberg, in *Strasberg at the Actors Studio*, pp. 316–7.

43 Susie Mee, 'Chekhov's *Three Sisters* and the Wooster Group's *Brace Up!*', in *The Drama Review*, vol. 36, no. 4 (T136), Winter 1992, p. 144.

44 Paul Schmidt, introduction to his translation of *Three Sisters*, New York, Theatre Communications Group, 1992, p. ix.
45 Harold Clurman, *Nation*, 27 July 1964, vol. 199, p. 38.
46 Geraldine Page, 'The bottomless cup' (interview with Richard Schechner), in Cole and Chinoy (eds), *Actors on Acting*, p. 637.
47 See Hirsch, *A Method*, p. 247, and Garfield, *A Player's Place*, p. 237.
48 Strasberg, in *Strasberg at the Actors Studio*, pp. 72–4.
49 Gerald Hiken, quoted by Victor Seymour in *Stage Directors' Workshop: A Descriptive Study of the Actors Studio Directors Unit, 1960–1964*, unpublished Ph.D. thesis, University of Wisconsin, 1965, p. 153.
50 Hiken, in Seymour, *Stage Directors'*, p. 132.
51 Hiken, in Seymour, *Stage Directors'*, p. 135.
52 Salem Ludwig, in Seymour, *Stage Directors'*, p. 133.
53 Seymour, *Stage Directors'*, p. 145.
54 John Strasberg, *Accidentally on Purpose*, New York, Applause, 1996, pp. 114–5. John Strasberg recalls that Kim Stanley, who was playing Masha, was not happy using sense memory, and asked if a bucket of ice could be left in the wings offstage in performance. Waiting for their entrances, the actors would gather around the bucket, and stick their hands into the ice. It is not clear, however, if Lee Strasberg himself approved of this procedure.
55 See Gordon Rogoff, 'Lee Strasberg: burning ice' in *Tulane Drama Review*, Winter 1964, vol. 9, no. 2, pp. 151–2.
56 Hiken, in Seymour, *Stage Directors'*, p. 137.
57 John Strasberg, *Accidentally*, p. 113.
58 Page, in Hirsch, *A Method*, p. 285.
59 Hiken, in Seymour, *Stage Directors'*, p. 137.
60 Page, 'Bottomless Cup', p. 636.
61 Strasberg, in Seymour, *Stage Directors'*, p. 149.
62 Hiken, in Seymour, *Stage Directors'*, p. 139.
63 John Strasberg, *Accidentally*, p. 111.
64 Page, 'Bottomless Cup', p. 636.
65 John Strasberg, *Accidentally*, p. 111.
66 *Newsweek*, 6 July 1964, p. 45.
67 Hiken, in Seymour, *Stage Directors'*, pp. 141–2.
68 A video of the film was released by Hen's Tooth Video in 1997.
69 Strasberg, in Hull, *Strasberg's Method*, p. 84.
70 Hiken, in Seymour, *Stage Directors'*, pp. 141–2.
71 Seymour, *Stage Directors'*, p. 146.
72 Kazan, *Elia Kazan*, p. 707.
73 Page, 'Bottomless cup', pp. 636–7.
74 McCarthy, in Adams, *Lee Strasberg*, p. 293.
75 John Strasberg, *Accidentally*, p. 114.
76 Clurman, *Nation*, 27 July 1964, p. 39.
77 In Garfield, *A Player's Place*, p. 237. Garfield suggests these comments applied to Act III, but this seems to be a mistake. In the film version, Stanley wears her hair long down her back in Act IV, not Act III; and it is in the final act that Stanley's Masha seems to come unhinged.
78 Hiken, in Seymour, *Stage Directors'*, p. 154.
79 See Seymour, *Stage Directors'*, pp. 152–3.

80 Jerry Talmer, *New York Post*, 23 June 1964; Henry Hewes, *Saturday Review*, 18 July 1964, vol. 47, p. 25.

81 Kazan, *Elia Kazan*, p. 708.

82 Olivier, quoted by Ronald Bergan in *Dustin Hoffman*, London, Virgin, 1991, p. 148.

83 Strasberg, in Adams, *Lee Strasberg*, p. 297.

84 In John Strasberg, *Accidentally*, p. 119.

85 Herbert Kretzmer, *Daily Express*, 14 May 1965; B.A. Young, *Financial Times*, 14 May 1965.

86 Peter Roberts, *Plays and Players*, July 1965, p. 34.

87 Strasberg in *The Evening Standard*, 14 May 1965.

88 Strasberg, in Adams, *Lee Strasberg*, p. 301.

89 Alan Brien, *Sunday Telegraph*, 16 May 1965.

90 Strasberg, in Adams, *Lee Strasberg*, p. 300. Sandy Dennis also played Irina in the film version of the production. Her performance is both thoughtful and moving; some of the nervous stumbles are there (as they always were in her performances), but they are slight. Her failure in London, then, seems to have been an aberration.

91 Robert Brustein, *Who Needs Theatre*, New York, Atlantic Monthly Press, 1987, p. 35.

92 Gordon Rogoff, 'The Moscow Art Theatre: surprises after Stanislavski' in *The Reporter*, 25 March 1965, p. 50. The Art Theatre tour also included Gogol's *Dead Souls* and Nikolai Pogodin's *Kremlin Chimes*.

93 Charles Marowitz, *The Act of Being*, London, Martin Secker & Warburg, 1978, p. 24.

94 Robert Brustein, *The New Republic*, 27 February 1965, vol. 152, pp. 26–8.

7 Andrei Serban: upstaging the playwright?

1 Richard Eder, *New York Times*, 10 March 1977.

2 Walter Kerr, *New York Times*, 27 February 1977; John Simon, 'Deadly Revivals' in *The New Leader*, 14 March 1977, p. 22.

3 Serban, interviewed by Arthur Bartow in *The Director's Voice*, New York, Theatre Communications Group, 1988, p. 296.

4 Serban, letter to the *New York Times*, 13 March 1977.

5 Kerr, *New York Times*, 27 February 1977. The lyrical charm of Loquasto's all-white set was later rejected by Serban: 'It really beautifies Russia, and I don't think there's anything beautiful about Russia in that way. I come from Romania and know what the countryside is like – the dust, the mud, the coarseness and poverty, it's nothing beautiful.' (Serban, interviewed by Laurence Shyer in 'Andrei Serban directs Chekhov: *The Seagull* in New York and Japan' in *Theater*, Winter 1981, p. 58.)

6 Kerr, *New York Times*, 27 February 1977.

7 Serban, in Shyer, 'Andrei Serban directs', p. 56.

8 Serban, letter to the *New York Times*, 13 March 1977.

9 Kerr, *New York Times*, 27 February 1977.

10 See Richard Eder, 'Andrei Serban's theatre of terror and beauty' in *New York Times Magazine*, 13 February 1977, p. 53.

11 See Ed Menta, *The Magic World Behind the Curtain: Andrei Serban in the American Theatre*, New York, Peter Lang, 1997, p. 156.

12 Strehler's production was staged in 1974 at the Piccolo Teatro di Milano.
13 Harold Clurman, *Nation*, 12 March 1977, vol. 224, p. 314.
14 Serban, in Bartow, *The Director's Voice*, p. 294.
15 See Ron Jenkins, *Theatre Journal*, June 1983, vol. 35, p. 243.
16 Menta, *The Magic World*, p. 52.
17 Stanislavski, *Rezhisserskie ekzemplyary K.S. Stanislavskogo*, vol. 3, Moscow, Iskusstvo, 1983, p. 427.
18 Stanley Kauffmann, *The New Republic*, 26 March 1977, p. 28.
19 Benedict Nightingale, 'Would Chekhov have embraced this *Vanya*?' in *New York Times*, 18 September 1983.
20 Serban, quoted by Mel Gussow in 'Serban, his *Vanya* and his Career' in *New York Times*, 6 September 1983.
21 Richard Gilman, 'How the new theatrical directors are upstaging the playwright' in *New York Times*, 31 July 1977.
22 Irene Worth, interviewed by Lally Weymouth in 'In order to achieve real wings in Chekhov, you just live it' in *New York Times*, 6 March 1977.
23 Rocco Landesman, 'Comrade Serban in *The Cherry Orchard*' in *Yale Theatre*, Spring 1977, vol. 8, p. 141.
24 Serban, in Shyer, 'Andrei Serban directs', p. 65.
25 Serban, in Shyer, 'Andrei Serban directs', p. 56.
26 Serban, in Bartow, *The Director's Voice*, p. 296. When Brook's production was revived in a more conventional theatre space, the Majestic Theater in Brooklyn, in 1988, it seemed to lose its charm.
27 Serban, in Shyer, 'Andrei Serban directs', p. 60.
28 Serban, in Shyer, 'Andrei Serban directs', p. 59. We might recall that Meyerhold criticised the Moscow Art Theatre's productions of Chekhov on similar lines – because the naturalistic detail in the settings stopped the imagination from seeing further. See Meyerhold, 'The naturalistic theatre and the theatre of mood' in Edward Braun (ed.), *Meyerhold on Theatre*, London, Methuen, 1969, pp. 23–34.
29 Serban, in Shyer, 'Andrei Serban directs', p. 66.
30 Shyer, 'Andrei Serban directs', p. 64.
31 Robert Asahina, *The Hudson Review*, Spring 1981, vol. xxxiv, no. 1, p. 99.
32 John Simon, 'Gulling the audience' in *New York*, 24 November 1980, p. 56.
33 Menta, *The Magic World*, p. 61.
34 Robert Brustein, 'A passion for the familiar' in *The New Republic*, 6 December 1980, vol. 183, p. 29.
35 Walter Kerr, *New York Times*, 23 November 1980.
36 Serban, in Shyer, 'Andrei Serban directs', p. 63.
37 Jack Kroll, 'A pair of *Three Sisters*' in *Newsweek*, 10 January 1983, p. 70.
38 Arthur Holmberg, *Performing Arts Journal*, 1983, part 7, pp. 71–2.
39 Holmberg, p. 71.
40 Holmberg, p. 71.
41 Reported by Ed Menta in *The Magic World*, p. 66.
42 Ron Jenkins, *Theatre Journal*, June 1983, vol. 35, p. 244.
43 Cherry Jones, quoted by Menta, *The Magic World*, p. 68.
44 Chekhov, letter to Knipper, 20 January 1901; in *Chekhov i tear*, E.D. Surkov (ed.), Moscow, Iskusstvo, 1961, p. 120.
45 Richard Schechner, 'We do Chekhov right' in *The Village Voice*, 4 October 1983, p. 121.

46 Albert E. Kalson, *Theatre Journal*, 1984, part 36, p. 108.

47 Nightingale, *New York Times*, 18 Sept. 1983.

48 Jack Kroll, '*Uncle Vanya* on the boards' in *Newsweek*, 26 September 1983, p. 93.

49 Nightingale, *New York Times*, 18 Sept. 1983; Schechner, *The Village Voice*, 4 October 1983, p. 121.

50 See Jenkins, *Theatre Journal*, June 1983, part 35, p. 243. The scene recalls the moment in *Waiting for Godot* when Estragon removes his belt in order to hang himself, and his trousers fall to his ankles.

51 Kerr, *New York Times*, 27 February 1977.

52 Bartow, *The Director's Voice*, p. 297.

53 Robert Brustein, *Who Needs Theatre*, New York, Atlantic Monthly Press, 1987, p. 118.

54 Brustein, *Who Needs Theatre*, p. 116.

55 Schechner, *The Village Voice*, 4 October 1983, p. 121.

56 Kroll, *Newsweek*, 26 September 1983, p. 93.

57 Julius Novick, 'Avanya Garde' in *The Village Voice*, 20 September 1983, p. 97.

58 Brustein, *Who Needs Theatre*, pp. 116–9.

59 Brustein, 'Reworking the classics: homage or ego trip?' in *New York Times*, 6 November 1988.

8 The Wooster Group: *Brace Up!*

1 David Savran, *Breaking the Rules: The Wooster Group*, New York, Theatre Communications Group, 1988, p. 194.

2 Savran, *Breaking the Rules*, p. 175.

3 Miller himself was not very happy with the results of The Wooster Group's work. 'The issue here is very simple: I don't want my play produced except in total agreement with the way I wrote it', he declared. (Quoted by Gerald Rabkin in 'Is there a text on this stage? Theatre/authorship/interpretation' in *Performing Arts Journal*, 1985, part 26/27, p. 144.)

4 Elizabeth LeCompte, quoted by Euridice Arratia in 'Island hopping: rehearsing the Wooster Group's *Brace Up!*' in *The Drama Review*, Winter 1992, vol. 36, no. 4, p. 121.

5 LeCompte, quoted Savran, *Breaking the Rules*, p. 50.

6 LeCompte, quoted Rabkin, 'Is there a text … ?', p. 145.

7 Savran, *Breaking the Rules*, p. 51.

8 Ron Vawter, quoted Savran, *Breaking the Rules*, pp. 53–4.

9 Paul Schmidt, 'The sounds of *Brace Up!*: translating the music of Chekhov' in *The Drama Review*, Winter 1992, vol. 36, no. 4, p. 157.

10 Kate Valk, interviewed by Susie Mee in 'Chekhov's *Three Sisters* and the Wooster Group's *Brace Up!*' in *The Drama Review*, Winter 1992, vol. 36, no. 4, p. 145.

11 LeCompte, interviewed by Mee, 'Chekhov's *Three Sisters* … ', p. 146.

12 Jim Clayburgh, quoted by Arratia, 'Island hopping', p. 124.

13 Marianne Weems, quoted by Arratia, 'Island hopping', p. 139.

14 Valk commented:

When we review the noh texts and the kyogen texts, when we watch Japanese theatre and Japanese movies, we are not going to try and walk as they walk in the noh theatre. We make our own Japan, our own Japanese style because it's culturally removed, it's existing in our heads ... We are not trying to live and work like they would to make Japanese theatre, it is not in us culturally. So it is our Japan.

(Quoted Arratia, 'Island hopping', p. 138.)

In rehearsal, LeCompte frequently referred to Roland Barthes' book, *Empire of Signs*, where Barthes argues that we, in the West, cannot 'know' Japan; any ideas we have of Japanese culture and society are simply our own constructs – we make our *own* 'Japan', existing in our heads. (See Barthes, *Empire of Signs*, New York, Hill and Wang, 1982.)

15 Weems, quoted by Mee, 'Chekhov's *Three Sisters* ... ', p. 148.
16 Kate Davy, 'Foreman's "vertical mobility" and "PAIN(T)"' in *The Drama Review*, vol. 18, no. 2 (T62), p. 35.
17 Arratia, 'Island hopping', p. 132.
18 Arratia, 'Island hopping', pp. 140–1.
19 Schmidt, 'The Sounds of *Brace Up!*', p. 157.
20 Dafoe, quoted by Philip Auslander, 'Task and vision: Willem Dafoe in LSD' in Phillip B. Zarrilli (ed.), *Acting (Re)Considered*, London, Routledge, 1995, p. 309.
21 Dafoe, in Auslander, 'Task and vision', p. 308.
22 LeCompte, in Arratia, 'Island hopping', p. 135.
23 Dafoe, in Auslander, 'Task and vision', p. 307.
24 LeCompte, in Arratia, 'Island hopping', p. 121.
25 LeCompte, in Arratia, 'Island hopping', p. 135. Philip Auslander has argued that the different styles of performance reflect the company's 'multi-tracked, polysemic production style'. (Auslander, 'Task and vision', p. 305.) In fact, different acting styles are incorporated or 'quoted', and even pastiched, in an eclectic, postmodern fashion. In *Brace Up!* for example, the company explored (or 'quoted') a 'soap-opera' style, which was used especially for the sequences performed to camera, and relayed on the TV monitors.
26 LeCompte, in Mee, 'Chekhov's *Three Sisters* ... ', p. 147.
27 LeCompte, in Arratia, 'Island hopping', pp. 132–3.
28 Weems, in Mee, 'Chekhov's *Three Sisters* ... ', pp. 151–2.
29 Weems, in Mee, 'Chekhov's *Three Sisters* ... ', p. 149.
30 Weems, in Mee, 'Chekhov's *Three Sisters* ... ', p. 149.
31 John Harrop, *Acting*, London, Routledge, 1992, p. 54.
32 Arratia, 'Island hopping', p. 135.
33 Alfred Nordmann, 'The actors' brief: experiences with Chekhov' in *Theatre Research International*, Summer 1994, vol. 19, no. 2, p. 141.
34 Kate Bassett, *The Times* (London), 6 July 1993.
35 Charles Marowitz, *Alarums and Excursions*, New York, Applause, 1996, p. 94.
36 Marowitz, *Alarums*, p. 94.
37 Gordon Rogoff, 'The Moscow Art Theatre: Surprises after Stanislavski', *The Reporter*, 25 March 1965, p. 49. Robert Lewis gave a series of talks in

1957, later assembled in his book, *Method – or Madness?* (London, Heinemann, 1960). See also 'Dialogue with Robert Lewis' in *Directing the Action* by Charles Marowitz (New York, Applause, 1986).

38 Phillip B. Zarrilli, introduction to *Acting (Re)Considered*, London, Routledge, 1995, p. 14.

Part IV: Chekhov in England

9 Theodore Komisarjevsky

1 Rodney Ackland, 'Anton Tchekov and the British public'. Unpublished manuscript, no date. Supplied by the author and used with permission.

2 Nigel Playfair recorded that *The Cherry Orchard* was 'probably put on to meet the wishes of G.B.S., who professed himself and certainly was a fervent admirer of the author'. (Playfair, *Hammersmith Hoy: A Book of Minor Revelations*, London, Faber & Faber, 1930, p. 260.)

3 *The Stage*, 1 June 1911.

4 Playfair, *Hammersmith Hoy*, p. 260.

5 Charles Morgan, *New York Times*, 21 June 1936.

6 Gielgud, interviewed by Lewis Funke and John E. Booth in *Actors Talk About Acting*, London, Thames & Hudson, 1961, p. 7.

7 John Gielgud, *Stage Directions*, London, Heinemann, 1963, p. 85.

8 Agate's talk was broadcast on BBC radio, 2 June 1925, and reprinted in Agate, *My Theatre Talks*, London, Arthur Baker Ltd, 1933, p. 15. Christine Gamble reports that Agate found himself involved in controversy when many listeners 'followed his advice and were thoroughly disenchanted with what they found at Hammersmith; Agate was even accused of having a financial interest in the production and broadcasting advice to line his own pocket' (Gamble, *The English Chekhovians*, unpublished Ph.D. thesis, University of London, 1979, p. 260).

9 Nigel Playfair, *The Story of the Lyric Theatre, Hammersmith*, London, Chatto & Windus, 1925, p. 216. The production was later revived in New York in 1928. American audiences, of course, had already seen the Moscow Art Theatre in Chekhov, and Fagan's actors just seemed so *English* in comparison. One critic wrote: 'I vow I thought that all Madame Ranevskaya's household would fall to playing cricket and then drift over to the vodka shop for a perfectly ripping lemon squash!' (*The Referee*, 1 April 1928).

10 Ackland, 'Anton Tchekov'.

11 St John Ervine, *Observer*, 29 September 1929.

12 John Gielgud, *Early Stages*, London, Heinemann Educational, 1974, p. 63.

13 The director's name was actually Fedor Komissarzhevski; Theodore Komisarjevsky was the Anglicised version.

14 *Evening Standard*, 1 September 1922.

15 Anthony Quayle, quoted by Michael Billington in *Peggy Ashcroft*, London, John Murray, 1988, pp. 52–3.

16 Theodore Komisarjevsky, *Myself and the Theatre*, London, Heinemann, 1929, p. 143 and p. 149. In 1917, Komisarjevsky was one of the founders, together with Meyerhold, Tairov and Evreinov, of the Union of Masters

of Theatre Productions. Their declared purpose was 'to imbue all the elements of a theatre production (acting, settings, lighting etc.) with a single artistic concept'. (Quoted by Alla Mikhailova in *Meierkhol'd i khudozhniki*, Moscow, Galart, 1995, p. 65.)

17 Komisarjevsky, *Myself*, p. 172.
18 Theodore Komisarjevsky, *The Theatre and a Changing Civilization*, London, John Lane, Bodley Head, 1935, p. 123.
19 Komisarjevsky, *Myself*, p. 138.
20

>   I worked at one time as an actor with Komisarjevsky, and I did not like him at all. I did not see any wonderful directorial qualities in him. He directed my dramatisation of *Crime and Punishment* in New York. He did not do much at all; he only paid attention to Gielgud [who played Raskolnikov]. When it came to the first dress rehearsal, Gielgud suddenly took over the whole production, saving it from being a disaster. I came to the conclusion that Komisarjevsky must simply have copied Stanislavski's productions of Chekhov. I realise that I am prejudiced, because I disliked him personally.
>
>   (Interview with Rodney Ackland, 25 February 1988)

21 F. Komissarzhevski, 'Iz pisem F.F. Komissarzhevskogo', *Vestnik teatra*, 9–17 October 1920, no. 70, p. 15.
22 Komisarjevsky, *Myself*, p. 67.
23 Komisarjevsky, *Myself*, pp. 41–2.
24 F. Komissarzhevski, *Tvorchestvo aktera i teoriya Stanislavskogo*, Petrograd, Svobodnoe Iskusstvo, 1917, p. 98.
25 Stanislavski, quoted by I. Vinogradskaya in *Zhizn' i tvorchestvo K.S. Stanislavskogo*, vol. 3, Moscow, VTO, 1973, p. 93.
26 Komisarjevsky, *Myself*, p. 126.
27 Komisarjevsky, quoted by Simon Callow in *Charles Laughton*, London, Methuen,1988, p. 14.
28 Komissarzhevski, *Tvorchestvo*, p. 9.
29 John Gielgud, interviewed by Carl Wildman, BBC Third Programme, 6 October 1965.
30 Komisarjevsky, *Myself*, p. 120.
31 Komisarjevsky, *Myself*, p. 123.
32 Warren Jenkins, interviewed by the author, 9 March 1986. All quotations from Jenkins are from this source.
33 Quayle, in Billington, *Peggy Ashcroft*, pp. 52–3.
34 Gielgud, *Stage Directions*, pp. 2–3.
35 Gielgud, in Funke and Booth, *Actors*, p. 7.
36 Charles Morgan, *New York Times*, 17 October 1926.
37 Gielgud, *Stage Directions*, pp. 87–8.
38 The promptbook is preserved as part of the Komisarjevsky collection in the Theatre Collection, Houghton Library, Harvard University. Stanislavski, of course, also created 'production plans' for his Chekhov productions which contained 'intricate patterns of movement'. He once told Gordon Craig that he included so much movement in Chekhov

'simply in order to make the audience follow and listen'. (Reported by Laurence Senelick in *Gordon Craig's Moscow 'Hamlet'*, Westport, CT, Greenwood Press, 1982, p. 77.)

39 Ivor Brown, *The Saturday Review*, 12 December 1925, vol. CXL, p. 699 (review of *Ivanov*). According to one critic, Komis 'set accomplished actors moving as though controlled by invisible elastic' – *The Times*, 16 January 1960.

40 Desmond MacCarthy, *Drama*, London, Putnam, 1940, p. 120.

41 Charles Morgan, *New York Times*, 17 October 1926.

42 Obituary, *The Times*, 19 April 1954.

43 James Agate, *James Agate: An Anthology*, London, Rupert Hart-Davis, 1961, p. 84.

44 Norman Marshall, quoted Callow, *Charles Laughton*, p. 14.

45 Komisarjevsky, *Myself*, p. 171. The actor in the 'Synthetic Theatre', Komis wrote,

> must be able to combine all the forms of expression he has to use, create a synthesis of them subordinating all of them to his conception of the part and to the single rhythm of his emotions. Without an understanding and practice of rhythm an actor cannot feel the text of the playwright and cannot achieve the necessary symmetry of the emotional movement in his mind with the movement of his speech and body.
>
> (pp. 143–4)

46 Komisarjevsky, quoted by Marc Slonim, *Russian Theater from the Empire to the Soviets*, London, Methuen, 1963, p. 208.

47 'On producing Tchehov: An interview with Theodore Komisarjevsky; February 1926', reproduced in *Drama*, 1989, no. 173, p. 17. Similarly, Stanislavski said that a sense of the rhythm of a play or a role 'can of itself, intuitively, unconsciously, at times automatically, take hold of the feelings of an actor and arouse a true sense of living the part'. (Stanislavski, *SS*, vol. 3, p. 208.) In his youth, Stanislavski trained with Komisarjevsky's father, who was an opera singer. Together they experimented in rhythm in movement, to a musical accompaniment. It is possible that Komisarjevsky's own 'musical' sense of rhythm, in movement and speech, also came from his father.

48 Peggy Ashcroft, in Billington, *Peggy Ashcroft*, p. 53; Gielgud, *Early Stages*, p. 65; Gielgud, *Backward Glances*, London, Hodder & Stoughton, 1989, p. 82.

49 See Irving Wardle, *The Theatres of George Devine*, London, Jonathan Cape, 1978, p. 54.

50 John Shand, *Adelphi*, December 1926, vol. 4, pp. 379–82; Agate, review of *Katerina* by Leonid Andreev, quoted Billington, *Peggy Ashcroft*, p. 21.

51 Komis observed that Stanislavski had found 'that the inner life of Chekhov's characters is intimately connected with the life of things and different sounds around them, and that these things and sounds must be made to live on the stage in harmony with the feelings of the players' – *Myself*, p. 137.

52 *Observer*, 9 October 1926. These sound-effects, the critic observed, were like 'familiar vanguards of the ineffable'.

53 Norman Marshall, *The Other Theatre*, London, John Lehmann, 1947, p. 219.
54 Shand, *Adelphi*, December 1926, pp. 379–82.
55 E.A. Baughan, *Daily News*, 17 February 1926.
56 John Shand, *Adelphi*, March 1926, vol. 3, p. 691.
57 'H.H.', *Observer*, 27 October 1929. Stanislavski, we should note, made a similar use of light from natural sources. In his plan for *Three Sisters*, at the start of Act II, the room was dark, and only a single shaft of light fell into the room through the door to Andrei's room. When Masha and Vershinin conversed, they sat down, stage left, in semi-darkness; the only source of light was two candles in the dining room, at the rear of the stage. See Stanislavski, *Rezhisserskie ekzemplyary K.S. Stanislavskogo*, vol. 3, Moscow, Iskusstvo, 1983, p. 132 and p. 145.
58 Agate, *James Agate*, pp. 84–5.
59 Harris Deans, *Illustrated Sporting and Dramatic News*, 2 November 1929, p. 294. Once again, Stanislavski's influence may be apparent here: in his production plan, Ol'ga extinguished all the lamps on the stage, and retired behind her screen, lighting a candle and presumably throwing her shadow against the back wall. See Stanislavski, *Rezhisserskie*, vol. 3, pp. 235–7.
60 'H.H.', *Observer*, 1 May 1928.
61 James Agate, *The Sunday Times*, 15 April 1928.
62 *Evening Standard*, quoted by Robert E. Tracy in *The Flight of the Seagull*, unpublished Ph.D. thesis, Harvard University, 1960, p. 163; C. Nabokoff, *Contemporary Review*, January–June 1926, vol. CXXIX, pp. 756–62, reproduced in Victor Emeljanow (ed.), *Chekhov: The Critical Heritage*, London, Routledge & Kegan Paul, 1981, p. 311.
63 Ivor Brown, 'Acting as a Fine Art', *The Saturday Review*, 27 February 1926, vol. CXLI, p. 258. Francis Birrell recalled that 'the audience were laughing most of the time' – *Nation and Athenaeum*, 27 February 1926, vol. XXXVIII, p. 745.
64 Ashcroft, in Billington, *Peggy Ashcroft*, p. 21; Rodney Ackland, interview with the author, 25 February 1988. In an article entitled 'From Komisarjevsky to Jonathan Miller', Ackland wrote:

> Half-way through the second act something happened to me that was to affect the whole of my life. It was during the impromptu party at the Prozorov's – but rather than get myself into Pseud's Corner by attempting to describe the indescribable, let me merely say that at a most unlikely moment during the performance a flash of illumination seemed to expand my seventeen-year-old consciousness and I experienced an epiphany. At the end of the play, I left the theatre and boarded a Number 9 bus for home in a state of exaltation.
>
> (*Spectator*, 18 September 1976, p. 34.)

Ackland told me that the 'epiphany' occurred in Act II, 'when Masha dances round the room saying, "The Baron is drunk, the Baron is drunk." It was a moment of incredible beauty to me. Whenever one sees a Chekhov play, there are moments like that.'
65 Komisarjevsky, *Myself*, p. 67.

66 Gielgud, *Early Stages*, p. 65.
67 Agate, *James Agate*, p. 85.
68 "R.J.", *Spectator*, 27 February 1926, p. 363; Ackland, 'From Komisarjevsky', *Spectator*, 18 September 1976, p. 34. Gwen Ffrangçon-Davies recalls that Beatrix Thomson was 'a very sensitive and slightly hysterical actress. Once during a matinee performance she cried so much they had to bring the curtain down' – interview with the author, 7 April 1988.
69 Brown, 'Acting', *Saturday Review*, 27 February 1926, p. 258.
70 Gielgud, *Early Stages*, p. 65.
71 'A.E.W.', *Star*, 17 February 1926.
72 Brown, 'Acting', *Saturday Review*, 27 February 1926, p. 258.
73 Michael Redgrave, *In My Mind's Eye*, London, Weidenfeld & Nicolson, 1983, p. 134.
74 *The Daily Mirror*, 21 May 1936.
75 *The Sphere*, 30 May 1936. Gielgud observes that Komis despised the commercial theatre, and when offered a job by a commercial producer, 'he would spend a great deal of money and do a rather, sometimes perverse, kind of job, whereas when we were at the Barnes with no money to spend at all, a few pounds on each production, he achieved miracles with the simplest possible means' – interviewed by Carl Wildman, BBC Third Programme, 6 October 1965.
76 'J.C.', *Daily Sketch*, 21 May 1936.
77 *Play Pictorial*, no date, no. 409, p. 1.
78 Ivor Brown, *Observer*, 24 May 1936.
79 Press cutting preserved in the Enthoven Collection, University of Birmingham. The name and date of the publication have unfortunately not been preserved.
80 Ronald Hayman, *Gielgud*, London, Heinemann Educational, 1971, p. 99; Stanislavski, *SS*, vol. 1, p. 298. It seems that Komis first saw *The Seagull* at the Art Theatre in 1898, when he was just 16. (See Komissarzhevski, *Tvorchestvo*, p. 99.)
81 Agate, *Sunday Times*, 24 May 1936.
82 Agate, *Sunday Times*, 24 May 1936; 'J.G.B.', *The Evening News*, 21 May 1936.
83 Bernard Shaw, letter to Edith Evans, quoted by Bryan Forbes in *Ned's Girl*, London, Elm Tree Books, 1977, p. 179.
84 Komisarjevsky, *Myself*, p. 88.
85 Peggy Ashcroft, quoted by Gordon McVay, 'Peggy Ashcroft and Chekhov', in Patrick Miles (ed.), *Chekhov on the British Stage*, Cambridge, CUP, 1993, p. 84.
86 Ivor Brown, *Illustrated London News*, 6 June 1936. Press cutting preserved in the Enthoven Collection, University of Birmingham. The original page number has unfortunately not been preserved.

10 Jonathan Miller

1 Rodney Ackland, 'From Komisarjevsky to Jonathan Miller', in *Spectator*, 18 September 1976, p. 34; Hilary Spurling, *Observer*, 27 June 1976.

2 Jonathan Miller, interview with the author, 17 September 1985. Unless otherwise specified, all quotations from Miller are from this source.
3 Jonathan Miller, *Subsequent Performances*, London, Faber & Faber, 1986, pp. 164–5.
4 Ars. Gurlyand, 'Iz vospominani ob A. P. Chekhove', in E.D. Surkov (ed.), *Chekhov i teatr*, Moscow, Iskusstvo, 1961, p. 206.
5 Miller, *Subsequent*, p. 165.
6 Miller, *Subsequent*, p. 167.
7 Miller, *Subsequent*, p. 168. In 1987, several actors from the Moscow Art Theatre visited Britain. At the time, Miller was working with the RSC. The company interrupted rehearsals to see the actors from the Art Theatre perform a scene from *Uncle Vanya*. The scene chosen was the encounter between Astrov and Elena in Act III, played by Oleg Borisov and Anastasya Vertinskaya. At the opening of the scene, the characters stood awkwardly, unsure quite how to begin.

ELENA: Yesterday, er, you promised to show me some of your work. Are you free now ?

ASTROV: Yes ... I don't suppose this will interest you ...

ELENA: Why not ? ... Er ... It's true I don't know the country, but I've read a great deal.

ASTROV: Mmm?

ELENA: Mmm.

The nervousness of the characters was both well-observed and comic. 'What was surprising and exciting for us,' Miller commented afterwards, 'was the relaxed manner in which things were happening, and the small-scale of the performances.' Alun Armstrong observed that the actors had frequently hesitated, 'ummed' and 'erred,' 'in a way that we, as English actors would tend to be shy of doing'; and this, Miller suggested, only added to the 'natural liveliness' of the performance. (A film of the visit of the Moscow Art Theatre, called *A Visit from Vanya*, was broadcast on BBC2, 21 October 1987.)

8 Miller, *Subsequent*, p. 171.
9 Robert Cushman, *First Night Impressions* (broadcast on BBC Radio 4, 28 May 1986).
10 Irving Wardle, *The Times*, 24 June 1976.
11 Miller, *Subsequent*, p. 165.
12 John Shrapnel, interviewed by Michael Romain in *A Profile of Jonathan Miller*, Cambridge, CUP, 1992, p. 128.
13 David Magarshack, *Chekhov the Dramatist*, London, Eyre Methuen, 1980, p. 247 and p. 257.
14 Miller, *Subsequent*, p. 171.
15 Wardle, *The Times*, 24 May, 1973.
16 Cushman, *First Night*.
17 Michael Billington, *Guardian*, 24 June 1976.
18 Ackland, 'From Komisarjevsky', p. 34.

19 Miller, *Subsequent*, p. 167. It appears that Komisarjevsky changed Irina's line when she hears of the Baron's death, softening it, from 'I knew it, I knew it', to 'I knew ... I knew something terrible was going to happen to him ... '. (See Victor Emeljanow, 'Komisarjevsky's *Three Sisters*: The Prompt Book', in *Theatre Notebook*, 1987, vol. XLI, no. 2, p. 65.)

20 Ackland, 'From Komisarjevsky', p. 34.

21 Magarshack, *Chekhov*, p. 249.

22 Romain, *A Profile*, p. 132.

23 Wardle, *Times*, 24 June 1976.

24 Miller, *Subsequent*, p. 165.

25 Sheridan Morley, *Punch*, 7 July 1976, p. 36.

26 Spurling, *Observer*, 27 June 1976.

27 Suzman, interviewed by Cushman, *First Night*. Suzman argues that the 'confession' scene in some ways caught 'the tone of the whole production'. It was 'the reverse of the way the scene is normally played – instead of being a great tragic confession, it simply became panic stricken' – interviewed by Romain, *A Profile*, p. 132.

28 Miller, *Subsequent*, p. 170.

29 Miller, *Subsequent*, pp. 170–1.

30 Miller, *Subsequent*, p. 171.

31 Irving Wardle, *The Times*, 24 May 1973.

32 Garry O'Conner, *Financial Times*, 24 May 1973.

33 Wardle, *The Times*, 24 May 1973.

34 Michael Billington, *Guardian*, 24 June 1976.

35 Wardle, *The Times*, 24 June 1976.

36 John Elsom, 'Touch of Instinct', *The Listener*, 1 July 1976, p. 848.

37 Michael Billington, *Guardian*, 24 May 1973.

38 Billington, *Guardian*, 24 May 1973.

39 Stanislavski observed that 'in real life many sublime moments of experience are often made manifest by the most ordinary, small, natural action'. (*SS*, vol. 2, p. 239.)

40 Elsom, 'Touch', p. 848.

41 'I never block a play in advance. I allow moves to develop, and then I crystallise, and perhaps add an element of formality or "choreography". I will slightly formalise it so that people fall into groupings and positions that are perhaps not altogether natural, although arrived at by natural means' – Miller.

42 Miller, *Subsequent*, pp. 165–6.

43 Spurling, *Observer*, 27 June 1976.

44 Miller, *Subsequent*, p. 166 & p. 171.

11 Mike Alfreds

1 Robert Cushman, introduction to *Shared Experience 1975–1984*, London, Shared Experience, 1985, p. 6.

2 I have interviewed Mike Alfreds about his work on Chekhov on numerous occasions since 1982. Unless otherwise specified, all quotations from Alfreds are from this source.

3 Spencer Golub, 'The theatre of Anatolij Efros', *Theatre Quarterly*, 1977, vol. 7, no. 26, p. 22.

4 Alfreds offers the following films as examples of what he means: *Cries and Whispers*, *Winter Night*, *The Silence*, and *Persona*. Interestingly, Andrei Serban has argued that 'in cinema Bergman comes closest to capturing the Chekhovian inner life'. (Serban, interviewed by Laurence Shyer in 'Andrei Serban Directs Chekhov', *Theater*, Winter 1981, p. 64.)

5 Anne McFerran, *Time Out*; reproduced in *London Theatre Record*, 8–21 October 1981, p. 542.

6 Robert Cushman, *Observer*, 15 August 1982.

7 Michael Billington, *Guardian*, 11 August 1982; Ned Chaillet, *The Times*, 10 August 1982; Michael Coveney, *Financial Times*, 10 August 1982.

8 David Jones, 'David Jones on Directing Gorky', in Simon Trussler (ed.), *New Theatre Voices of the Seventies*, London, Methuen, 1982, p. 39.

9 Alfreds, production notes for *The Cherry Orchard*; quoted by Stuart Young, 'Changes of Direction: Mike Alfreds' Methods with Chekhov', in Patrick Miles (ed.), *Chekhov on the British Stage*, Cambridge, CUP, 1993, p. 175.

10 My wife, who is Russian, thinks that *Italians* are too 'temperamental'.

11 Quoted by Kenneth Rea, 'The theatre of Mike Alfreds', *Drama*, 1987, no. 163, p. 6.

12 Sheila Hancock, *Ramblings of an Actress*, London, Hutchinson, 1987, p. 202.

13 Hancock, *Ramblings*, p. 203.

14 Milton Shulman, *London Standard*, 11 December 1985.

15 Hancock, *Ramblings*, pp. 204–5.

16 Michael Billington, *Guardian*, 12 December 1985.

17 Billington, *Guardian*, 12 December 1985.

18 Young, 'Changes', p. 176.

19 Young, 'Changes', p. 176.

20 *Actors' Workshop*, BBC Radio 4, 25 June 1988.

21 Laban defined eight different 'efforts,' or types of movement: pressing, flicking, wringing, dabbing, slashing, gliding, punching, and floating. For a further explanation, see Jean Newlove, *Laban for Actors and Dancers*, London, Nick Hern Books, 1993.

22 *Shared Experience*, p. 43.

23 Alfreds, *Actors' Workshop*.

24 Hancock, *Ramblings*, pp. 202–3.

25 Young, 'Changes', p. 172.

26 Michael Ratcliffe, *Observer*, 15 December 1985.

27 Hancock, *Ramblings*, p. 208.

28 Alfreds, quoted by Hancock, *Ramblings*, pp. 214–5.

29 Nigel Andrews, speaking on *Critics' Forum*, BBC Radio 3, 19 April 1986.

30 Charles Spencer, *The Stage*, 10 April 1986.

31 Michael Billington, speaking on 'Critics' forum', BBC Radio 3, 19 April 1986.

32 Billington, *Guardian*, 3 April 1986.

33 Chekhov, letter to Komissarzhevskaya, 13 November 1900; in E.D. Surkov (ed.), *Chekhov i teatr*, Moscow, Iskusstvo, 1961, p. 117.

34 Andrews, *Critics' Forum*.

35 Helen Rose, *Time Out*, 9 April 1986; in *London Theatre Record*, 26 March–8 April 1986, vol. 6, no. 7, p. 321.

36 Benedict Nightingale, *The Times*, 25 April 1991.
37 I saw the production on four occasions: at the Northcott Theatre, Exeter, 6 February 1998; at the Oxford Playhouse, 3 June 1998; at the Everyman Theatre, Cheltenham, 12 September 1998; and at the Theatre Royal, Bury St Edmunds, 29 January 1999.

Conclusion

1 Laurence Senelick, *The Chekhov Theatre*, Cambridge, CUP, 1997, pp. 3–4.
2 Chekhov, 'Opyat' o Sare Bernar', written 1881; in E.D. Surkov (ed.), *Chekhov i teatr*, Moscow, Iskusstvo, 1961, pp. 171–2.
3 Chekhov, reported by Evtikhi Karpov, 'Istoriya pervogo predstavleniya *Chaiki*', in *Chekhov i teatr*, p. 238.
4 Maurice Baring, *The Puppet Show of Memory*, London, W. Heinemann, 1922, p. 266.
5 Stanislavski, *SS*, vol.1, p. 292.
6 Stanislavski, 'Otchet o desyatiletnei khudozhestvennoi deyatel'nosti Moskovskogo khudozhestvennogo teatra', *SS*, vol. 5, p. 142.
7 Stanislavski, *SS*, vol. 4, p. 351–2.
8 N. Chushkin, introduction to V. Toporkov, *Stanislavski na repetitsii*, Moscow, Iskusstvo, 1950, p.11.
9 Stanislavski, quoted by Sharon M. Carnicke in *Stanislavski in Focus*, Amsterdam, Harwood Academic Publishers, 1998.
10 See N. Gorchakov, *Rezhisserskie uroki K.S. Stanislavskogo: besedy i zapisi repetitsi*, Moscow, Iskusstvo, 1951, p. 152.
11 D. Gorodetski, 'Iz vospominani ob A. P. Chekhove', in *Chekhov i teatr*, pp. 208–9; A. Gurlyand, 'Iz vospominani ob A. P. Chekhove', *Chekhov i teatr*, p. 206.
12 Stanislavski, *SS*, vol.1, p.353.

References

Works in Russian

Anikst, A., *Teoriya dramy v Rossii ot Pushkina do Chekhova*, Moscow, Nauka, 1972.

Balukhaty, S.D., *Problemy dramaturgicheskogo analiza Chekhova*, Leningrad, Academia, 1927; repr. Munich, Wilhelm Fink, 1969.

—— *'Chaika' v postanovke Moskovskogo khudozhestvennogo teatra: rezhisserskaya partitura K.S. Stanislavskogo*, Leningrad and Moscow, Iskusstvo, 1938.

.Bryusov, Valeri, *Sobranie sochineni*, vol. 6, *Stat'i i retsensii 1893–1924; iz knigi 'Dalekie i blizkie'; miscellanea*, ed. D.E. Maksimov, Moscow, Khudozhestvennaya literatura, 1975.

Chekhov, A.P., *Polnoe sobranie sochineni i pisem v tridtsati tomakh* (Collected Works in Thirty Volumes), Moscow, Nauka, 1974–83.

Demidova, Alla, *Teni zazerkal'ya: rol' aktera: tema zhizni i tvorchestva*, Moscow, Prosveshchenie, 1993.

Efros, Anatoli, *Repetitsiya – lyubov' moya*, vol. 1 of a four-volume edition of Efros' writings, Moscow, Panas, 1993.

—— *Professiya: rezhisser*, vol. 2, Moscow, Panas, 1993.

—— *Prodolzhenie teatral'nogo romana*, vol 3, Panas, 1993.

Efros, Nikolai, *Moskovski khudozhestvenny teatr: 1898–1923*, Moscow, Gosudarstvennoe izdatel'stvo, 1924.

Ezhegodnik Moskovskogo khudozhestvennogo teatra 1943, Moscow, Iskusstvo, 1945.

Gershkovich, Aleksandr, *Izbrannoe*, Moscow, ULISS/ Teatral'naya zhizn', 1994.

—— *Teatre na Taganke (1964–1984)*, Moscow, Solyaris, 1993.

Gitovich, N.I. (ed.), *A.P. Chekhov v vospominaniyakh sovremennikov*, Moscow, Khudozhestvennaya literatura, 1986.

Gladkov, Aleksandr, *Meierkhol'd*, 2 vols, ed. V.V. Zabrodina, Moscow, STD RSFSR, 1990.

Gogol', N.V., *Sobranie sochineni*, eds S.I. Mashinski and M.B. Khrapchenko, vol. 6, Moscow, Khudozhestvennaya literatura, 1978.

Gorchakov, N., *Rezhisserskie uroki Stanislavskogo: besedy i zapisi repetitsi*, Moscow, Iskusstvo, 1951.

—— *Rezhisserskie uroki Vakhtangova*, Moscow, Iskusstvo, 1957.

Il'inski, Igor, *Sam o sebe*, Moscow, Iskusstvo, 1984.

Komissarzhevski, F., *Tvorchestvo aktera i teoriya Stanislavskago*, Petrograd, Svobodnoe iskusstvo, 1917.

Mal'tseva, O., *Akter teatra Lyubimova*, St. Petersburg, LenNar, 1994.

Meierkhol'd, V.E., *V.E. Meierkhol'd: stat'i, pis'ma, rechi, besedy*, ed. A.V. Fevral'ski, 2 vols, Moscow, Iskusstvo, 1968.

—— *Meierkhol'd repetiryet*, ed. M.M. Sitkovetskaya, 2 vols, Moscow, ART, 1993.

Mikhailova, Alla, *Meierkhol'd i khudozhniki*, Moscow, Galart, 1995.

Nemirovich-Danchenko, Vl. I., *Izbrannye pis'ma*, vol. 1 (1879–1909), Moscow, Iskusstvo, 1979.

—— *Rozhdenie teatra: vospominaniya, stat'i, zametki, pis'ma*, ed. M.N. Lyubomudrov, Moscow, Pravda, 1989.

Radishcheva, O.A., *Stanislavski i Nemirovich-Danchenko: istoriya teatral'nyx otnosheni. 1897–1908*, Moscow, ART, 1997.

Rudnitski, K., *Rezhisser Meierkhol'd*, Moscow, Nauka, 1969.

Simonov, Ruben, *S Vakhtangovym*, Moscow, Iskusstvo, 1959.

Smelyanski, Anatoli, *Nashi sobesedniki: Russkaya klassicheskaya dramaturgiya na stsene sovetskogo teatra 70-x godov*, Moscow, Iskusstvo, 1981.

Stanislavski, K.S., *Rezhisserskie ekzemplyary K.S. Stanislavskogo*, vol. 2, *1898–1901: 'Chaika' A.P. Chekhova, 'Mikhail' Kramer' G. Hauptmanna*, ed. I.N. Vinogradskaya and I.N. Solov'eva, Moscow, Iskusstvo, 1981.

—— *Rezhisserskie ekzemplyary K. S. Stanislavskogo*, vol. 3, *1901–1904: p'esy A.P. Chekhova 'Tri sestry', 'Vishnevy sad'*, ed. I.N. Solov'eva and N.N. Chushkina, Moscow, Iskusstvo, 1983.

—— *Sobranie sochineni v devyati tomax* (Collected Works in Nine Volumes), Moscow, Iskusstvo, vols 1–7, 1988–95.

—— *Moe grazhdanskoe slyzhenie Rossii*, ed. M.N. Lyubomudrova, Moscow, Pravda, 1990.

—— *Rezhisserskie ekzemplyary Stanislavskogo 1898–1930: 'Dyadya Vanya' A.P. Chekhova, 1899*, ed. I.N. Solov'eva, Moscow, Phoenix, 1994.

Stanislavski v menyayushchemsya mire: sbornik materialov Mezhdunarodnogo simpoziuma 27 Fevralya–10 Marta 1989 g., Moskva, Moscow, Blagotvoritel'ni fond Stanislavskogo, 1994.

Stroeva, M. *Chekhov i khudozhestvenny teatr: rabota K.S. Stanislavskogo i Vl. I. Nemirovich-Danchenko nad p'esami A.P. Chekhova*, Moscow, Iskusstvo, 1955.

—— *Rezhisserskie iskaniya Stanislavskogo, 1898–1917*, Moscow, Nauka, 1973.

—— *Rezhisserskie iskaniya Stanislavskogo, 1917–1938*, Moscow, Nauka, 1977.

Surkov, E.D. (ed.), *Chekhov i teatr*, Moscow, Iskusstvo, 1961.

Suvorin, A.S., *Dnevnik A. S. Suvorina*, ed. M. Kricheski, Moscow and Petrograd, L.D. Frenkel', 1923.

Toporkov, V., *Stanislavski na repetitsii: vospominaniya*, Moscow, Iskusstvo, 1950.

Vakhtangov, E., *Evg. Vakhtangov: materialy i stat'i*, eds L.D. Vendrovskaya and G.P. Kaptereva, Moscow, VTO, 1959.

Vendrovskaya, L.D. (ed.), *Vstrechi s Meierkhol'dom: sbornik vospominani*, Moscow, VTO, 1967.

Vilenkin, V. Ya. (ed.), *Ol'ga Leonardovna Knipper-Chekhova: vospominaniya i stat'i; perepiska s A. P. Chekhovym (1902–1904)*, 2 vols, Moscow, Iskusstvo, 1972.

Vinogradskaya, I.N., *Zhizn' i tvorchestvo K.S. Stanislavskogo: letopis'*, 4 vols, Moscow, VTO, 1971–6.

—— *Stanislavski repetiruet: zapisi i stenogrammy repetitsi*, Moscow, STD RSFSR, 1987.

Books in other languages

Adams, Cindy, *Lee Strasberg: The Imperfect Genius of the Actors Studio*, New York, Doubleday, 1980.

Agate, James, *My Theatre Talks*, London, Arthur Barker Ltd, 1933.

—— *James Agate: An Anthology*, London, Rupert Hart-Davis, 1961.

Ahrends, Günter (ed.), *Konstantin Stanislawski: Neue Aspekte und Perspektiven*, Tübingen, Gunter Narr Verlag, 1992.

Baring, Maurice, *The Puppet Show of Memory*, London, W. Heinmann, 1922.

Barthes, Roland, *Empire of Signs*, New York, Hill & Wang, 1982.

Bartow, Arthur, *The Director's Voice: Twenty-one Interviews*, New York, Theatre Communications, 1988.

Benedetti, Jean, *Stanislavski: A Biography*, London, Methuen, 1988.

—— *The Moscow Art Theatre Letters*, London, Methuen, 1991.

Bergan, Ronald, *Dustin Hoffman*, London, Virgin, 1991.

Beumers, Birgit, *Yuri Lyubimov at the Taganka Theatre 1964–1994*, Amsterdam, Harwood Academic Publishers, 1997.

Billington, Michael, *Peggy Ashcroft*, London, John Murray, 1988.

Boleslavsky, Richard, *Acting: The First Six Lessons*, New York, Theatre Arts Books, 1933.

Braun, Edward (ed.), *Meyerhold on Theatre*, New York, Hill & Wang, 1969.

—— *The Director and the Stage*, London, Methuen, 1982.

Brecht, Bertolt, *Brecht on Theatre: The Development of an Aesthetic*, ed. John Willett, London, Methuen, 1978.

Bristow, Eugene K. (ed.), *Anton Chekhov's Plays*, New York, W.W. Norton, 1977.

Brustein, Robert, *Who Needs Theatre: Dramatic Opinions*, New York, Atlantic Monthly Press, 1987.

Callow, Simon, *Charles Laughton: A Difficult Actor*, London, Methuen, 1988.

Carnicke, Sharon M., *Stranislavski in Focus*, Amsterdam, Harwood Academic Publishers, 1998.

Clark, Barrett H. (ed.), *European Theories of the Drama*, New York, Crown Publishers, 1965.

Clayton, J. Douglas (ed.), *Chekhov Then and Now: The Reception of Chekhov in World Culture*, New York, Peter Lang, 1997.

Clurman, Harold, *The Fervent Years: The Group Theatre and the 30s*, New York, Da Capo Press, 1983.

Cole, Toby (ed.), *Acting: A Handbook of the Stanislavski Method*, New York, Three Rivers Press, 1995.

Cole, Toby and Chinoy, Helen Krich (eds), *Actors on Acting: The Theories, Techniques, and Practices of the World's Great Actors, Told in Their Own Words*, New York, Three Rivers Press, 1970.

Dukore, Bernard F. (ed.), *Dramatic Theory and Criticism: Greeks to Grotowski*, New York, Holt, Rinehart & Winston, 1974.

Edwards, Christine, *The Stanislavsky Heritage*, London, Owen, 1966.

Emeljanow, Victor (ed.), *Chekhov: The Critical Heritage*, London, Routledge & Kegan Paul, 1981.

Forbes, Bryan, *Ned's Girl*, London, Elm Tree Books, 1977.

Funke, Lewis and Booth, John E., *Actors Talk about Acting*, London, Thames & Hudson, 1961.

Gamble, C.E., *The English Chekhovians: The Influence of Anton Chekhov on the Short Story and Drama in England*, unpublished Ph.D. thesis, University of London, 1979.

Garfield, David, *A Player's Place: The Story of The Actors Studio*, New York, Macmillan, 1980.

Gassner, John (ed.), *Producing the Play*, New York, Holt, Rinehart, & Winston, 1941.

Gershkovich, Alexander, *The Theater of Yuri Lyubimov: Art and Politics at the Taganka Theater in Moscow*, translated by Michael Yurieff, New York, Paragon House, 1989.

Gielgud, John, *Stage Directions*, London, Heinemann, 1963.

—— *Early Stages*, London, Heinemann Educational, 1974.

—— *Backward Glances*, London, Hodder & Stoughton, 1989.

Gorchakov, Nikolai A., *The Theater in Soviet Russia*, translated by Edgar Lehrman, New York, Columbia University Press, 1957.

Gordon, Mel, *The Stanislavsky Technique: Russia – A Handbook for Actors*, New York, Applause, 1987.

Gottlieb, Vera, *Chekhov in Performance in Russia and Soviet Russia*, Cambridge, Chadwyck–Healey, 1984.

Hancock, Sheila, *Ramblings of an Actress*, London, Hutchinson, 1987.

Harrop, John, *Acting*, London, Routledge, 1992.

Hayman, Ronald, *Gielgud*, London, Heinemann Educational, 1971.

Hethmon, Robert H. (ed.), *Strasberg at the Actors Studio*, New York, Theatre Communications Group, 1991.

Hirsch, Foster, *A Method to their Madness: The History of the Actors Studio*, New York, Da Capo Press, 1984.

Houghton, Norris, *Moscow Rehearsals: An Account of Methods of Production in the Soviet Theatre*, London, George Allen & Unwin, 1938.

Hull, Lorrie, *Strasberg's Method as Taught by Lorrie Hull: A Practical Guide for Actors, Teachers and Directors*, Woodbridge, Connecticut, Ox Bow Publishing, 1985.

Jackson, Robert Louis (ed.), *Chekhov: A Collection of Critical Essays*, Englewood Cliffs, NJ, Prentice–Hall, 1967.

Jones, David Richard, *Great Directors at Work*, Berkeley, University of California Press, 1986.

Kazan, Elia, *Elia Kazan: A Life*, London, Andre Deutsch, 1988.

Kluge, Rolf-Dieter, *Anton P. Čechov: Eine Einführung in Leben und Werk*, Darmstadt, Wissenschaftliche Buchgesellschaft, 1995.

Komisarjevsky, Theodore, *Myself and the Theatre*, London, Heinemann, 1929.

—— *The Theatre and a Changing Civilization*, London, John Lane, Bodley Head, 1935.

Komissarjevsky, V., *Inside Moscow Theatres*, Moscow, 1959 (publisher unknown).

Lewis, Robert, *Method – or Madness?*, London, Heinemann, 1960.

Lyubimov, Yuri, *Le Feu Sacré*, Paris, Fayard, 1985.

MacCarthy, Desmond, *Drama*, London, Putnam, 1940.

Magarshack, David, *Stanislavsky: A Life*, London, MacGibbon & Kee, 1950.

—— *Chekhov the Dramatist*, London, Eyre Methuen, 1980.

Marowitz, Charles, *The Act of Being*, London, Martin Secker & Warburg, 1978.

—— *Directing the Action: Acting and Directing in the Contemporary Theatre*, New York, Applause, 1986.

—— *Alarums and Excursions: Our Theatre in the 90s*, New York, Applause, 1996.

Marshall, Norman, *The Other Theatre*, London, John Lehmann, 1947.

Miles, Patrick (ed.), *Chekhov on the British Stage*, Cambridge, Cambridge University Press, 1993.

Miller, Jonathan, *Subsequent Performances*, London, Faber & Faber, 1986.

Newlove, Jean, *Laban for Actors and Dancers*, London, Nick Hern Books, 1993.

Playfair, Nigel, *Hammersmith Hoy: A Book of Minor Revelations*, London, Faber and Faber, 1930.

—— *The Story of the Lyric Theatre, Hammersmith*, London, Chatto & Windus, 1925.

Redgrave, Michael, *In My Mind's Eye*, London, Weidenfeld & Nicolson, 1983.

Roberts, J.W., *Richard Boleslavsky: His Life and Work in the Theatre*, Ann Arbor, UMI Research Press, 1981.

Romain, Michael, *A Profile of Jonathan Miller*, Cambridge, Cambridge University Press, 1992.

Rudnitsky, Konstantin, *Meyerhold the Director*, translated by George Petrov, Ann Arbor, MI, Ardis, 1981.

—— *Russian and Soviet Theatre: Tradition and the Avant-Garde*, translated by Roxane Permar, London, Thames & Hudson, 1988.

Saint-Denis, Michel, *Theatre: The Rediscovery of Style*, London, Heinemann, 1960.

Savran, David, *Breaking the Rules: The Wooster Group*, New York, Theatre Communications Group, 1988.

Sayler, Oliver M., *The Russian Theatre*, London, Bretano's, 1923

Schmidt, Paul, *Three Sisters* (translation), New York, Theatre Communications Group, 1992.

Senelick, Laurence (ed.), *Russian Dramatic Theory from Pushkin to the Symbolists*, Austin, University of Texas Press, 1981.

—— *Gordon Craig's Moscow 'Hamlet'*, Westport, CT, Greenwood Press, 1982.

—— (ed.) *Wandering Stars: Russian Emigre Theatre 1905–1940*, Iowa City, University of Iowa Press, 1992.

—— *The Chekhov Theatre: A Century of the Plays in Performance*, Cambridge, CUP, 1997.

Seymour, Victor, *Stage Directors' Workshop: A Descriptive Study of the Actors Studio Directors Unit, 1960–1964*, unpublished Ph.D thesis, University of Wisconsin, 1965.

Shared Experience 1975–1984 (no named author), London, Shared Experience, 1985.

Simmons, Ernest J., *Chekhov: A Biography*, Chicago, The University of Chicago Press, 1962.

Simonov, Ruben, *Stanislavsky's Protégé: Eugene Vakhtangov*, translated and adapted by Miriam Goldina, New York, DRS Publications, 1969.

Slonim, Marc, *Russian Theater from the Empire to the Soviets*, London, Methuen, 1963.

Smeliansky, Anatoly, *Is Comrade Bulgakov Dead?: Mikhail Bulgakov at the Moscow Art Theatre*, London, Methuen, 1993.

Stanislavski, Constantin, *My Life in Art*, translated by J.J. Robbins, Harmondsworth, Penguin Books, 1967.

Strasberg, John, *Accidentally on Purpose: Reflections on Life, Acting, and the Nine Natural Laws of Creativity*, New York, Applause, 1996.

Tracy, Robert E., *The Flight of the Seagull: Chekhov's Plays on the English Stage*, unpublished Ph.D thesis, Harvard University, 1960.

Trussler, Simon (ed.), *New Theatre Voices of the Seventies*, London, Methuen, 1982.

Vakhtangov, E., *Evgeny Vakhtangov*, ed. by Lyubov Vendrovskaya and Galina Kaptereva, translated by Doris Bradbury, Moscow, Progress, 1982.

—— *Jewgeni B. Wachtangow: Schriften*, ed. Dieter Wardetzky, Berlin, Henschelverlag, 1982.

Wardle, Irving, *The Theatres of George Devine*, London, Jonathan Cape, 1978.

Wellek, René and Nonna, D. (eds), *Chekhov : New Perspectives*, Englewood Cliffs, NJ, Prentice Hall, 1984.

Williams, Raymond, *Drama in Performance*, Harmondsworth, Pelican Books, 1972.

Worrall, Nick, *Modernism to Realism on the Soviet Stage: Tairov, Vakhtangov, Okhlopkov*, Cambridge, CUP, 1989.

—— *The Moscow Art Theatre*, London, Methuen, 1996.

Zarrilli, Phillip B. (ed.), *Acting (Re)Considered*, London, Routledge, 1995.

Index of Chekhov's works: titles and characters

Index of names, places and topics

Yavorskaya, Lidya 4, 5
Yeargan, Michael 135
Yezhov [Ezhov], Nikolai 87
Young, B.A. 125
Yvonne Arnaud Theatre, Guildford
187

Zakhava, Boris 71, 73, 76
Zamkovets, G. 101
Zavadski, Yuri 76